GREENING ASIA

Cover
Circles represent emerging intensities of Green activity over an implied map of Asia. The pattern is adapted from the map on pages 28 to 29.

Disclaimers
The information and arguments presented in this book have been assembled, derived and developed from various sources including textbooks, academic papers, news media, reports, standards, guidelines, professional firms, and the Internet. These are presented in good faith. The author and publisher have made every reasonable effort to ensure that information presented is accurate. It is the responsibility of all users to utilise professional judgement, experience and common sense when applying information presented in this book. This responsibility extends to verification of local codes, standards and climate data.

Every effort has been made to ensure that intellectual property rights are rightfully acknowledged. Omissions or errors, if any, are unintended. Where the publisher or author is notified of an omission or error, these will be corrected in subsequent editions.

Publisher
BCI Asia
Construction Information Pte Ltd
371 Beach Road
#02-25 Keypoint
Singapore 199597

Editor
J.B. Bungar

Design
Atelier MNN

Printer
Tien Wah Press Pte Ltd
4 Pandan Crescent
Singapore 128475

Every effort was made to seek out and adhere to environmentally-sound materials and practices during the production of this book.

Paper was purchased from reputable mills that are endorsed with Forest (FC) and Chain-of-Custody (CoC) certifications. Paper selected was sourced from well-managed forests with verification systems that track raw materials from forest to finished product. These systems include the Forest Stewardship Council™ (FSC™) and the Programme for Endorsement of Forest Certification Schemes (PEFC).

The book was sized to minimise waste during production.

Only 100% soya-based ink, free of volatile organic compounds, was used.

Only water-based varnish was used.

Only glue that is free of hazardous chemicals was used.

The cover is laminated with Thermal OPP film, a precoated grade that does not rely on solvent or water-based additives.

FSC
www.fsc.org
MIX
Paper from
responsible sources
FSC™ C019704

This publication is supported by
Autodesk Asia Pte Ltd
3 Fusionopolis Way
#10-21 Symbiosis
Singapore 138633
www.facebook.com/Autodeskedcommunity
students.autodesk.com

Autodesk·

Printed and bound in Singapore

ISBN 978-981-07-0116-1

GREENING ASIA

EMERGING PRINCIPLES FOR SUSTAINABLE ARCHITECTURE

Nirmal Kishnani

CONTENTS

113
The Projects

PREAMBLE

In its present form the Green building in Asia is in urgent need of scrutiny. At the heart of the problem underlying Greening is a fragmentation of thinking – good ideas coexisting with bad ones – that leads to conflicting, sometimes meaningless, outcomes. This is what permits a building to be declared Green if it has an energy-efficient cooling system even though it is wrapped in a glass envelope that increases its cooling load measurably. It is what allows a building to be unexceptional in its day-to-day performance, yet continue to be regarded Green because it was certified such on the drawing board. Something in industry mind-sets enables the acceptance of these outcomes. As Asia embraces the Green building – using *sustainable* interchangeably with the term *Green* – this trend is increasingly troubling.

Greening Asia starts by questioning the placebo effect of Green, the widespread acceptance of conventions of Greening. It then looks to several new developments that buck the trend and extracts from them principles for what might be an emerging approach to sustainable design.

The antecedents of Green in Asia – bioclimaticism, tropicality, regionalism – were around in the 1960s, 70s and 80s, in part a reaction to the forces of urbanisation and globalisation that were sweeping the region.[1] The 1990s brought with them market reform and privatisation that accelerated change in many Asian societies, particularly in the once state-controlled economies of China and India. Negative social and environmental impacts of this transformation have led to questions about the part played by buildings and cities. The vulnerability of national and global economies to fluctuating oil prices and effects of climate change drove home the point that buildings, as key consumers and emitters, must be more efficient and responsible.

The convergence of thought on what constitutes a Green building has been rapid and widespread; in Asia the pace of

6

1_ Steele, J. (2005)

adoption has picked up since 2005. There were, at last count, 13 Green building assessment tools offering third-party audits and certification. There is much overlap in the way these tools are structured and administered. Each has near identical categories of assessment – energy, water, site, indoor environment – representing opportunities for impact mitigation. Credits earned for compliance are aggregated into a score that then becomes the basis for a project's rating.

Almost all Asian tools have been adapted from a few parent tools that were formulated for conditions in North America and the United Kingdom (UK).[2] As tools are tailored to a particular context, the score assigned to each category of compliance is altered to reflect local priorities. There are other attempts to indigenise a tool (for instance, inclusion of local codes) but the overarching goal is essentially the same: reduce resource use and adverse environmental effect, improve health and comfort of occupants. The case for Green is almost always made in the language of numbers – coefficients, concentrations, efficiencies, payback – argued as optimisation on the drawing board.

The question that few tools ask – one that is particularly important to the Asian condition – is what is to be done for communities that do not consume much to start with. What if the pressing problem is not yet consumption but, really, quality of life? There are criticisms that the tool-based approach to Greening does not address "regional distinctions and cultural differences enough", that tools are largely a "technocratic, top-down approach lacking specificity and social-ecological engagement".[3] Does Green, with emphasis on technology and optimisation, offer a perspective on what it means to be sustainable in Asia?

It should be said that Green is not, by definition, the same as sustainable. Green is a relative measure, an argument to *do less harm*. A building is deemed Green if it consumes or emits less than a predetermined benchmark. Sustainability is harder to

2_ Fowler, K.M. & Rauch, E.M. (2006)
3_ Cole, R.J. (2012a), p. 3

measure. There is no simple metric that sums up sustainability in buildings. To be sustainable is to live within the carrying capacity of our planet, consuming or emitting no faster than what can be replaced or repaired naturally. In other words, to *do no harm*. Sustainable design starts with an understanding of the exchange between buildings and the environment at large. Sustainability calls for a holistic and interconnected worldview in which ecological concerns take their place alongside the social and economic needs of communities.

The operative difference between Green and sustainable is the *system boundary* within which a building is said to operate. A system is defined by boundaries within which its elements interact. If the goal of Greening is to balance comfort and consumption over *five years* (time as the boundary for an exchange) one option would be to procure energy-efficient air conditioning equipment since this offers a calculable drop in energy use and operational costs. Were this increased to *20 years*, there would be less certainty, more risk, since we cannot pin down the availability or price of energy. It becomes necessary then to design for contingencies, to ask how indoor comfort would be sustained if reliance on mechanical cooling is compromised. The installed system might still be air conditioning, only now backed up with a hybrid, low-energy mode or natural ventilation that allows the building to continue to function without having to be retrofitted or rebuilt. The value proposition with an expanded time boundary is not just energy savings; it is *resilience* and *adaptation*. Changing the boundary dramatically changes how we estimate success and the course of action.

This book owes an intellectual debt to Peter Buchanan. *Ten Shades of Green* was an exhibition curated by Buchanan in 2000, and later a book of the same name. His remarkable, seemingly naïve descriptors of Green were published some years before assessment tools became synonymous with the subject. Buchanan picked ten high-performance buildings in Europe and North America from which he extracted ten characteristics of Green. Some were prescient of what is now central to the Green agenda: *low energy/high performance, recycling, health*. Some did not catch on: *embeddedness in place, happiness, long life/loose fit*. What is compelling about his take on the subject was the interconnectedness of ideas in service of a larger whole. *Long life/loose fit*, for instance, speaks of the building as a set of changing conditions across its lifespan. There was also an implicit refusal to limit the discourse to quantitative metrics. *Occupant well-being* meant more than setting the *right* indoor temperature; it was also about an individual's place in the community. *Ten Shades of Green* was, in that sense, truer to the triple bottom line of sustainability – *people, planet, profit* – than most present-day frameworks. In the decade since the exhibition and book, we have forgotten how to integrate. Greening has become an act of deconstruction with no game plan on how to put it back together again.

There were criticisms of the Buchanan approach that could be levelled at this book as well. It is worth starting with a few qualifiers on the road taken.

First, discussing sustainability on the scale of buildings is problematic. Much that happens at the level of the neighbourhood and city is important; much that governments do matters. There are many research institutions and professional associations dedicated to the larger question of the Asian city. They model the future in a manner that links urban and architectural typologies to consumption and quality of life. That said, very few projects built today are situated in an idealised eco-city. Project teams still take on one building at a time, often within poorly designed settings with no long-term vision. The stand-alone building – the unit of discussion in this book – may pose limits to the theory of future cities but it continues to be a fact of life on the drawing board. This book will be most useful to practitioners and other industry stakeholders engaged in the business of making buildings, and to educators who must teach the same.

Second, this book situates itself within a complex and rapid change sweeping Asia. The drivers of this change, as we know it, are the quest for growth – the year-on-year increments of national gross domestic product (GDP) – and the ensuing expectation of improved well-being. This dialogue, mostly between markets and governments, is conflicted between the short-term value of buildings as vehicles for capital investment, and their long-term impact and opportunity cost to community and nation. This book offers a critique of this rhetoric, of the language that is used, and its bias towards the interest of some players. A new lexicon is needed that will enable other stakeholders to be heard.

Third, there is risk in presenting a shortlist of projects from a region that is so vast and dynamic. I concede that for each project discussed here, there are many noteworthy examples that are not. It has been difficult getting in-depth information *and* broad-based representation, particularly from projects that have little documentation. The mix presented here represents the diversity of Asia, as much as possible. Five of the 13 projects in the latter part of this book are low-budget buildings that do not have the luxury of technology and tools. Eight of the 13 are not certified by an assessment tool; in effect they lie beneath the radar of Greening today. It is my hope that despite context – urban or rural, high-tech or low-tech, certified or not – the principles and their implementation shine through. The ecological site planning of the Vanke Centre could, for instance, be applied to other projects even where the budget is tight. The adaptation of vernacular solutions in the Pearl Academy of Fashion is a lesson for other developments, even those with bigger budgets.

A shared understanding of Green was and continues to be important. This is what this book is about, really. Assessment tools, as one such framework, provide a semblance of order today. In the 1990s the discourse on Green was a babble of confusing words and conflicting agendas. Tools like LEED and others that followed were an act of distillation. They collapsed complex ideas into simple structures, making possible new dialogue between stakeholders in the building sector. Having got here, the question we now face is how to leverage on market awareness and the acceptance of Greening towards less certain, more probing questions about sustainability. It is time to step out of our comfort zone again, this time to ask if the conventions of Greening are enough.

My roles as design practitioner and environmental consultant in Southeast Asia, coupled with teaching and editorial work that connects me to other parts of Asia, influence what is said here. The six principles proposed represent both a fundamental shift in ideology *and* continued concerns about the design-construction process. This middle ground between theory and practice will not be comfortable to many. Some will think *Greening Asia* goes too far in the change that it advocates; others will argue that it does not go far enough.

Whatever the reaction, this book will be deemed successful if it provokes a discussion on sustainability in Asia. This is not the last word; I fully expect others to weigh in with their ideas and perspectives.

Nirmal Kishnani, 2012

GREENING ASIA
REBOOTING THE CONVERSATION

The case for Greening is quite suddenly heard across Asia. This is paradoxical since most of Asia lives within its ecological limits; many of its buildings do not (as yet) consume excessive resources. Most are made with low-impact materials, built with local knowledge generations old. Yet we speak of Green buildings as something new.

The Green building in Asia, as we know it, needs a couple of qualifications.

First, Green has come to mean *certification* with a Green building assessment tool. It is not uncommon now, from Delhi to Bali to Beijing, for a discussion on Green to veer towards a particular tool. To earn a certificate, a building must secure credits for compliance with a checklist of stipulations that make up the tool. Certification costs money and takes time; it also promises savings and a measure of status. This appeals to some more than others, primarily developers catering to the rising middle class of Asian cities. The list of certified buildings confirms this trend: shopping centres, hotels, corporate headquarters, residential developments and institutional buildings.

Second, Greening is predicated on improving building performance in relation to known costs. Almost all decisions made in the name of Greening are tied to costs – a key consideration for a developer or owner. The building sector concerns itself really with the *conventions of Greening*, a reductive logic with emphasis on features and technologies that can be assessed for their short-term gains.

Green Buildings in Asia
Birth of a movement

The first decade of this century saw considerable activity on the Green building front, much of this spurred on by the formation of Green building councils (GBCs).[4] In 2001 there were four active GBCs (or equivalent) in Asia: Hong Kong, South Korea, India and Japan. There were several assessment tools in play – LEED,[5] BREEAM,[6] CASBEE,[7] HK-BEAM,[8] EEWH[9] – tied to growing industry awareness of the environmental impact of buildings. Because of their origins, LEED and BREEAM were regarded as imported impositions on the design-construction process. On the other hand, CASBEE, HK-BEAM and EEWH kept within the national boundaries for which they had been written.

Since 2004 Asia has seen the birth of new and emerging GBCs – Indonesia, Malaysia, Philippines, Singapore, Taiwan – and related

13

4_ Green Building Councils (GBC) are non-profit organisations affiliated with the World Green Building Council. Green building assessment tools are audit protocols for the assessment of buildings; these are typically owned and administered by GBCs. A building is awarded a rating on the basis of compliance with requirements stipulated by the tool.

5_ Leadership in Energy and Environmental Design; 1998, US | US Green Building Council. www.usgbc.org

6_ Building Research Establishment Environmental Assessment Method; 1990, UK | BREEAM, UK. www.breeam.org

7_ Comprehensive Assessment System for Building Environmental Efficiency; 2001, Japan | Institute of Building Environment and Energy Conservation, Japan. www.ibec.or.jp

8_ Hong Kong Building Environment Assessment Method; 1996, Hong Kong, People's Republic of China | BEAM Society, Hong Kong. www.beamsociety.org.hk

9_ Ecology, Energy, Waste and Health; 1999, Taiwan | Architecture and Building Research Institute, Ministry of Interior, Taiwan. www.abri.gov.tw

groups in China, Hong Kong, Sri Lanka, Thailand and Vietnam. Some assessment tools have become game changers in their markets. Singapore's Green Mark,[10] launched in 2005, is one of several in Asia that is government-owned; in 2008 it became mandatory for all new buildings in Singapore to be certified. By 2011 there were 25 million m² of Green Mark-certified space in Singapore, accounting for about 12% of all built-up space,[11] plus 12 million m² certified by the Singapore authorities in Vietnam, China and Malaysia. Other tools – such as LOTUS (Vietnam),[12] Green Building Index (Malaysia),[13] Green Building Evaluation Standard (China),[14] and LEED-India[15] – continue to be voluntary and confined to national boundaries.

The year-on-year reporting on certification numbers is, without fail, upbeat. In 2011 China announced that it had over 200 certified buildings plus another 300 on the way.[16] India had 200 certified buildings with some 1,300 in the pipeline.[17] In 2010 LEED-certified space in India added up to over 2,300,000 m² of built floor area, a jump from 1,800 m² in 2003. In 2009 nearly 200 Hong Kong properties were HK-BEAM certified, accounting for more than 37% of commercial space and 28% of homes built in that year. By 2030 Singapore aims to have 80% of its building stock certified – one of the most ambitious national targets to date. The region-wide surge is due in part to the successful marketing of tools as a way of differentiating a development and unlocking its latent value – *more savings*, *less waste* – promising a quick return on investment.

14

The question of opportunity cost interests another key stakeholder: the government. Over 40% of all energy and 25% of water consumed within a country is by its building sector. Eighty per cent of all energy used by a building is in its operations.[18] An industry-wide drop in consumption, however modest, can alter national dependency on imports, potentially deferring or eliminating the need for expanded utilities infrastructure. Governments are starting to see buildings as part of a strategy for coping with questions of energy and water security.

10_ Green Mark; 2005, Singapore | Building and Construction Authority, Singapore. www.bca.gov.sg
11_ Keung, J. (2011, 13–16 September)
12_ LOTUS; 2010, Vietnam | Vietnam Green Building Council. www.vgbc.org.vn
13_ Green Building Index; 2009, Malaysia | Green Building Index, Malaysia. www.greenbuildingindex.org
14_ Ministry of Construction of the People's Republic of China & National Head Office for Quality Supervision, Inspection and Quarantine of the People's Republic of China. (2006, 7 March)

15_ Leadership in Energy and Environmental Design, India; 2007, India | Indian Green Building Council. www.igbc.in
16_ Li, B. (2011, 13–16 September)
17_ Indian Green Building Council. www.igbc.in
18_ Life cycle analyses of buildings carried out in two Asian countries – Thailand and Japan – showed that operational energy accounts for some 80% of total energy used over a 50-year lifespan. Embedded energy in materials is next, accounting for approximately 15–17%. | Kofoworola, O.F. & Gheewala, S.H. (2009) and Michiya, S.T. & Tatsuo, O. (1998)

The politics of climate change is another important government concern today. The United Nations Intergovernmental Panel on Climate Change (IPCC)[19] and McKinsey report[20] both speak of buildings as a low-hanging fruit for greenhouse gas abatement. Buildings account for a third of all emissions and change that is needed to reduce emissions is straightforward and inexpensive.

With climate change on the negotiating table, governments feel the pressure to declare targets for abatement. India has committed to reducing its carbon intensity by 24% by 2020, against the year 2005. Within that same time frame, the Chinese government has promised a 40% reduction while the Taiwanese legislature has called for the creation of four low-carbon regions.[21] None of these targets can be met without involving the building sector.[22]

Despite their proclamations, Asian governments are also cautious about over-regulating their economies. Singapore, a front-runner in legislative control, only recently announced mandatory disclosure of energy use by all building owners,[23] a move that initially was feared to ride against market sentiment. In most of Asia, the situation is lax. Sixty-five per cent of all Green building-related activity in Southeast Asia, for instance, is voluntary or market-based; only 32% is driven by regulation.[24]

Governments are cautious for other reasons as well. In Vietnam, for instance, there was initial suspicion of LOTUS, the tool launched by the Vietnam Green Building Council, which was seen to be in competition with national standards and codes. The government of India went so far as to launch its own tool, GRIHA,[25] partly in response to what was seen to be the influence of LEED-India, which had been adapted by the Indian Green Building Council from the tool of the same name in the United States (US). In places where statutory codes and voluntary tools have worked in tandem – the former prescribing minimum standards, the latter describing best practice – the market moves ahead. Where the gap between the two is wide and enforcement lax, industry is slow to respond.

19_ IPCC. (2007)
20_ McKinsey & Company. (2008)
21_ Lewis, R. & Carmody, L. (2010, March) and Environmental Protection Administration, R.O.C. (Taiwan) (2009)
22_ United Nations Human Settlements Programme. (2010)
23_ Keung, J. (2011, 13-16 September)
24_ Anggadjaja, E. (2011, 13-16 September)
25_ Green Rating for Integrated Habitat Assessment, India. www.grihaindia.org

Few in the building sector today will openly admit that they do not care about Greening. As early as 2007, in a survey of 1,200 building professionals in Asia, 45% of all respondents said that they had high to very high levels of commitment to Green. Nearly all said that they wanted to be a part of an industry that valued the environment.[26] This was remarkable since many of them had probably only just heard of Green buildings. In another survey, the number of firms in Asia dedicated to Greening – defined as having no less than two-thirds of their projects seeking Green outcomes – was predicted to double from 36% in 2008 to 73% in 2013.[27]

Public declarations of Green buy-in are countered by scepticism in private. The argument for operational savings mostly benefits projects where such costs – utilities, maintenance, labour – are high and the developer is also the owner-occupier. There is less incentive when budgets are tight, labour costs low, and speculative forces rampant. The *business case* for Greening – that a Green building is a better investment with quicker returns – fails to find an audience in parts of developing Asia where the challenge is not just cost and investment but also quality of life and livelihood.

An Asian Conundrum
When more becomes less

Asia is in search of a better life. This means different things to different groups since there are vast disparities of wealth and well-being in the region.[28] It is home to half of the world's absolute poor living on less than US$1.25 a day. It has the largest share of the world's slum population – more than half, about 505.5 million people.[29] Asia is also home to the world's fastest growing club of millionaires. In 2011 Singapore was reported to have the highest number of millionaires per head in the world; one in every six households had assets in excess of one million dollars.[30]

En route to a better – or the good – life Asia finds itself confronted with escalating environmental costs. China is now the world's

26_ Kerr, T. (2008)
27_ McGraw Hill Construction. (2008)
28_ In 2010, Asia accounted for 30% of the world's land mass but 60% of its population or 1.76 billion people. | United Nations Human Settlements Programme. (2010)
29_ United Nations Human Settlements Programme. (2010)
30_ "As the financial markets improved (in 2010), global wealth grew in nearly every region in the world. The fastest, at 17.1%, came in the Asia Pacific region (excluding Japan), followed by North America at 10.2%... While China and India are driving wealth creation in Asia, Singapore also grew at a fast pace. The number of millionaire households in Singapore jumped about 38.6% in 2010, to 170,000, from nearly 123,000 in 2009... The country has had the largest proportion of millionaire households for several years and the share continues to grow. Singapore's millionaire households increased to 15.5% of total households in 2010 from 11.4% in 2009." | Wong, V. (2011, 2 June)

36

PERCENTAGE OF FIRMS SURVEYED IN THE ASIAN BUILDING SECTOR IN 2008
THAT REPORTED THEY WERE DEDICATED TO GREENING

73

PERCENTAGE OF FIRMS IN THE SAME 2008 SURVEY THAT DECLARED THEIR INTENTION
TO BE DEDICATED TO GREENING BY 2013

largest emitter of greenhouse gases[31] even though its emissions
per head are below the world average. Between 1990 and 2007,
which saw rapid growth, China's gross domestic product (GDP) per
head increased almost eightfold[32] while its emissions per head
increased by over 160%. Over the same period India's GDP per head
tripled as its emissions increased by 130%.

The link between wealth and environmental impact is found in
other metrics. Countries with the largest ecological footprints,
for instance, are also the ones with the highest GDP and Human
Development Index (the inverse is also true). The richest countries
are also the most urbanised. In 2010 42.2% of Asia's population
lived in cities; cities accounted for 80% of its GDP.[33] Read together,
these numbers suggest that wealth is linked to urban living and
the pursuit of well-being is contingent on being part of the urban
economy. This perception fuels migration to cities.

Since 2005 Asia's urban population has increased by 37 million
each year, exceeding 100,000 a day. In 2010 it had seven of the

17

31_ "China emits more CO_2 than the US and
Canada put together – up by 171% since
the year 2000... India is now the world's
third biggest emitter of CO_2 – pushing
Russia into fourth place... For comparison,
the whole world emits 4.49 tonnes per
person. China, by contrast, emits under
6 tones per person, India only 1.38." |
Roger, S. and Evans, L. (2011)

32_ www.imf.org

33_ United Nations Human Settlements
Programme (UN-HABITAT) (2010)

42.2

PERCENTAGE OF ASIAN POPULATION
LIVING IN CITIES IN 2010

80

PERCENTAGE OF REGION'S GDP
ATTRIBUTED TO URBAN ECONOMIES
IN 2010

ten most populous cities in the world.[34] By 2025 China will have
221 cities with populations in excess of one million; Europe by
contrast will have 25.[35] In 2011, India was reported to have
350 million living in cities, a figure expected to reach 600 million
by 2030.[36] It is predicted that by 2050, 64% of Asia's population
will be living in cities.[37] This surge will have a ripple effect, pushing
housing, industry and agriculture further out into periurban and
rural areas where they in turn will displace smaller settlements
and ecosytems.

34_ United Nations Human Settlements
     Programme. (2010)
35_ Economist Intelligence Unit. (2011)
36_ Gopal, K. (2011)
37_ ADB. (2011, August)

100,000

NUMBER OF PERSONS PER DAY
THAT MOVED INTO A CITY IN ASIA IN 2011;
A TOTAL OF 37 MILLION PER YEAR

1,000

HECTARES OF PRODUCTIVE AGRICULTURAL
LAND THAT ARE CONVERTED TO URBAN USE
EVERY DAY IN ASIA

20,000

NUMBER OF NEW HOMES NEEDED EVERY DAY
TO ACCOMMODATE THE INFLUX OF MIGRANTS
INTO ASIA'S CITIES

64

PERCENTAGE OF ASIA'S POPULATION
LIVING IN CITIES BY 2050, AN INCREASE OF
23.5% OVER 2011 FIGURES

19

Every day in Asia some 1,000 hectares of productive agricultural
land are converted to urban use.[38] Southeast Asia, in particular, has
also seen wide scale loss of rainforests as land is cleared to make
way for agriculture and biofuels, which in turn has had a direct,
measurable impact on climate change.[39] From 2000 to 2005,
for instance, Vietnam lost more than 50% of its primary forests,
placing it amongst countries with the worst deforestation rate.[40]
More than 366,400 hectares of agricultural land along coastal
plains and the delta bordering Ho Chi Minh City were turned into

38_ United Nations Human Settlements
Programme. (2010)

39_ "Southeast Asia, with 203 million hectares
of forests, accounts for 5.2% of the global
total. Expansion of large-scale commercial
crops is a significant driver of deforestation
in the region, especially as food grain
prices rise and oil palm cultivation grows
to meet the rising demand for biodiesel.
In the early 2000s, about 3 million hectares
of peat land in Southeast Asia had been
burnt, releasing between 3–5 petagrams
of carbon (PgC). Draining of peat lands
has affected an additional 6 million hectares
and released a further 1–2 PgC." | ADB.
(2010a, November)

40_ Butler, R.A. (2005, 16 November)

industrial parks and urban areas.[41] In the 2010 master plan for Hanoi, 110 km² of agricultural land was converted for urban-related use,[42] resulting in loss of livelihood for more than 150,000 farmers, many of whom migrated to the city, adding to its congestion.

As more opt for the urban life, the Asian city starts to fray. Social inequity becomes entrenched and self-perpetuating; many of the poor and poorly-educated who move into urban ghettoes find it difficult to escape the poverty trap. Their well-being is affected by failures of the physical environment – density, crowding, pollution – and compounded by social fragmentation and isolation.

With urban densities reaching as high as 20,000 people per km²,[43] public infrastructure struggles to keep up as the upkeep and administration of cities become increasingly complex.[44] The influx of migrants leads to a vicious cycle of expansion and degradation where a city's waterways double up as open sewers and its outdoor air quality deteriorates to the extent that natural ventilation is a health hazard. Poor air quality, for instance, causes over half a million deaths each year across Asia.[45]

As a city expands, so does its ecological footprint. In most Asian cities, this is some 5 global hectares per head. Against current population numbers, each person on the planet should average no more than 1.7 global hectares.

20

The overcrowded city with stretched infrastructure is particularly vulnerable to extreme weather and other natural vectors. The 2011 floods in Bangkok were a textbook example of a city's interdependence with the countryside and its connectivity to the global economy. By year's end, over 600 persons in various parts of Thailand that were affected by floods had died and over 5,000 jobs had been lost. Some 790,000 people employed by 20,000 firms were affected in one way or another and 70% of flood-hit areas experienced a rise in food prices. It was predicted that long after the flood waters had receded, consumers around the world would

41_ ADB, HCMC People's Committee & DONRE. (2009, 25 April)

42_ Nguyen, V.S. (2009, January)

43_ Urban densities in Asia are double that of Latin America, triple that of Europe and ten times higher than the US. | United Nations Human Settlements Programme. (2010)

44_ "Rapid urbanisation is something that India was not prepared to deal with... The second largest urban system in the world was characterised by rickety infrastructure, lopsided development, slum proliferation, traffic congestion, as well as water and sanitation deficits. Cities have started merging with surrounding municipalities and villages to become greater cities. Mumbai, Delhi, Bangalore and Hyderabad grew to anywhere between three to four times... Hyderabad, the capital city of Andhra Pradesh, was declared a greater city in 2007. As the population doubled, the city swelled from 174–625 km². The city as such was experiencing difficulties in providing water supply and sewerage services to areas in the old municipal limits – the "Hi-tech City" that boasts state-of-the-art infrastructure and iconic buildings had a maze of fibre optic lines for communication but had no underground sewer lines." | Gopal, K. (2011)

45_ United Nations Human Settlements Programme. (2010)

16/20

16 OUT OF 20 MOST DENSE CITIES IN THE WORLD ARE IN ASIA

10,000 -20,000

NUMBER OF PERSONS PER KM^2 IN ASIAN CITIES

519,000

PREMATURE DEATHS EACH YEAR RESULTING FROM POOR AIR QUALITY IN ASIAN CITIES

15/20

15 OUT OF 20 CITIES MOST VULNERABLE TO SEA LEVEL RISE IN THE WORLD ARE IN ASIA

95,000,000

NUMBER OF PEOPLE IN ASIA AFFECTED BY RISING SEA LEVELS BY 2070

22

see a spike in the price of external hard drives, due to production slowdowns in Bangkok's industrial parks.[46]

The double whammy of surging urban density and looming climate change is set to worsen. Experts predict that by 2050, 15 out of the 20 cities most vulnerable to climate change will be in Asia. A sea level rise of 1 m will, for instance, result in land losses of up to 25,000 km^2 in Vietnam and 34,000 km^2 in Indonesia.[47] By 2070, it is predicted that 95,000,000 people in Asia will be adversely affected by sea level rise.[48]

46_ Various online news agencies: BBC, Xinhua, Reuters and Associate Press
47_ United Nations Human Settlements Programme. (2010)
48_ Nicholls, R.J., Hanson, S., Herweijer, C., Patmore, N., Hallegatte, S., Jan Corfee-Morlot, Jean Chateau & Muir-Wood, R. (2007)

Is Greening Enough?
Questioning the questions

There are, it seems, two ongoing discourses – one making the case for Green buildings, the other arguing for sustainable development. The disparity between the two is wide enough for concern.

Green assessment tools in Asia, for instance, stipulate that a 30–45% improvement in energy efficiency must be attained before a project can qualify for a high tier of certification.[49] Experts estimate that a *net* 50–80% reduction in greenhouse gas emissions is needed if global warming is to stabilise by 2100 (the lower figure applicable to developing countries, the upper to developed countries[50]). Given that energy use and emissions in Asia are interlinked – 80% of all primary energy in 2006 was from the burning of fossil fuels – there is a mismatch here. The top-rated Green buildings in Asia are on a less strict diet, so to speak, than what the experts say is necessary. Equally disturbing is that there are no prescribed energy targets for low to mid tiers of certification to meet.

Compounding the low expectations of Green building performance are low numbers of certification relative to the pace of development. China's 200 certified buildings, for instance, represent a negligible fraction of the 2 billion m² of new floor area that is added each year to an existing stock of 44 billion m². Even if regulation kicks in – with the prospect of 1,000 new certifications a year – it will not be enough to mitigate climate change.

49_ The five Asian assessment tools that are the point of reference here and in subsequent sections are: [1] LEED-India, Abridged Reference Guide for New Construction and Major Renovations, Version 1.0, 2007; [2] HK-BEAM Version 4.04 New Buildings, 2004; [3] BCA Green Mark for New Non-Residential Buildings, Version 4.0, 2010; [4] Green Building Index Assessment Criteria for Non-Residential New Construction Version 1.0, 2009; [5] LOTUS Sustainable Building Assessment System Version 1.5.5, 2008.

50_ ADB. (2011, August)

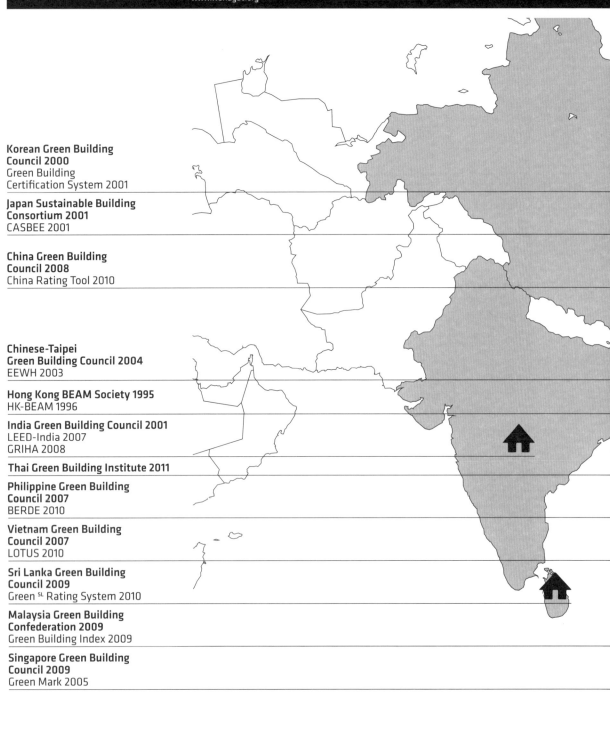

Korean Green Building Council 2000
Green Building Certification System 2001

Japan Sustainable Building Consortium 2001
CASBEE 2001

China Green Building Council 2008
China Rating Tool 2010

Chinese-Taipei Green Building Council 2004
EEWH 2003

Hong Kong BEAM Society 1995
HK-BEAM 1996

India Green Building Council 2001
LEED-India 2007
GRIHA 2008

Thai Green Building Institute 2011

Philippine Green Building Council 2007
BERDE 2010

Vietnam Green Building Council 2007
LOTUS 2010

Sri Lanka Green Building Council 2009
Green SL Rating System 2010

Malaysia Green Building Confederation 2009
Green Building Index 2009

Singapore Green Building Council 2009
Green Mark 2005

Indonesia Green Building Council 2008
Green Ship 2010

1990 | Intergovernmental Panel on Climate Change (IPCC), First Assessment Report

1992 | Earth Summit Rio, United Nations Conference on Environment and Development

1995 | IPCC Second Assessment Report: Climate Change 1995
1996 | COP1 Berlin
1996 | COP2 Geneva
1997 | COP3 Kyoto
1998 | COP4 Buenos Aires
1999 | COP5 Bonn
2000 | COP6 The Hague

19 90

19 95

20 00

US Green Building Council | **1993**

Hong Kong BEAM Society | **1995**

World Green Building Council | **1999**

Korea Green Building Council | **2000**

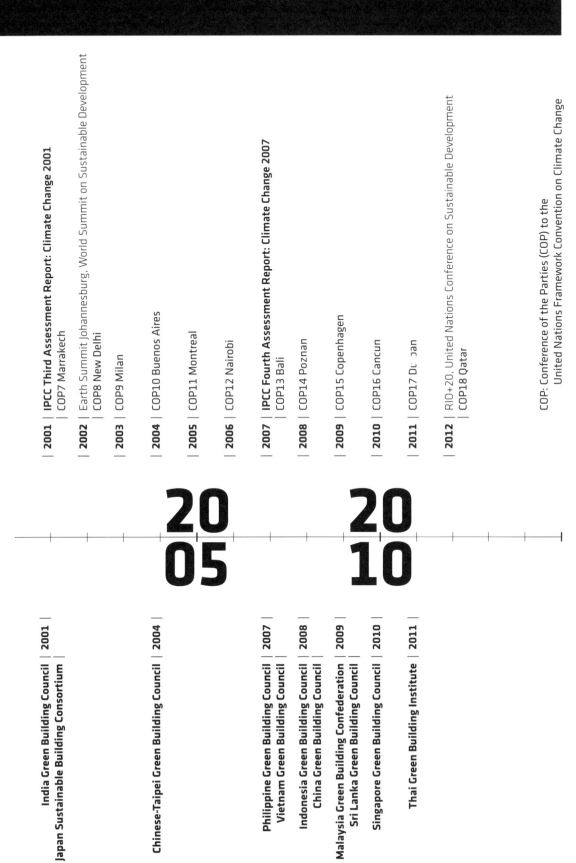

2001 | IPCC Third Assessment Report: Climate Change 2001 | COP7 Marrakech

2002 | Earth Summit Johannesburg, World Summit on Sustainable Development | COP8 New Delhi

2003 | COP9 Milan

2004 | COP10 Buenos Aires

2005 | COP11 Montreal

2006 | COP12 Nairobi

2007 | IPCC Fourth Assessment Report: Climate Change 2007 | COP13 Bali

2008 | COP14 Poznan

2009 | COP15 Copenhagen

2010 | COP16 Cancun

2011 | COP17 Durban

2012 | RIO+20, United Nations Conference on Sustainable Development | COP18 Qatar

COP: Conference of the Parties (COP) to the
United Nations Framework Convention on Climate Change

2005
2010

India Green Building Council | 2001 |
Japan Sustainable Building Consortium |

Chinese-Taipei Green Building Council | 2004 |

Philippine Green Building Council | 2007 |
Vietnam Green Building Council |

Indonesia Green Building Council | 2008 |
China Green Building Council |

Malaysia Green Building Confederation | 2009 |
Sri Lanka Green Building Council |

Singapore Green Building Council | 2010 |

Thai Green Building Institute | 2011 |

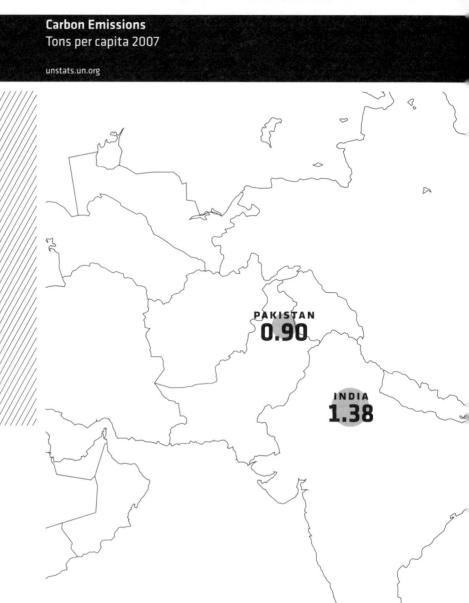

28

United States	19.74
Australia	19.00
Canada	17.91
Germany	10.22
United Kingdom	8.97
France	6.50

PAKISTAN
0.90

INDIA
1.38

SRI LANKA
0.62

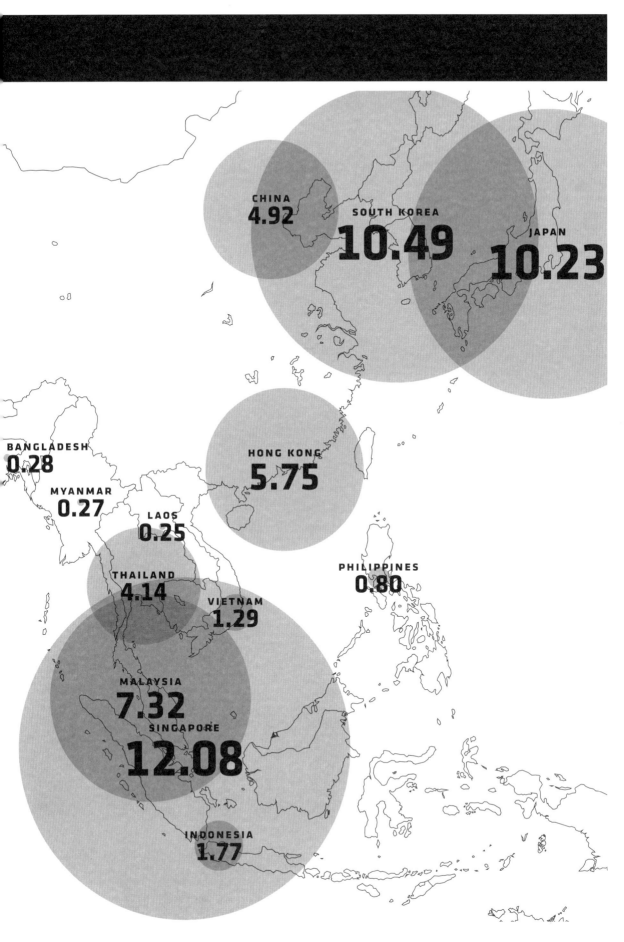

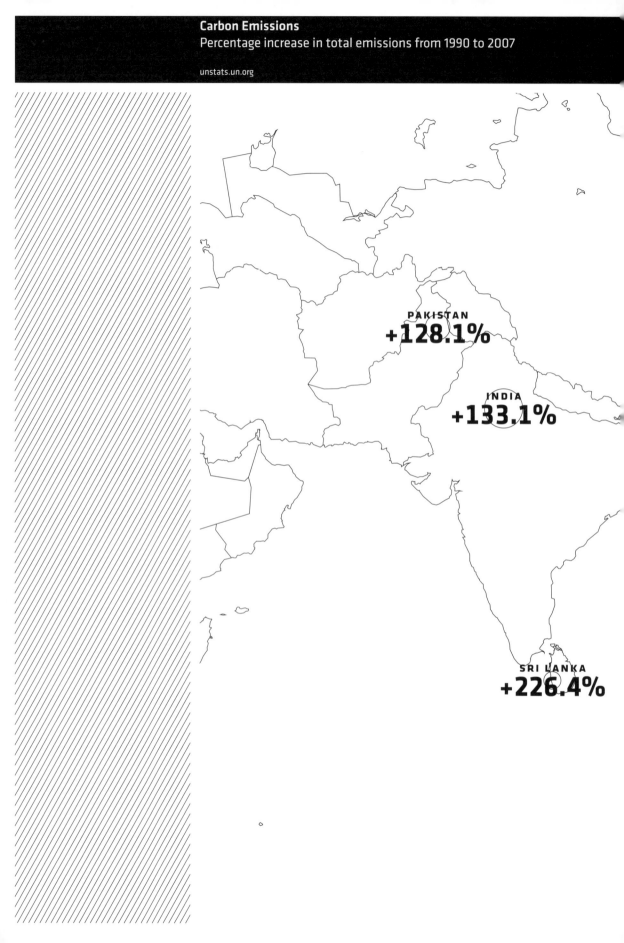

Carbon Emissions
Percentage increase in total emissions from 1990 to 2007

unstats.un.org

PAKISTAN
+128.1%

INDIA
+133.1%

SRI LANKA
+226.4%

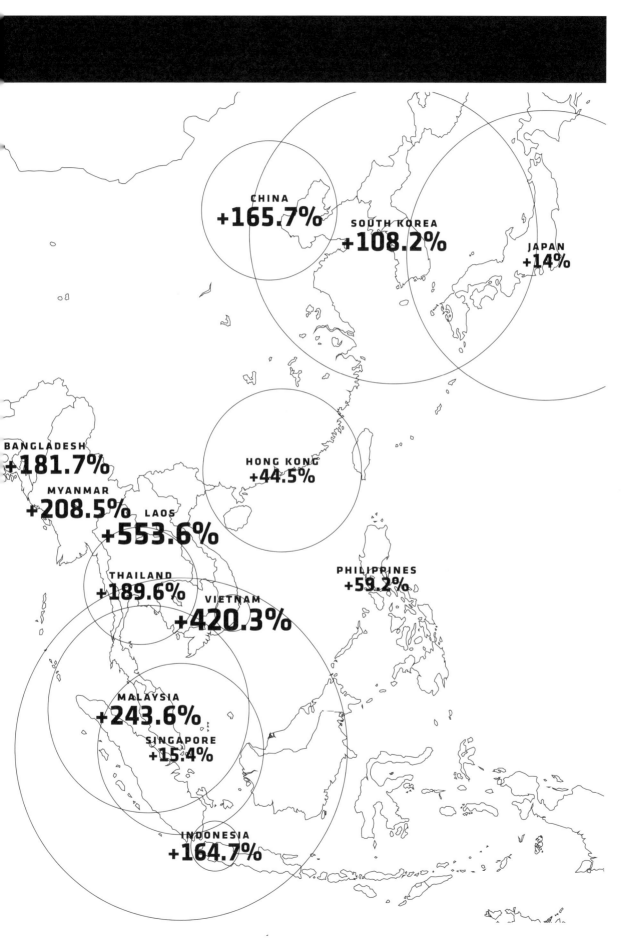

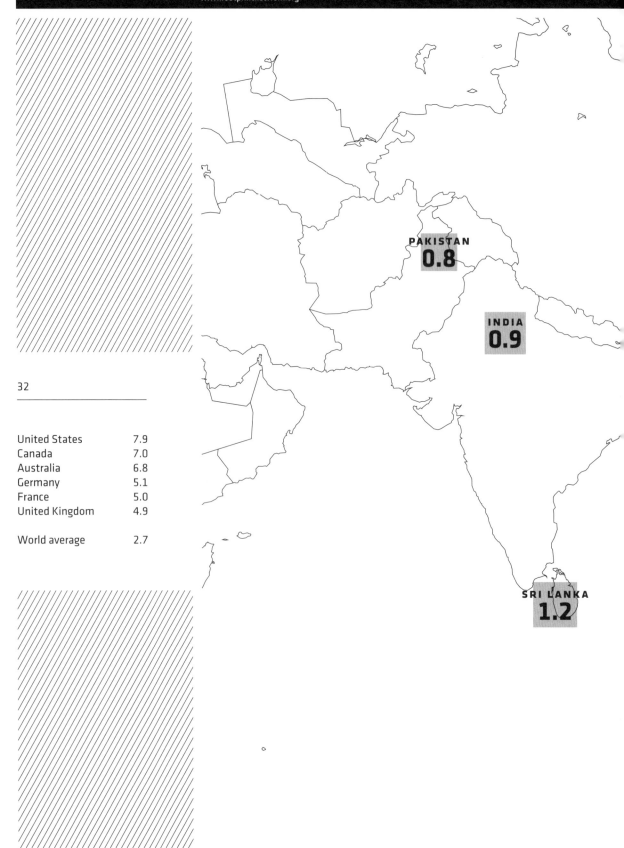

32

United States	7.9
Canada	7.0
Australia	6.8
Germany	5.1
France	5.0
United Kingdom	4.9
World average	2.7

PAKISTAN
0.8

INDIA
0.9

SRI LANKA
1.2

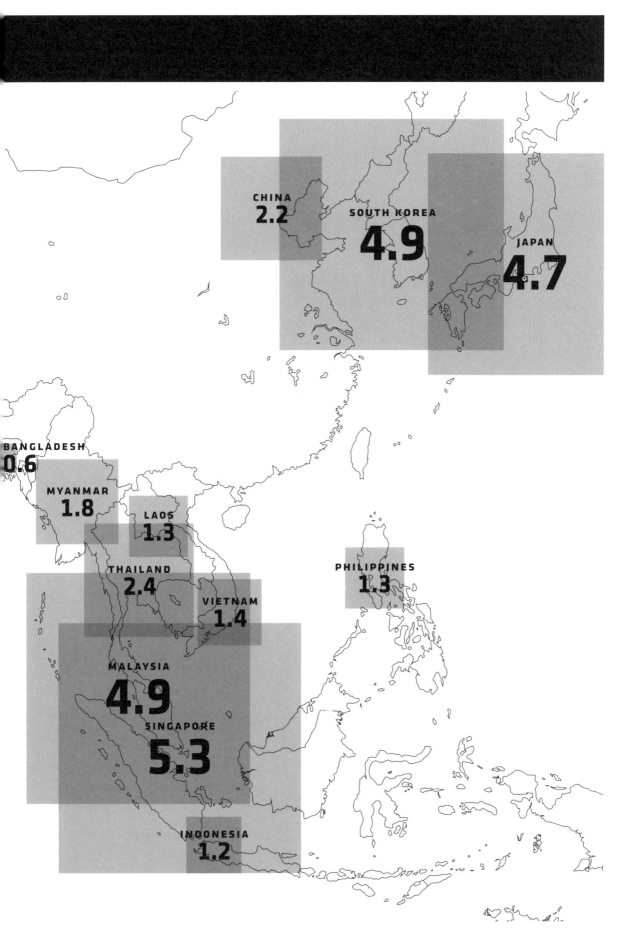

■ 1990
■ 2007

SINGAPORE

3.1 | 5.3

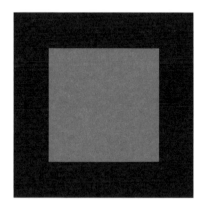

SOUTH KOREA

3.0 | 4.9

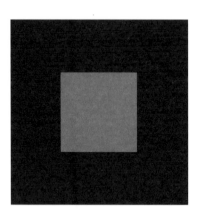

MALAYSIA

2.1 | 4.9

JAPAN

4.5 | 4.7

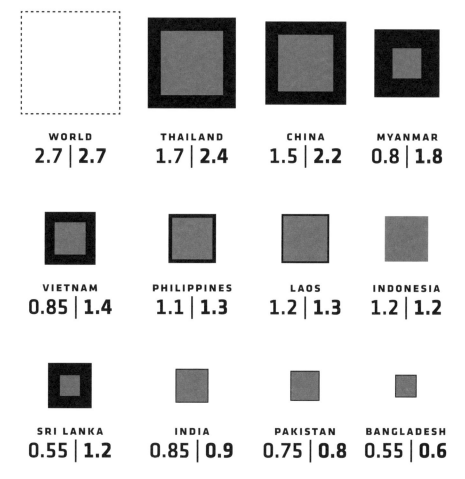

WORLD
2.7 | 2.7

THAILAND
1.7 | 2.4

CHINA
1.5 | 2.2

MYANMAR
0.8 | 1.8

VIETNAM
0.85 | 1.4

PHILIPPINES
1.1 | 1.3

LAOS
1.2 | 1.3

INDONESIA
1.2 | 1.2

SRI LANKA
0.55 | 1.2

INDIA
0.85 | 0.9

PAKISTAN
0.75 | 0.8

BANGLADESH
0.55 | 0.6

Wealth

Gross national income per capita 2010

data.worldbank.org/indicator

$ = US$500

36

	US$
United States	47,140
Australia	43,740
Germany	43,330
France	42,390
Canada	41,950
United Kingdom	38,540
World average	9,097

MALAYSIA

US$7,900

$$$$$$$$$$
$$$$$$

INDONESIA

US$2,580

$$$$$

INDIA

US$1,350

$$$

LAOS

US$1,010

$$

JAPAN

US$42,150

$$$$$$$$$
$$$$$$$$$
$$$$$$$$$
$$$$$$$$$
$$$$$$$$$
$$$$$$$$$
$$$$$$$$$
$$$$$$$$$
$$$$

SINGAPORE

US$40,920

$$$$$$$$$
$$$$$$$$$
$$$$$$$$$
$$$$$$$$$
$$$$$$$$$
$$$$$$$$$
$$$$$$$$$
$$$$$$$$$
$$

HONG KONG

US$32,900

$$$$$$$$$
$$$$$$$$$
$$$$$$$$$
$$$$$$$$$
$$$$$$$$$
$$$$$$$$$
$$$$$

SOUTH KOREA

US$19,980

$$$$$$$$$
$$$$$$$$$
$$$$$$$$$
$$$$$$$$$

CHINA

US$4,260

$$$$$$$$

THAILAND

US$4,210

$$$$$$$

SRI LANKA

US$2,290

$$$$$

PHILIPPINES

US$2,050

$$$$

VIETNAM

US$1,100

$$

PAKISTAN

US$1,050

$$

BANGLADESH

US$640

$

JAPAN HONG KONG SOUTH KOREA SINGAPORE MALAYSIA SRI LANKA

Human Development Index 2010

Average achievement in three basic dimensions of human development: long and healthy life, knowledge and a decent standard of living

hdr.undp.org

Threshold of very high human development (2011)

0.889

Threshold of low human development (2011)

0.456

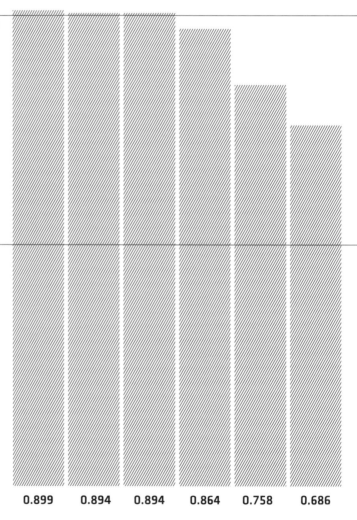

JAPAN	HONG KONG	SOUTH KOREA	SINGAPORE	MALAYSIA	SRI LANKA
0.899	0.894	0.894	0.864	0.758	0.686

Urbanisation

Percentage of population living in cities in 2010

www.unstats.un.org

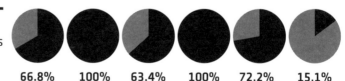

| 66.8% | 100% | 63.4% | 100% | 72.2% | 15.1% |

 Urban population    Rural population

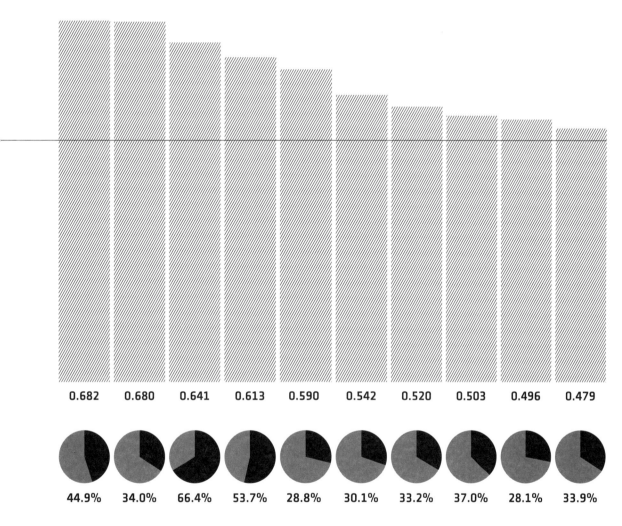

CHINA	THAILAND	PHILIPPINES	INDONESIA	VIETNAM	INDIA	LAOS	PAKISTAN	BANGLADESH	MYANMAR
0.682	0.680	0.641	0.613	0.590	0.542	0.520	0.503	0.496	0.479
44.9%	34.0%	66.4%	53.7%	28.8%	30.1%	33.2%	37.0%	28.1%	33.9%

EN I

T ENOUGH?

LDINGS

LL-BEING?

JNIVERSAL

TO GREENI

UTCOMES

ABLE?

E VALUE

r.?

CONVENTIONS
OF GREENING
FIVE
QUESTIONS

Across the region, the *conventions of Greening* are proving to be insufficient. This may be because a good deal of what is done in the name of Green conforms to industry mindsets that were in place before Green made inroads into mainstream thinking. To bring about the needed paradigm shift towards sustainable architecture, there must be critical reflection of what is deemed Green and why. Equally important is understanding how the building sector knows when it has done enough. The following questions probe these conventions and the *system boundaries* that frame them.

Q1   How efficient is efficient enough?
      Are we getting false comfort from numbers?

      Efficiency is at the heart of Greening in Asia. This is borne out by the fact that in most assessment tools, project teams are prompted to select resource-efficient fittings and technologies and, where components come together to form a system, they aim for systemic optimisation.

The most common efficiency index is kilowatt hours (kWh) per m^2 of gross floor area (GFA).[51] This amalgamates all energy used by the building (cooling, heating, lighting, plug loads), normalising it to floor area and operational hours. Targets for energy efficiency vary across rating tools; Singapore's Green Mark specifies a prerequisite 30% reduction for its highest rating[52] while HK-BEAM requires 45%.

This approach raises several questions. Should, for instance, efficiency be estimated on the basis of unit floor area[53] or should it account for consumption per occupant? Should there be continued reliance on kWh as the unit of measure, given that greenhouse gas emissions are the real concern?

There are ongoing discussions on what a low-carbon economy might mean in Asia but most assessment tools continue to rely on units of electrical power at point of use. Experts complain also of how poorly performance is measured, if and when it is measured at all.[54] A building that is certified might, in the years that follow its completion, consume more than its neighbours and yet continue to bear the Green label.[55]

Many tools ask that energy demand be estimated using modelling software in which a virtual model is generated, describing a building's geometry and layout, its reliance on electro-mechanical systems and operational hours. This is then compared to a second computation featuring the same building with beyond code-compliant fittings and systems and added Green technologies

43

51_ Energy Efficiency Index (EEI) is also normalised to an average number of hours the building is in operation each year.

52_ Prerequisite for Platinum rating for Green Mark, Non-Residential New Buildings, Version 4.0. | Building and Construction Authority, Singapore. www.bca.gov.sg

53_ "Kilowatt hour per m^2 is a measure of usage, not efficiency. You cannot conflate the two. An effective use of a building (should be its) embedded energy... divided by all these people working there... So when the LEO building in Malaysia claims to be 100 kWh/m^2/year, you have to compare it against equivalent density of people... Using (the metric of) energy per m^2... what can be even more efficient than... an abandoned warehouse? There is no water, electricity, there's nothing. It's totally green!" | Lee, E.L. (2011)

54_ "The thing that speaks loudest is measured performance. What is not subjective is high accuracy measurement... Measure accurately and let that be the bottom line. But nobody likes that (because) everything that consumes energy must be considered... nobody thinks issues through in detail." | Lee, E.L. (2011)

55_ "The best data available shows that on average, (LEED buildings) use more energy than comparable buildings. What has been created is the image of energy-efficient buildings, but not actual energy efficiency... The LEED system does this by rewarding designers for predicting that a building will save energy, not for proving that a building actually saves energy." | Gifford, H. (2008)

and features. Efficiency is the difference between the two models. This approach has its critics. Efficiency here depends in part on how poorly designed the initial model is; in part it depends on how many add-ons are procured. It does not address strategies for demand reduction. A project, for instance, might be rewarded for use of high-performance glass but not penalised for having large windows facing west. Some tools are moving away from this comparison with self, asking instead for comparison with industry averages. Malaysia's Green Building Index (GBI) and Vietnam's LOTUS, for instance, stipulate benchmarks of energy use by typical buildings.

There is also concern that the emphasis on electro-mechanical efficiency encourages reliance on these same systems. Credits for daylight versus energy-efficient electrical lighting and controls, for instance, are skewed in favour of the latter. While LOTUS gives equal credits to either, Malaysia's GBI and HK-BEAM offer more to the latter (four credits for electrical lighting, three for daylight). Singapore's Green Mark offers twice as many for electrical lighting than daylight (12 versus six). Is there enough incentive here for a project team to take on daylight design – a front-end decision affecting a building's form, orientation, openings – when electrical lighting and the procurement of energy-efficient equipment gets the same or more credits?

//

Efficiency is defined as the rate of consumption within site and shell. The approach to estimating efficiency reinforces the notion of a building as an assembly of parts, each with its own short-term returns. Technology is the enabler of performance. Passive strategies which lower reliance on electro-mechanical systems are undervalued. There are industry concerns about how consumption is measured and benchmarked, bringing into question the useful-ness of post-occupancy data.

Q2 How do buildings foster well-being?
Is this enough to describe what occupants need?

Occupant well-being in buildings is gauged using metrics afforded by the science of comfort and health. These assume that well-being takes place within bandwidths describing certain ambient conditions – thermal, visual, acoustical, chemical, biological – collectively known as Indoor Environmental Quality (IEQ). Straying from prescribed bandwidths can lead to health problems, or at the least, discomfort and dissatisfaction which can in turn affect productivity. These symptoms, where they occur, can often be traced to decisions made on the drawing board or at the construction site. Certain pathogens and smells, for instance, are linked to particular materials and finishes or the operation of electro-mechanical systems.

Assessment tools in Asia differ considerably on the number of credits assigned to well-being. Green Mark, Singapore, assigns 8% of achievable credits to IEQ. For LEED-India the figure is 21.7%; GBI Malaysia, 24.4% and LOTUS, Vietnam, 27%. With the exception of HK-BEAM – which requires its platinum winners to show at least a 65% compliance with listed IEQ requirements – it is not difficult in practice to play down well-being and still be certified.

Credit weightage is only part of the problem. There are also questions about the assumptions that drive these requirements. Conditions for comfort, in particular, are neither universal nor solely physiological. An occupant's response to an ambient condition is affected by his/her expectations that are in part about preferences and needs. Experts talk about *adaptive comfort*,[56] the process by which occupants actively manage their own comfort. The adaptive theory of comfort has led to interest in the building-occupant interface. Personalised lighting and cooling controls, for instance, permit occupants to decide how much they need and when they need it. This is a noteworthy shift away from the *principle of avoidance* – where indoor conditions are designed to *not exceed* prescribed limits – towards *affordance*, where the

56_ Nicol, J.F. & Humphreys, M.A. (2002)

attributes and interfaces that address individual needs and preferences are made available.

Another problem with the IEQ approach is that it is often associated with the design of *electro-mechanical systems*. To stipulate that comfort is attained at about 25°C air temperature is to say that air conditioning is needed in many parts of Asia most of the time. Critics argue that the emphasis on these international standards of comfort within assessment tools favour a reliance on electro-mechanical systems over passive strategies or low-energy cooling systems that are indigenous to a place.[57]

//

Well-being, like efficiency, adopts an approach in which technology becomes an enabler. This framing of well-being as a physiological response to indoor attributes is incomplete since well-being is also psychological and therefore cannot be reduced to a set of universal IEQ prescriptions. The principle of avoidance that underpins well-being requirements does not encourage the consideration of what different people, living and working in different conditions in Asia, might need or prefer.

57_ "Most of the architecture in India prior to '91... was by its very nature, Green. It responded to the sun, had shading devices, thermal mass, courtyards, etc. Post '91, there was a dramatic shift; we started getting buildings designed by a variety of international architects which had a big influence on domestic architects and clients. Clients started perceiving all-glass buildings as a symbol of corporate power even though most of India is in a hot climate. Along came LEED at that point in time, bringing with it a mechanism for rating buildings Silver, Gold or Platinum without due consideration of climate, of where the project was in India, whether it was in a warm-humid, or in a hot-dry or composite climate with stringent requirements on indoor air quality which necessitated hermetically sealed air-conditioned buildings. There was no emphasis on passive and low-energy architecture which further gave license to these high energy-consuming, modernist, non-climate responsive blocks to further percolate through the country, qualifying themselves as Green architecture. It also gave license to a lot of engineering firms to proclaim themselves as masters of Green. Within a short span of 20 years, we disbanded thousands of years of knowledge of passive and low-energy architecture. In a country where a large portion of buildings is still naturally ventilated – and you can't achieve a LEED rating for a naturally ventilated building – this rating tool has caused, I think, severe, irreversible damage." | Rastogi, M. (2011)

Q3 **Is there a universal approach to Greening?**
Should Greening not depend on where a building is?

Why do so many buildings across Asia – despite differences of climate and context – look the *same*? And why is it hard to differentiate the Green-certified ones from the rest? How a building looks says something of how it functions. How it functions should say something of where it is. Does the proliferation of glass-clad, climate-controlled buildings across Asia suggest there is a universal template at work?

The building sector in Asia has for decades been powered by the flow of ideas and products via global networks and supply chains that connect continents. The widespread availability of curtain wall systems, for instance, means that an architect in Manila will have the same envelope options as another in, say, Guangzhou. If both share a predilection for sharp lines and clean geometry, it is likely that they will design two similar-looking buildings resembling something they might admire in New York.

This overlap of technological availability and stylistic preference is powered by potent media coverage in Asia. This coverage depicts modernity as an act of acquisition, typically from more developed nations. In this context the question of how glass skin performs in the climates of Manila or Guangzhou becomes a secondary consideration.

Electro-mechanical systems – easily available worldwide – reinforce this view. They delimit plan depth (thereby allowing an architect to pursue any form or style) since there is no need to ventilate or illuminate through the building skin. Deep-plan and compact buildings cost less per unit envelope surface area (for a given built-up floor area) and they make more efficient use of central support services, such as lifts. Bigger floor plates can also be divided into any configuration of units for sale or rental. Air conditioning ensures a higher sale or rental price since many buyers in Asia expect this from a better class of buildings.

In this context it is hard to make a case for passive design, the climate-moderating principles that offer a different kind of comfort. Assessment tools provide no incentive to weigh, say, traditional shading devices against imported low-e glass. Both are seen to moderate solar heat gain. It does not matter if a building uses ground cooling tubes – that use little or no energy – or energy-efficient air conditioning. Some tools, in fact, offer credits to the latter but not the former.

It should be said that there is some recognition in Greening for local sourcing which connects a building to site and location. Almost all tools offer credits for renewable energy, the on-site use of wind or solar technologies. Many encourage the use of regional materials. A few reward rainwater collection. But these continue to be lightweight considerations. Malaysia's GBI gives local or regional sourcing up to eight credit points from a maximum of 100. For renewable energy, which almost all tools mention, the expectation is relatively modest: that up to 7% plus of the total energy needs will be met with renewables.

//

The building sector in Asia is locked into a dependence on global supply chains that influences how buildings are designed and relate to climate and locale. In years to come, these supply chains will be disrupted by the undersupply or overpricing of resources, much of it contingent on availability of fossil fuels.[58] The reliance on globally sourced hardware is deepened by a preference for certain architectural styles and consumer trends in real estate. Collectively, these undervalue local resources and knowledge.

58_ "We grow our food with oil, we make clothing with oil, and we certainly build, light, cool and heat our buildings with oil. You are probably wearing petrochemical clothing, recently ate food grown with natural gas fertilisers, will soon use a gas powered vehicle, and will sleep tonight in a climate controlled with fossil fuel energy. All of this might be fine except for a few problems only recently coming to light: the many and huge toxic hazards to people and environment that are an oil-based economy and its by-products, the abrupt and unpredictable changes to global climate caused by the recent increase of carbon and other substances in the air, and, last but certainly not least, the fact that supply is limited: we've already used up half the oil we ever had." | King, B. (2008), p. 97

Q4   Must all outcomes be measurable?
    Is a building not also a cultural object?
    Quantification is critical to Greening. By extension, precision and certainty become necessary. There is an implicit belief here that if performance can be scientifically estimated at the drawing board stage, the building will function as planned.

Menara UMNO is an office building on an island off the west coast of Malaysia that was built in the 1990s. It was the first to offer its occupants two modes for thermal comfort. They could, when the day was warm, switch to air conditioning, and when the day cooled, open windows. This was aided by wind-channelling walls, *brise-soleil* and sky gardens. It was also one of the first projects to use simulation software to model airflow around a building.

On moving in, tenants put up partitions – as they often do in leased office spaces – sealing off pathways for airflow. Their reluctance to rely on natural ventilation and daylighting was compounded by the fact that the building's skin let in more heat than had been predicted. The building in operation consumed more than twice the energy estimated on the drawing board.[59]

It is highly likely that the same building, if assessed today using the assessment tools that exist in Asia, would be certified. These tools continue to reward drawing board assumptions, especially if these are backed by scientific modelling.

49

The confounding variable here is the occupant. Occupants are not passive recipients. They have expectations and preferences and they behave in ways that are hard to model. When the interface between a building and its occupants is not well designed, performance veers far from initial estimates.

Even though Menara UMNO did not connect well with its occupants, it received extensive coverage in architecture

59_ Kishnani, N. (2002)

magazines and books. This skyscraper for the tropics became a symbol of bioclimatic design that spoke of aspirations to connect with *place*, climatically and culturally. In attempting this, it spoke to a generation of architects in Southeast Asia.

No Green building today in Asia attempts to articulate its aspirations or position. Most appear utilitarian or at best ordinary. This is not to say there are no iconic buildings in Asia that speak to the masses. The CCTV Headquarters in Beijing and Petronas Towers in Kuala Lumpur speak of Asia's rise on the global stage, its assertiveness and wealth.

None however speak of Asia's role as a responsible global citizen. Architects seem to struggle to express themselves when crafting a Green language. And when buildings are reduced to technical entities they cease to be instruments of communication. Without communication, there can be no buy-in; without buy-in, Green cannot live up to its promise.

//

A Green building is discussed mostly as a technical object with measurable outcomes, rarely as a cultural force shaping society. There is some attempt by assessment tools to shape behaviour (say, the provision of bicycle racks) but there is little to suggest this is effective or meaningful in Asia. Where there is no occupant buy-in – or a lack of attention to the building-occupant interface – a building will not be used in the way it was designed. A Green building without buy-in is a missed opportunity to engage the occupant as a stakeholder.

Q5   What is the value of Greening?
Does value depend on priorities of the design process?

Value is defined by the building sector in Asia primarily in terms of cost and profit. The discussions tend to revolve around how much *more* a Green building costs and how quickly that added investment will be recovered.[60] Cost is discussed as capital expenditure, money spent before a building is completed. In a recent survey of stakeholders in the Asian building sector,[61] *increase in capital expenditure* was cited as the single biggest concern hindering adoption of Green practices and systems. The single most important reason for *wanting to go Green* was also cost, described as *lower operational expenditure*. When asked what they thought would be the likely cost increase due to Greening, most said *don't know*. When asked what might be the likely savings, the majority again responded *don't know*. Cost appears to be the most persistent cause of uncertainty in Greening.

In that same survey, the firms that expressed lower levels of commitment to Greening were also the ones that wanted to know more about Green technologies and were likely to start thinking about Greening midstream in the design-construction process. Firms with higher levels of commitment expressed interest in the long-term value of a Green building and were likely to start earlier. This suggests that there is an intersection between how value is defined and how process is managed.

There is little incentive in Asia to rethink the design-construction process even in projects where certification is sought. In many instances the lead time for upstream thinking – brief formulation and sketch design – can be absurdly short. Builders are often asked to price works and commence construction even when the design is not yet finalised, creating a high likelihood of pricing error, and with it, an equally high likelihood that ideas will be amended or jettisoned as the project moves ahead. This acceptance of a high risk of error is linked to low labour costs and high interest rates. The clock starts ticking the day that land is acquired, often with

51

60_ Green Mark-rated buildings reportedly show a return on investment. Capital cost increments of 2–8% for Platinum rating are recovered in 2–8 years, 1–3% for Gold Plus in 2–6 years, 1–2% for Gold in 2–6 years, 0.3–1% for Certified in 2–5 years. | Keung, J. (2011, 13-16 September)
61_ BCI Asia. (2008)

penalties for delay. In this context, the jackhammer is also the eraser.[62]

The design-construction process is typically linear and fragmented. Once an architectural concept is approved by a developer, it gets locked in. Consultants weigh in and contribute to the next stage of development. The concept is tweaked to make room for structure, equipment and change-of-mind. But rarely, at any point, is that first sketch thrown out completely. Greening here is a layering of technologies and features. Assessment tools are generally process-neutral; in other words, they do not reward a rethink of how things are done. There is, in rare cases, a nod to process; HK-BEAM, for instance, is one of few that rewards modularisation and prefabrication of building components.

//

The primary yardstick of value in the Asian building sector is the return on capital investment, pegged to a timeframe that is significantly shorter than the life of a building. This fragments the design process and limits long-term thinking where competing priorities and potential synergies – arising from an inter-relatedness of parts over time – might otherwise be considered. Project teams in Asia, almost always in haste, look for 'value-add' features but not value as such. The typical design process, on to which Greening becomes an additional layer, does not afford them time to ask how things connect and why a building matters to a particular context or community.

62_ "In the Western world, where Building Information Modelling (BIM) originated, a major portion of construction cost is from labour. Idle workers as a result of coordination errors are expensive, and a need for improved productivity on-site created a drive to find a better way of documenting and coordinating design... In Asia, the complete opposite is true. Foreign construction workers are inexpensive and plentiful. Site errors are often rectified with either a jackhammer or shrug of the shoulders and a bit of adjustment to the design. In architectural and engineering practice, legions of 2D draftsmen are readily available and a business model of throwing bodies at a job until all the drawings are completed is commonplace. Thorough coordination is not overly important; speed of production drives the process. This doesn't happen on its own. In Asia, clients want to start their piling before the ink is dry on their title to the site. Project schedules often don't allow for a meticulous, coordination process. Clients and builders want the drawings yesterday, but insist on putting off crucial design decisions for as long as possible." | Lazarus, P. (2012)

LIMITS OF GREENING

RETHINKING SYSTEM BOUNDARIES

The conventions of Greening today do not question the precepts of conventional building design that preceded the birth of Green. Like its conventional neighbour, the Green building is designed to operate within a set of physical and temporal boundaries. These describe the Green building as a system that can be quantitatively measured and benchmarked against self or an equivalent, for which cost and investment return are the primary yardsticks of value. Components within this system are seen to be discrete entities with their own performance metrics. The aggregated performance of components is assumed to be the performance of the building as a whole.

Three system boundaries define the limits of Greening: *Space*, *Time* and *Exchange*.

Space | Beyond site and shell

A building is not an isolated entity even when it is privately owned. It engages with the neighbourhood, with the urban economy and within man-made and natural ecologies. It can connect (or isolate) people and communities. Expanding the boundary of physical space – from site and shell to neighbourhood and city – offers an opportunity to address wider contexts on which the building depends. *Place* was a term used by Buchanan[63] to describe the nexus of conditions that buildings operate in: climatic, social, cultural, urban and ecological. Designing for Place begins with a mapping of existing networks or grids with the aim of limiting disruption and enhancing connectivity. Its prime concern is *embeddedness*. This is contingent on local sourcing and reliance on indigenous know-how – particular to a locale – that covers construction craft and climatic response.

Time | Beyond short-term fiscal gains

The building sector is in the habit of seeking certainty and short-term fiscal gains which in Greening results in a culture of *short-termism*. In an imprecise, uncertain world, short-termism creates inaction on many fronts. A project team might opt for a solar hot water system if it offers a payback on investment within five years. It will rarely consider photovoltaic technology, which at current prices, does not. If the timescale for assessment were upped to 50 years, renewables take on a different significance. The question then is not if but *when* and *how* to adopt and adapt. Understanding long-term outcome is critical to unlocking the value of buildings and cities.[64] *Long-termism* – where the boundary of time is stretched to at least the predicted life of a building – looks for gains and confronts risks, seeking where possible to extend the

55

63_ "Instead of being conceived of as a self-contained object, design focuses on elaborating a dense web of complex symbiotic relationships with all aspects of the building's setting. The inspirational ideal is to imagine a building that seems to have grown in place in intimate interaction with its surroundings, and often also with deep roots in the accumulated wisdom of the local culture and its vernacular buildings." | Buchanan, P. (2000)

64_ "Time is a necessary ingredient of building a good city. But profit actually works the other way. The faster you build something, the more money you make. And I think China is a classic example of the dichotomy of the pursuit of profit versus the pursuit of good city building. The idea of an eco-city is fine but it would be interesting to see how it's actually inhabited, what it looks like 30 to 50 years from now. That's the minimum time frame of a city; it has to go through a few generations to know whether the city's adapted to the people or the people have adapted to the city." | Rastogi, M. (2011)

life of a building, its components and materials. It takes a broader view of well-being – incorporating productivity and satisfaction of occupants, community ties and connectivity with nature. It looks to the principles of resilience and adaptation, and deals with risk and uncertainty linked to climate change and urbanisation.

Exchange | Beyond quantitative, aggregated outcomes

A building is commonly seen as a set of discrete elements – envelope, structure, electro-mechanical systems – assembled around a design idea that satisfies a specific programmatic need. Consultants are responsible for a part of the whole and assigned a budget and schedule. In this context, Greenness is the aggregated performance of parts.

This approach of assessment, as bottom-up aggregation, often leads to outcomes that are less than the sum of their parts because design teams cherry-pick what they want to do and leave out what they don't. A project is rewarded for what it does *right*; it is rarely penalised for what it does not do or does *wrong*.[65] The exchange between parts and stakeholders is ignored or under valued. The conventions of Greening do not encourage integration. There is also a conspicuous absence of the consideration of qualitative outcomes.

65.. There are very few exceptions to this. The Japanese rating tool – CASBEE – is the only rating tool in Asia where the final score is a ratio, not an aggregate. Greening here becomes an act of managing tradeoffs – some factors are to be minimised (consumption, waste, emissions, etc.), others must be maximised (comfort, community, functionality, etc.). This makes for complex calculations but it allows the same tool to be applied to diverse building types and conditions, from new office buildings in Tokyo to vernacular housing in Malaysia (Murakami, S. & Ikaga, T., 2008). In North America, the Living Building Challenge (International Living Buildings Institute, 2008) is the only tool that demands all 20 imperatives be met, making it impossible for teams to pick what they find easy or profitable. This is also the only tool where subjective attributes of beauty and inspiration are requirements.

The real difficulty in changing any enterprise lies not in developing new ideas but in escaping from the old ones.

John Maynard Keynes

SIX PRINCIPLES OF SUSTAINABLE ARCHITECTURE EMERGING IDEAS FOR ASIA

The Green building in Asia has, in a short space of time, become the orthodoxy; a set of precepts that represents a barrier to sustainable design.

A lot of what we know of Green is the result of conversations taking place between markets and governments. These exchanges tell us what a Green building is and how to value it with prescribed metrics of performance. Greening nomenclature, like efficiency and indoor environmental quality, describe what is administrable today and profitable in the short-term. They delineate the space for action that is linked to principles of technical optimisation and return on investment. The problem with this is that it continues to describe where we are, not where we want to be.

The transition from Green to sustainable needs new tools for thinking. Asia needs a new *vocabulary* to reboot the conversation, language that embraces both the qualitative and quantitative dimensions of the built environment; words that can trigger a response that is aligned with the vectors of sustainability.

A number of Asian projects are thinking beyond Green. Collectively they manifest six principles that could be the bridge to sustainability.

EFFICACY

SEEKING LONG-TERM EFFECTIVENESS

Whereas efficiency describes the input-to-output ratio of a process, efficacy is *effectiveness* of an action against its stated intent. Efficacy asks the question: what is the intent? A building envelope in a warm climate is said to be more efficient than another if it slows the passage of heat from outside to inside. If the envelope was intended to better comfort indoors, other attributes (beside thermal transmittance) come into play since comfort also depends on daylight, air and views. Efficacy, unlike efficiency, is an act of integration managing tradeoffs and synergies within a whole.

To work, efficacy must be ascribed the vector of time since effectiveness can only be gauged if there is a stipulated time frame. To assess efficacy is to understand throughputs and exchanges over the life of the building. There are many unknowns that inhibit the adoption of this idea: the future cost of energy, the various scenarios of climate change, the behaviour of a building's occupants. But there is also a growing sentiment in Green circles that it is the building-in-use that is important, not simply the building-as-designed.

Attempts to influence building-in-use are sometimes seen in Asia. These can be the result of statutory codes or a condition for recertification under an assessment tool.[66] Asia is also seeing new types of tenancy agreements – known as *Green leasing* – that bind occupant and landlord to shared environmental goals.[67]

Efficacy as a whole (building) life proposition is almost never seen. Were it considered, it might open up the possibility that resource flows are designed as closed loops or for synergies. Conventional wisdom has it that each piece of equipment should do one thing well. In sustainable thinking, a single element might do several things well (*the envelope can keep the rain out and generate electrical power*); a single resource can be used several times over (*waste from one process becomes a resource in another*). In combined heat and power (CHP) systems, for instance, both the electrical power and thermal energy produced are utilised. The energy that might otherwise be discharged into the atmosphere as waste heat is captured and channeled towards air conditioning or hot water equipment.

Efficacy of water use is equally important. Rainwater collection systems and grey water recycling can be looped to reduce demand for potable water from the city grid.

66_ Building owners in Singapore, for instance, are now obliged by law to disclose energy use. The Singapore Green Mark is subject to recertification every three years. If a building fails to meet its performance targets, it can be stripped of its rating.

67_ Lim, C. & Lee, B.L. (2012), pp. 72–73

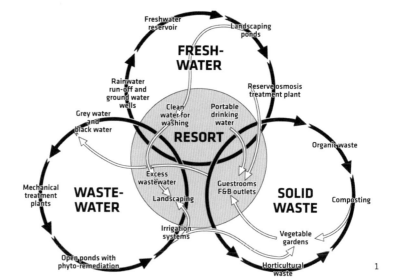

FRESH-WATER

Freshwater reservoir

Landscaping ponds

Rainwater run-off and ground water wells

Reserve osmosis treatment plant

Grey water and black water

Clean water for washing

Portable drinking water

RESORT

Organic waste

Excess wastewater

Guestrooms F&B outlets

Mechanical treatment plants

WASTE-WATER

Landscaping

SOLID WASTE

Composting

Irrigation systems

Vegetable gardens

Open ponds with phyto-remediation

Horticultural waste

1

2

3

4

66

2001   Phuket,
        Thailand

Evason Resort
Waste-to-resource loops

Large tracts of the Evason estate are dedicated to water capture and recycling. Grey and black water from 260 guest rooms and several restaurant kitchens is treated in mechanical systems and then in open ponds filled with water hyacinth and lotus plants, a natural cleansing technique known as phyto-remediation. The treated, now clean water is returned to the water table via irrigation systems that support the resort's greenery, almost all of which consists of plant species native to the locale. The resort also has its own freshwater reservoir. From here, water is piped into a reverse osmosis plant that produces potable water. All of the resort's solid waste is separated for recycling. Besides paper, plastic, metal and glass, there is also capture of used cooking oil, food and garden waste. A converter turns oil (from Evason's kitchens and restaurants on Phuket) into biodiesel fuel. A shredder breaks down garden waste. Soft material from this is mixed in with food waste to make compost that is then used in its herb and vegetable gardens. The resort is 100% self-sufficient in its water needs. Its gardens contribute as much as 30% of employees' and 5% of guests' dietary needs. The waste recycling efforts lessen the resort's footprint by 15 tonnes of CO_2e per year.

5 Perimeter walls and facades
  made with rescued bottles
6 Bottle House exterior
7 Bottle facade serves to moderate ingress of light and heat
  into the building

2007   Bandung,
        Indonesia

Bottle House
Consumer waste turned into building material

In a salvage operation lasting over six months, 30,000 bottles were collected from dumping grounds in and around Bandung. These were cleaned and then used as a facade material in this residential development. This resulted in a lower demand for new construction materials; the bottles that would have gone to a landfill were also given an extended lifespan. This substantially reduced the embedded energy of the development, which is the energy consumed in manufacturing and transporting materials to site. The bottles are deployed in a manner that augments the building's environmental goals. The split-level courtyard house, with a gross floor area of 320 m², has an open layout with minimal wall partitions that promote the flow of light and air. The bottles make up a part of the building skin that interfaces between outdoor and indoor conditions. Acting as an environmental filter the bottle wall lets in only diffused natural light, even at times when there is low-angle sun. Air trapped within the bottles creates a thermal buffer that reduces heat transmission. Sliding doors and windows next to the bottle walls can be fully opened when needed. With three internal courtyards, fresh air circulates freely. Water features and a swimming pool situated at the periphery of the house offer relief on hot days; evaporative losses moderate the microclimate of the site, bringing cool air into the heart of this home. As a result no air conditioning is needed in the house; there is minimal reliance on artificial lighting during the day.

8 Corridors are naturally ventilated and protected from solar
  exposure
9 Classroom interior with light
  shelves
10 Exterior, UWC campus
11 Configuration of teaching
   block with double-loaded
   corridors and interstitial
   spaces
12 Classroom interior where
   air supplied at lower speeds
   and higher temperature set
   points is backed up by ceiling
   fans

2011   Singapore

United World College of South East Asia
Energy flows and air quality

The United World College (UWC) campus is a 76,000 m² school built on a 5.2-hectare site for a population of 2,500 students. Its teaching blocks have double-loaded corridors – two rows of classrooms with a shared circulation access – to make the building compact enough to fit onto a tight site. This configuration resulted in increased demand for mechanical cooling. A number of questions were asked early in the design process about the efficacy of conventional air conditioning systems. For instance, must cooled air be recirculated? Is there a more effective way to move the huge volumes of air needed? In a seemingly counter-intuitive twist to air conditioning in the hot-humid tropics, the UWC system operates with 100% fresh air. That is to say, there is no recirculated air. This should have substantially increased energy consumption but it did not. Instead it had several multiplier effects. It eliminated all return air ducts and fans, almost half the air-side equipment. This reduced the energy load of the air conditioning system by about 30%, which offset the increase in latent load. It ensured high indoor air quality, benefiting occupant health. All that fresh air meant that rooms could be supplied air at a lower flow rate. Instead of high-speed cold air, low-speed air is ducted in at higher temperatures. Slow-moving ceiling fans increase air movement when this is needed by the occupants. Air discharged from classrooms seeps into corridors and then into gathering spaces such as foyers. Eight hundred square metres of primary air-conditioned space – mainly classrooms – is

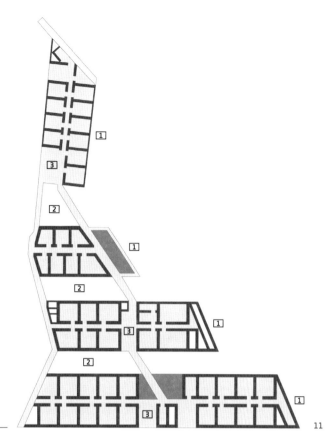

11

used to co-cool another 300 m² of secondary circulation space. The cumulative effect of all Green ideas put in place – and there are many besides cooling – is that the uwc campus cost significantly less to build. It was completed within a 24-month construction period and it saves over 60% energy compared with equivalent developments in Singapore. This translates into annual operational savings of S$1 million at 2011 energy prices, equal to reduced emissions of about 2,200 tonnes of CO_2e/year.

ECOLOGY

RESPECTING AND REPAIRING NETWORKS

Ecology refers to networks of living communities. An ecosystem is a network of plant and animal life coexisting alongside active food chains, supported by abiotic resources. Ecological balance is the stable but dynamic exchange between inhabitants of a network. Human beings are an integral part of ecosystems; any action by humans that affects ecosystems in turn affects humans.[68]

As human settlements expand, their geographical and ecological footprints widen. Swaths of peri-urban zones are displaced further

68_ "People are integral parts of ecosystems and that a dynamic interaction exists between them and other parts of ecosystems, with the changing human condition driving, both directly and indirectly, changes in ecosystems and thereby causing changes in human well-being." | World Resources Institute. (2005), p. v

afield. Industry and commercial agriculture strip forest cover and destroy habitats. It is predicted that up to 70% of the original biomes across Earth's ecosystems will, as result of human actions, be lost by 2050.[69] The most vulnerable regions are in the tropical and subtropical belts of Asia. This loss signals a corresponding disappearance of biodiversity, destabilised ecologies and climate change. Forests are one of the most important global carbon sinks; fewer forests – due to land clearance and logging – equal greater build-up of atmospheric concentrations of carbon dioxide resulting in accelerated global warming.

Current models of development are largely *exploitative*: human actions take place at the expense of the ecosystems that support life on Earth.[70] Critics of this have argued for new ways of seeing and valuing nature.[71] The thrust of their argument is that any reshaping of the natural world or built intervention must be supportive of processes and flows that already exist. This idea is finding form in Asia[72] where two approaches are seen.

Living Networks | Coexistence

This is an argument to tread lightly. Every site is part of hydrological, carbon and nutrient cycles. Some sites sustain flora and fauna that are part of food chains; all are subject to seasonal changes and thermal flows.[73] The design team starts by describing the network – the cycles and flows of energy and materials – and then seeks to position the new development such that it causes little or no disruption. Rain, for instance, is allowed to naturally recharge a water table. Newly planted greenery offers continued refuge and food for insects and animals.

Depending on the scale of the development and surrounding ecology, the principle of *living networks* can be widened beyond site boundaries. *Ecological urbanism* starts by describing the broader natural system of a region – for instance, the watershed around a river – that then becomes the organising structure that shapes the new development. The process would include the identification

69_ World Resources Institute. (2005)
70_ "Continuous growth of the human eco-footprint on a finite planet has dramatic consequences for other organisms. Habitat and bio-productivity appropriated for human use is irreversibly unavailable to other species. Therefore, contrary to popular mythology, the continuous growth of the human enterprise necessarily means the depletion of nature." | Rees, W.E. (2008)
71_ du Plessis, C. (2012)
72_ "Some Asian cities, like Singapore, having lost much of their ecosystems are seeking a new equilibrium between nature and the city. Singapore has seen an increase of over 10% in its green cover from 1986 to 2007, despite almost a doubling of the population in the same period. Some 100 km of green corridors link parks and green spaces; this figure is expected to reach 360 km by 2020. Southeast Asia's first ecological corridor is underway; the bridge, when completed in 2013, will reconnect two of Singapore's nature reserves, separated by a highway. The national blueprint for sustainability stipulates that 50 hectares of skyrise greenery – roof gardens and green facades – will be built by year 2030. In 2010, The United Nations Convention on Biological Diversity, together with Singapore, launched the first self assessment tool for cities that measures biodiversity – the Singapore Index on Cities' Biodiversity – formally endorsed by 10th Conference of Parties in Nagoya, Japan, that same year." | Koh, H.Y. & Kishnani, N. (2009)
73_ Yeang, K. (2006)

of species, processes and events with survival and continuity as stated goals.[74] This begins with a mapping of patterns – flows, migration, pollination, dispersal – that the intervention must consider. The spatial and formal qualities resulting from this approach are substantially different from orthogonal grids seen in conventional master plans.

Regenerative Design | Partnership
Regenerative design places importance on both the social and natural capitals of a locale. This has its roots in the argument – some decades old – that cities and buildings should be designed in ways that restore or regenerate lost ecosystems.[75] This act of regeneration might involve the removal of contaminants from soil or water using plants (phyto-remediation). A project could incorporate permaculture as a way of restoring nutrient balance. Some developments introduce biodiversity – plants, insects, birds, fish – that become part of a food chain that exists alongside human activities.

A new strand of regenerative thinking is emerging, one that probes deeper into the humans versus nature dialectic. It argues that human beings, their "artefacts and cultural constructs are inherent parts of an ecosystem", and that all "actions should contribute positively to the functioning and evolution of ecosystems and biogeological cycles... enabling self-healing".[76] What differentiates this from earlier arguments on regeneration is it seeks a co-evolution of human culture and life. It aspires "not just to preserve and protect, it serves to restore lost plenitude".[77]

74_ Forman, R.T. (2002)
75_ Lyle, J.T. (1994)
76_ du Plessis, C. (2012)
77_ Van der Ryn, S. & Cowan, S. (2007), p. 37

ECOLOGICAL BALANCE IS THE STABLE BUT
DYNAMIC EXCHANGE BETWEEN INHABITANTS OF
A NETWORK. HUMAN BEINGS ARE AN INTEGRAL
PART OF ECOSYSTEMS; ANY ACTION BY HUMANS
THAT AFFECTS ECOSYSTEMS IN TURN AFFECTS
HUMANS.

74

2009   Hong Kong,
        People's Republic of China

Hong Kong Wetland Park
Conservation and restoration

Located in the northern part of Tin Shui Wai in the New Territories, this 61-hectare site is an ecological undertaking that restores wetlands compromised by a nearby new town development. Augmenting the conservation efforts, the authorities added several amenities that cater to local and overseas visitors. The main building, as gateway to the park, comprises a visitor centre with three main galleries, a resource centre, a discovery centre, a children's play area, offices, a café and a shop. There is also a satellite building and three bird hides along walking trails from which visitors can discretely observe the park's wildlife. All new buildings are designed to minimise impact. Sustainably sourced timber was used throughout. Seventy-five per cent of the total concrete volume contains recycled aggregates or pulverised fuel ash as partial cement replacement. The satellite building collects rainwater for flushing. Native plant species are used in all new land-scaping. The wetlands and recreated habitats are the heart of the park which aims to conserve the diversity of Hong Kong's ecosystems. Based on figures from initial monitoring, the park is succeeding where it matters: a total of 129 bird species, 32 odonate species, 55 butterfly species, nine fish species, nine amphibian species, seven reptile species and five mammal species were spotted.

4 Crafting an oasis for people and nature
5 Integrating site hydrology and wastewater treatment
6 Building-integrated greenery
7 Aerial view, clusters of buildings set in a verdant landscape

2003   Singapore

CleanTech Park
Partnering nature

The day-to-day business needs of this industrial park will be met by clusters of buildings on a 50-hectare site in Singapore which, when completed, will be home to a working population of 20,000. It is what happens between these buildings that differentiates this development from others of its kind. The master plan commits to conservation and regeneration of biodiversity. The site will be a refuge to the area's existing wildlife including the native Sunda pangolin and harlequin butterflies. The landscape design adapts to the undulating terrain and mature greenery with natural streams, and incorporates tropical freshwater wetland forest which will include endangered tree species native to Singapore. These species and certain other fruit-producing plants will draw in more wildlife. Site planning addresses existing hydrological cycles. Property-wide rainwater capture and filtration is planned for: rainwater from kerbside drains will be treated in bioretention swales, retained in ponds and wetlands and then purified by a cleansing biotope.

Grey water from the buildings will be recycled and, with the rainwater that is collected, is expected to satisfy an estimated 38% of the development's non-potable needs. The design of hydrological flows and capture follows new Singapore guidelines[78] for making waterways accessible to the public, incorporating lookout decks, pavilions and boardwalks.

78. Singapore has over 7,000 km of canals and drains that channel storm water into 15 reservoirs and 32 rivers. The Active, Beautiful, Clean (ABC) Waters Programme, launched in 2007, is set to transform all hydrological channels and water bodies on the island into public attractions, going beyond their present role as infrastructure for flood control and freshwater storage. These transformations adopt Water Sensitive Urban Design (WSUD) measures, integrating natural hydrological processes. Concrete canals and storage basins are converted into naturalised channels, bioswales and wetlands. This new Green infrastructure will double up as social and leisure settings for the community. | Public Utilities Board, Singapore. (2011, July)

Moist warm air expelled

Hot air from conservatory purged to supertrees and atmosphere

Wildlife connections

Glasshouse shading performed by the supporting beams

Hot air purged to atmosphere

50% sunshaded by beams

Rainwater collection and reuse

Fans located under walkways to create air movement

Breeze created at ground

Flue gases drive ventilation in supertrees

Electricity generated for site and conservatory

Irrigation to conservatory

Heat for dehumidifier

Water storage and cleaning

Clean water discharged to reservoir

Irrigation

New plant material for gardens and market

Biowaste from gardens burnt to create power

Green waste from gardens

Fertiliser

Ash from biomass furnace used for fertiliser

Seedings and cuttings

8

2012   Singapore

Gardens by the Bay
Nature as urban oasis

Gardens by the Bay (GB) is an exemplar of reconstructed nature within a high-density urban setting. Designed as a horticultural attraction on land reclaimed from the sea, GB is a functioning, living network of flora and fauna. It comprises three waterfront gardens – Bay South, Bay East and Bay Central – which cover a total of 101 hectares in the Marina Bay downtown area. The site incorporates several ecosystems: aquatic and tropical rainforest, plus two cool-house biomes that contain temperate and tropical montane

plant collections. The Gardens' lake acts as a natural water filtration system and provides an aquatic habitat for biodiversity such as fish and dragonflies. Water run-off from within the Gardens is captured by the lake and cleansed by aquatic plants before being discharged into the adjacent Marina Reservoir. The naturally cleansed water is also used for the irrigation of the Gardens. The two biomes are supported by mechanical cooling systems that are energy-efficient and mimic natural flows. Their domes are fitted with glass that

allows optimal light entry but cuts out a substantial amount of heat. Cooling is delivered only to occupied zones thereby reducing the volume of air to be cooled. Envelope flaps on the roofs open up when there is excessive heat build-up; retractable sunscreens slide out from under the structural skeleton when there is too much sun. To trim down the amount of energy required in the cooling process, air is dehumidified with liquid desiccant before it is cooled by chillers. These chillers are powered by a steam turbine run on horticultural waste.

Based on early energy modelling studies, this suite of energy-efficient technologies can help to achieve at least 30% savings in energy consumption, compared to conventional cooling technologies. Towering above the natural trees in the Gardens are 18 *supertrees* that act as vertical gardens, supporting a living skin of epiphytes, ferns and flowering climbers. A number of them are fitted with environmental features that mimic the ecological functions of trees. Photovoltaic cells, for instance, harvest solar energy to light up the supertrees at night; others are linked to the biomes and serve as air exhaust outlets. The manner in which these systems are designed and integrated – based on lessons learnt from nature – is a key part of GB's advocacy.

WELLNESS

CONNECTION WITH OUTDOORS, COMMUNITY, NATURE

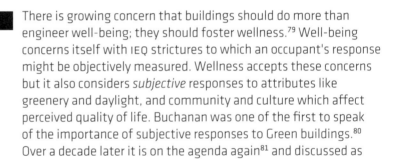

There is growing concern that buildings should do more than engineer well-being; they should foster wellness.[79] Well-being concerns itself with IEQ strictures to which an occupant's response might be objectively measured. Wellness accepts these concerns but it also considers *subjective* responses to attributes like greenery and daylight, and community and culture which affect perceived quality of life. Buchanan was one of the first to speak of the importance of subjective responses to Green buildings.[80] Over a decade later it is on the agenda again[81] and discussed as

79_ "Wellness is the optimal state of health of individuals and groups. There are two focal concerns: the realisation of the fullest potential of an individual physically, psychologically, socially, spiritually and economically, and the fulfillment of one's role expectations in the family, community, place of worship, workplace and other settings." | Smith, B.J., Tang K.C. & Nutbeam, D. (2006)

80_ "Occupants are often not only deprived of the joys of fresh air and natural light, and do not have personal control over the artificial substitutes for them, but they are without even a view to the outside. Designed only for efficiency, as defined in the most squalidly narrow terms, such buildings do nothing to foster any sort of community life within them. They do nothing to ground or expand people in a sense of contact with the surroundings and nature, with each other or even with the building itself. But such buildings are not only profoundly alienating and joyless, and so psychologically unhealthy, they are bad for people's physical health too... The creation of a Green architecture, then, is much more than a merely technical issue: it is essentially concerned with delivering a much-enhanced quality of life, to be enjoyed now and capable of continuing into the future. It is only this broader vision of cultural transformation promised by a truly green architecture that will convince people to move forward to sustainable lifestyles." | Buchanan, P. (2000)

81_ "Can we learn how to measure happiness? The Centre for Bhutan Studies, set up by the Bhutanese government 12 years ago, is currently processing the results of interviews with more than 8,000 Bhutanese. The interviews recorded both subjective factors, such as how satisfied respondents are with their lives, and objective factors, like standard of living, health and education, as well as participation in culture, community

a counterpoint to material wealth and the negative impact of urbanisation.[82] This acceptance of the subjective permits a rethink of how buildings are valued.

The argument for preserving old buildings, for instance, is rarely made on grounds that their IEQ is optimal. Their value lies in how people see them as part of a continuum of community and history. Studies also indicate that an appreciation of the building in entirety often translates into acceptance for what it does in parts, even if the latter is a suboptimal condition.[83]

Vectors of human *satisfaction* or *acceptance* suggest that the sustainable building is not just about physiological needs; it aims to connect with occupants at psychological and emotional levels as well. It could be argued, by extension, that the best defense against obsolescence of buildings – the unsustainable spectacle of build-and-tear-down that is seen all over Asia – is people emotionally invested in what they have. To be sustainable is to increase perceived value so that owners and occupants are less inclined to tear down existing buildings or retrofit them. Several attributes of a building relate to wellness.

Connectivity with outdoors
Visual access to weather and natural light affect how individuals feel and perform. In an oft-cited study on post-operative recovery period in hospital wards, patients with views to the outdoors were discharged sooner than those who did not have the same;[84] evidence that a link with the outdoors can affect the mind and body. For this connectivity to have a positive outcome there must be a well-designed interface between indoors and outdoors in which the form and envelope of a building come together to moderate daylight, solar heat gain, airflow and view.

Access to nature
Biophilia is an intuitive need for contact with things natural.[85] If a site has pre-existing natural elements – mature trees,

79

vitality, ecological health, and the balance between work and other activities. It remains to be seen whether such diverse factors correlate well with each other. Trying to reduce them to a single number will require some difficult value judgments." | Singer, P. (2011)

82_ "The question... is how to achieve happiness in a world that is characterised by rapid urbanisation, mass media, global capitalism, and environmental degradation. How can our economic life be re-ordered to recreate a sense of community, trust, and environmental sustainability? First, we should not denigrate the value of economic progress. When people

are hungry, deprived of basic needs such as clean water, health care and education, and without meaningful employment, they suffer. Economic development that alleviates poverty is a vital step in boosting happiness. Second, relentless pursuit of GNP to the exclusion of other goals is also no path to happiness. In the US, GNP has risen sharply in the past 40 years, but happiness has not. Instead, single-minded pursuit of GNP has led to great inequalities of wealth and power, fueled the growth of a vast underclass, trapped millions of children in poverty, and caused serious environmental degradation. Third, happiness is achieved through a balanced

approach to life by both individuals and societies. As individuals, we are unhappy if we are denied our basic material needs, but we are also unhappy if the pursuit of higher incomes replaces our focus on family, friends, community, compassion, and maintaining internal balance. As a society, it is one thing to organise economic policies to keep living standards on the rise, but quite another to subordinate all of society's values to the pursuit of profit." | Sachs J.D. (2011, 29 August)

83_ Deuble, M. & de Dear, R. (2010, 9–11 April)
84_ Ulrich, R.S. (1984)
85_ Bell, P.A., Greene, T.C., Fisher, J.D. & Baum, A. (1996)

water bodies – it has strong potential to address this need. Where there is little or none, gardens, green roofs and planted facades are a common proxy for nature. A study in Singapore found that the presence of these elements in buildings positively affects wellness even where they are man-made.[86]

Links to community and place

Many people in Asian cities experience isolation and feel disconnected from community and culture. Demolition of old buildings to make way for new real estate further depletes a sense of place, the physical and social attributes of an environment that speaks of where one is and how a location has evolved over time. Sustainable design is concerned with the protection or creation of community ties, typically by valuing community interaction where it exists. It also affirms connections to culture and place. Vietnam's LOTUS is the only Asian tool that explicitly lists *cultural heritage and community* as a requirement. This concerns itself with the recognition that certain buildings and spaces should be conserved for the continuity and connectivity they offer. Other assessment tools, by and large, are silent on socio-cultural attributes of a locale.

86_ Sng P.L. (2011)

WELL-BEING CONCERNS ITSELF WITH IEQ STRICTURES TO WHICH AN OCCUPANT'S RESPONSE MIGHT BE OBJECTIVELY MEASURED. WELLNESS ACCEPTS THESE CONCERNS BUT IT ALSO CONSIDERS SUBJECTIVE RESPONSES TO ATTRIBUTES LIKE GREENERY AND DAYLIGHT, AND COMMUNITY AND CULTURE WHICH AFFECT PERCEIVED QUALITY OF LIFE.

1 Interior view of atrium roof
  after retrofit
2 Detail of clerestory window
  with mirrors
3 Section across atrium
4 Exterior view of an atrium roof
  with mirrors
5 Performance modelling
  showing daylight distribution
  within an atrium

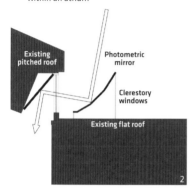

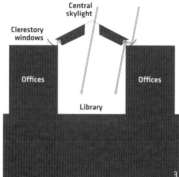

2006   Manila,
        Philippines

Asian Development Bank Headquarters
Daylight access and connectivity with outdoors

The Asian Development Bank (ADB) headquarters is a nine-storey office building, built in 1991, with more than 143,000 m² of space. Staff complained that the building's interior had too little natural light which in turn affected their mood and comfort. A retrofit of its two atria was commissioned in 2006. The daylight enhancement system that was installed consisted of large mirror reflectors placed on the roof along existing clerestory windows. Each reflector is about 2 m high. The cumulative length of all

reflectors is almost a quarter kilometre, making this one of the largest daylight enhancement systems ever installed in Asia. Prior to the retrofit, on a sunny day, natural light levels at the base of the atria were less than 100 lux. Following the retrofit light levels shot up sixfold under sunny skies, fourfold on overcast days. At the atria floors, light levels of 300 lux and more were recorded for 75% of the day, enough to read unaided by electrical light (one of the atria floors is used as a library, the other as a staff lounge). A survey

of occupants confirmed that with a brighter daylit atrium, 66% of staff said that having an office facing the atrium had become more acceptable, 63% said their morale had improved, and 61% felt that they were more productive. The overall satisfaction levels with the indoor environment increased to over 90% with almost all staff saying that they preferred the retrofitted atria to the original. The project has since become a symbol of the Bank's commitment to Green, reinforcing ADB's mission in Asia as an advocate and facilitator of change.

6 Central courtyard and link
  bridge
7 Section showing courtyards,
  green roofs and terrace
  gardens
8 Indoor-outdoor connectivity
9 Morphology of 8 m-wide
  stacked blocks

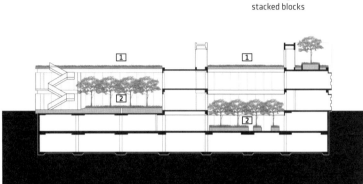

6

7

8

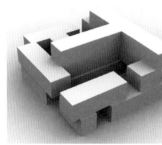

9

1 Green roof
2 Landscaped courtyard

83

2009   Delhi,
       India

Corporate Office for India Glycols Limited
Form as maker of microclimate

The difference between this and
other corporate buildings in India
is immediately apparent. Whereas
the latter have deep plans and exces-
sively glazed facades, the Glycols
building has opaque external facades
with fluid, transparent and permeable interiors. The building appears
to be a series of stacked blocks.
Workspaces are housed within
each of the 8 m-wide blocks, a plan
depth that ensures ventilation and
daylight access for all its occupants.
The seemingly random stacking
is in fact a conscious attempt to

create interstitial spaces – courtyards, verandas, terraces, green
roofs – that link inside with outside,
blurring boundaries between building
and landscape. This configuration,
so different from the monolithic,
central-core typology of its neighbours, does several things at once.
During the cool months windows
can be opened to let breezes through.
These outdoor spaces then act as
extensions of the building's interior.
When the hot summers of Delhi kick
in, air conditioning can be switched
on and all activity retreats indoors.

Occupants are never far from a vista
or view, though. Having daylight
means that reliance on artificial
lighting is substantially reduced.
The green roofs and terrace gardens
provide good thermal insulation.
Mist gardens, water bodies and
plants aid in evaporative cooling
that enhances the site microclimate, particularly in summer when
dependence on mechanical cooling is
substantially less here than in other
equivalent buildings.

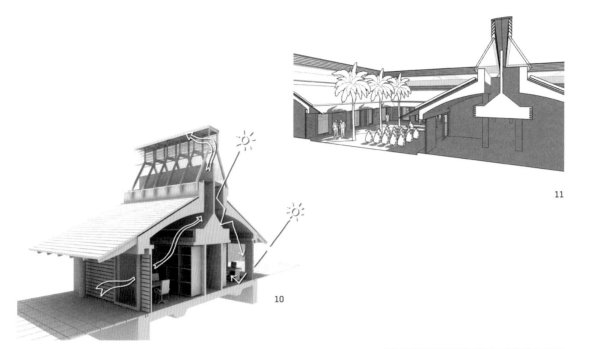

11

10

12

2009	Colombo, Sri Lanka

British High Commission
Courtyards for connectivity to climate and place

In a layout that harks back to traditional Sri Lankan architecture, this consular building is built around a series of courtyards with a total of 16 partially enclosed and open spaces that are designed to maximise connectivity with the outdoors. These courtyards act as interstitial lungs permitting its indoor spaces to *breathe* fresh air and draw in natural light. All workspaces and meeting rooms are located within the fish-bone-shaped building made up of a central spine and projecting ribs. This permits a hierarchical arrangement

of spaces: one end of the spine is accessible to the public, the other contains more private consular activities. No occupant, at either end of that divide, is deprived of daylight or far from a view of water and plants. To make certain that its double-loaded corridors do not cut off airflow, spaces within the building's ribs are topped with a jack roof that functions as a solar chimney and clerestory window. When air conditioning is switched on, a damper stops airflow into the chimney. When sliding glass doors –

found in every office – are opened to an adjacent courtyard, the damper opens and air is drawn through. As the sun heats the top of the chimney, warm air is expelled. This in turns pulls air up from the space beneath facilitating a convective flow. Water is used extensively in pools and fountains creating a microclimate within the courtyards, tempering the heat of Colombo summers. The High Commission's perimeter wall is made from local granite, relying on traditional methods of construction. Deep overhanging roofs are made from

10 Jack roof with solar chimney and clerestory window
11 Courtyards as interstitial lungs
12 Night view of courtyard
13 Architecture of climate and place
14 Perimeter wall built using traditional construction methods
15 Water and plants moderate site microclimate

traditional Sri Lankan terracotta tiles; coconut timber panels are used as walls. The combined effect of climatic response and materiality is an architecture that feels profoundly tropical and local.

EMBEDDEDNESS

LOCAL RELIANCE AND SELF-SUFFICIENCY

To be embedded is to attain a measure of self-sufficiency by becoming partly (if not fully) reliant on local resources. Resource here refers to what is needed in construction or during operation – energy, water, materials and food. Local sourcing is already practised in parts of Asia, particularly where imports are deemed expensive, but there are other equally compelling reasons for going local.

The use of local materials in construction, for instance, can produce an architecture that connects people with craft and tradition. It can also help sustain local industries and skills. Local sourcing reduces greenhouse gas emissions due to the transport of materials from point of origin to the project site (referred to as *carbon miles*). Local knowledge of climatic response can moderate reliance on electro-mechanical systems. In the long run, self-sufficiency can temper the shock of overpricing or undersupply of resources that often occurs in global markets.

Food, for now, is the least considered of local resources in Asia even though there is ongoing research into how high-density cities like Bangkok,[87] Hong Kong[88] and Singapore[89] might someday integrate agriculture within the urban fabric. Energy sourcing is the most discussed. On-site use of renewable technologies – solar, wind and geothermal – is found in a number of projects across the region. There is also interest in on-site power generation with increasing reliance on generators, particularly in places where the power grid is unreliable. For the same reason, water is sourced locally as well. Some Asian cities are now mandating on-site capture of rainwater and management of hydrological flows to reduce the carrying capacity of water infrastructure.[90]

On-site capture of energy and water earn credits with some assessment tools. Some tools also reward local material sourcing. The latter is, in part, about procuring materials with lower environmental impact and, in part, reducing carbon miles. The problem with these tools is that they hedge their bets. They reward the use of materials from near the site *and* those with third-party certification which in parts of Asia means *import*. The advantage accrued with one action might cancel out the other. With energy and water sourcing there is also an implicit preference for technology. The use of photovoltaics, for instance, is rewarded with credits; reliance on ground cooling (based on vernacular precedents) is not, even though the latter – as a site-specific, climate-moderating solution – might reduce cooling demand more efficaciously than the energy produced by a photo-voltaic array.

87_ Suteethorn, K. (2009)
88_ Hui, C.M.S. (2011, 18–21 March)
89_ Lim, Y.A. & Kishnani, N.T. (2010)
90_ "In 2009... Bangalore finally resorted to mandating rainwater collection on both commercial and residential plots larger than 223 m². In less than two years, half of the 60,000 households covered by the order began harvesting rainwater on their properties... (the) rate of compliance can be attributed to government threats to cut off water supply, a rather draconian step... The Singapore solution has four main faucets. Most impressive (of these) is a $3 billion waste water recycling system which channels all water from toilets and other household uses (which is) sent to four water recycling plants that use reverse osmosis and ultra-light for purification... The government's tiered pricing structure penalises those who use too much water." | Hamilton, A. (2011), pp. 47–50

1 Daylight ingress into atrium
2 Fabric sunshades over external windows
3 Central courtyard with evaporative cooling. Photovoltaic panels are visible through roof opening

88

2008   Gurgaon,
        India

Institute of Rural Research and Development
Regionalism meets certification

The new headquarters for the Institute of Rural Research and Development (IRRAD) is a hybrid of regionalist outlook and assessment tool mantra. Its architect is well-known for designing context-sensitive buildings in the tradition of Indian regionalism. The developer meanwhile wanted LEED certification as a way of positioning the building at the forefront of the Indian Green building movement.[91] The two approaches had a good deal of overlap. Local timbers, such as bamboo and rubberwood, were used extensively, along with stone and brick. One hundred per cent of all materials used are local – much of it from within 800 km of the project site which is a LEED-related obligation. The architectural design permits the building to be passive-run, relying wholly on natural light and wind when possible. Natural ventilation is in some places aided by evaporative cooling, a technique commonly used when the Indian summer is both dry and hot. The building's occupants also have access to air conditioning which is reportedly used for only 60 to 70 days a year. The one feature that is clearly LEED-inspired is the array of photovoltaic panels on the roof: 35 kWp that offset over 20% of the building's overall energy needs.

91_ Jayaraman, V. (2011)

4 Pearl River Tower in the final
stages of construction
5 Artist impression of Pearl
River Tower
6 Performance modelling
showing air flowing past wind
turbines

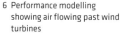

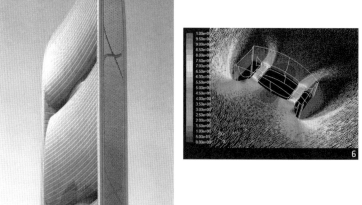

89

2011   Guangzhou,
        People's Republic of China

Pearl River Tower
Powered by wind and sun

Prior to its completion the 71-storey Pearl River Tower (PRT) was heralded as the most progressive clean energy skyscraper in the world.[92] The 204,000 m² office tower is designed to be a (near) net zero energy building, situated in one of most populated and polluted cities in China. The development adopts multiple strategies for on-site sourcing, including wind energy, facade-integrated photovoltaics, microturbines, geothermal cooling and daylight reliance. The most striking of these are two wind turbines

installed in gaps midway up the tower height. The slightly curved profile of the envelope propels air through these gaps, increasing air speed by 2.5 times, generating 15 times more power than a stand-alone turbine in the same location. Over 65% of the building's load is reduced by demand manage-ment and systemic integration. This includes adoption of passive strategies such as solar orientation, daylighting and a double-skin facade that lessens heat gain. The design process sought integration through

multiplier effects. The double-skin facade, for instance, keeps the heat out by channelling it away from the inner skin. The same rising hot air is used to dehumidify incoming fresh air for the air conditioning system, thereby reducing energy needs. The concrete structure inside the tower doubles up as part of the cool-ing system. Floor slabs are fitted with chilled water pipes that cool the structure allowing it to act as a source of radiant cooling.

92_ Low, C. (2008)

| 2010 | Suoi Re Village, Vietnam |

This community house is designed to provide a gathering space and amenities for villagers in a rural part of North Vietnam, not far from Hanoi. The architectural typology borrows from traditional houses of the Kinh and Muong people who are native to this part of Vietnam. The building's open court is used for games and performances. Spread over two floors, the centre's indoor spaces are used for kindergarten classes and as gathering places. An elliptical void connects the two floors; grass steps and slopes connect front

Suoi Re Multi-Functional Community House
Site and climate

to back, interior to exterior, creating a continuous chain of spaces. This promotes a feeling of openness and connectivity throughout. The building capitalises on the topography of the site which is sheltered from northeast winds that can be dry and cold in the winter, but takes advantage of the southeast winds that are cooling in the summer. Built with local materials and labour, the ground floor was constructed with stone. Bamboo is used extensively on the building shell. A rammed earth wall with heavy stones makes up the

base structure. The roof is finished with thatched palm leaves. What is unusual about this modest structure is the integration of technology that gives a unique spin to the principle of embeddedness in the rural context. Solar cells, rainwater collection tanks and a geothermal system keep the centre connected to the land and sky. The design process relied on performance modelling of airflow and daylight ingress.

10

11

12

13

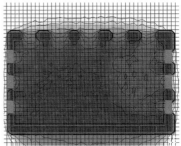

7 Kindergarten
8 Forecourt
9 Back of house
10 Exterior, day
11 Exterior, night
12 Palette of local materials
13 Local labour during
    construction
14 Perspective of building
    exterior
15 Performance modelling show-
    ing daylight entry on ground
    floor
16 Performance modelling show-
    ing airflow through building
    interior

91

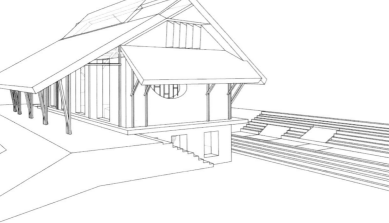

14

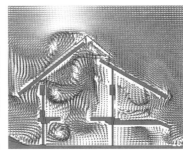

ADVOCACY

BUILDINGS AS A CULTURAL FORCE

Buildings communicate. They speak implicitly or explicitly to their occupants and those that encounter them. The skyscrapers of Asian cities, for instance, are symbols of corporate assertiveness. The icons of Asia – sports stadia, art centres, hotels – speak of the region's newfound influence and wealth. In this milieu, the potential of Green design as an act of advocacy – representing collaboration, restraint and responsibility – is undervalued. Instead a Green building is often perceived as a dull object that is designed to be functional and efficient.

Advocacy is necessary if there is to be occupant or public awareness of the ecological role of buildings. A Green building that is not understood will not be used as designed nor will it be valued over time. With awareness there is the possibility that human behaviour will align itself to set goals.

There are two shades of advocacy: explicit and implicit. Explicit advocacy relies on information that is packaged for a specific audience, typically the building's occupants. At its most literal, this can be visual *prompts*. Recycling bins become reminders of the need to manage waste; signs that tell us to switch off lights also tell us to conserve a valuable resource; smart meters that report on how much is consumed indicate how far we are from a goal. It is assumed here that when occupants encounter a prompt, they act accordingly.

The prompt as message is sometimes pitched to a wider audience beyond a building's occupants. Several buildings in Asia aim to educate and transform the industry at large. In these, there is an overt display of Green technologies and strategies, sometimes with real-time feedback on consumption such that a visitor understands performance. Examples of this include the CII-Sohrabji Godrej Green Business Centre in India[93] and the Green Energy Office Building in Malaysia.[94]

Implicit advocacy relies on *signals*, sensorial or experiential, that create awareness of what the building does. Daylight sensors that self-adjust the brightness of electrical lights, for instance, tell us something of the way a building responds to climate. The exaggerated size of sunshades on the facade of the National Library in Singapore speaks of where the building is climatically. These signals are important to the way a Green building is *read*. A study in Singapore[95] found that architects – when reading a Green design – look for elements of climatic response. A layperson without any building-related background seeks out natural features such as gardens and water features. This may be why Green-certified

93_ CII-Sohrabji Godrej Green Business Centre.
      www.greenbusinesscentre.com
94_ Yoong, E. (2008)
95_ Fa'atulo, W.R. (2010)

buildings, many with emphasis on systems and electro-mechanical efficiency, often do not elicit a positive response from either group.

Another important avenue for advocacy is community engagement. Some projects – particularly social housing – involve their future users in decision-making during design and construction. This may be in the form of feedback on ideas or workshops to determine what is needed or how an element might be designed. The assumption here is that when users are involved, it strengthens their awareness and increases their commitment to a building's eventual performance. The case for *participatory design*, avidly discussed in the 1960s and 70s, is finding a new role in the sustainability discourse especially among those who see building performance as being contingent on occupant buy-in.

ADVOCACY IS NECESSARY IF THERE IS TO BE
OCCUPANT OR PUBLIC AWARENESS OF THE
ECOLOGICAL ROLE OF BUILDINGS. A GREEN BUILDING
THAT IS NOT UNDERSTOOD WILL NOT BE USED AS
DESIGNED NOR WILL IT BE VALUED OVER TIME.
WITH AWARENESS THERE IS THE POSSIBILITY THAT
HUMAN BEHAVIOUR WILL ALIGN ITSELF TO SET GOALS.

1 Village house under
  construction
2 Reliance on local labour
  and materials
3 Veranda as extension of
  living space
4 Exterior, side view
5 Exterior, front view

2008	Rudrapur, Bangladesh

HOMEmade DESI
Community engagement in a rural setting

Three village homes were built by a group of Austrian and Bangladeshi students led by their teachers and a non-government organisation. The process became a quest to redefine *home* within a community with very few resources. The battle for stakeholders' hearts began with the question of how to build. Locals used to seeing the village elite build with bricks and concrete aspired to emulate the better-off and more powerful. The project team argued instead for mud, a building material commonly used in this part of the country, seeking to reconnect people with traditional craft and skills. Arguments on durability and the cost-effectiveness of mud were not enough to persuade the hosts.[96] The team turned to several ideas that made them see the material in a new way. Focusing on strategies for passive comfort – a cool interior in tropical heat – the design team made the case that the new homes would be unlike the mud homes they knew. The newer ones would have coconut fibre insulation, glass windows for daylight and openings for cross-ventilation. Mud construction done right could be taken up to two storeys instead of the one-storey structures that the village was used to seeing. This meant that land could be freed up for crop cultivation, a key to survival in periods of shortage.

96_ Heringer, A. (2008)

6 Aerial view of completed estate

7 Future residents engaged in feedback sessions during design process

8 *Care-for-Seedlings* campaign

2009	Hong Kong, People's Republic of China

Redevelopment of Lam Tin Estate, Phase 7
Community engagement

This residential estate occupies a site area of 2.7 hectares and consists of four 40-storey blocks with over 3,000 units. The theme that was adopted at the start of the design process – *Green living* – suggested intent to influence the lifestyles of future residents. This intent translated into a series of community workshops during the design process. Early in the schematic design phase, the project team met with residents and solicited their views on ideas that were on the drawing board. When the building commenced construction,

the team again involved residents in workshops that focused on the design of a key shared space – a two-storey landscape area for community activities called the Deck Garden. Participants were also asked to decide on content for a heritage trail that would tell the story of the estate. Engagement continued through the construction stage with school visits, art workshops and writing competitions. The residents' sense of becoming stakeholders was further heightened when they were asked to care for seedlings

during the construction stage. Upon completion, the seedlings were permanently planted around the estate. This meant that each resident could point to a plant or a tree on the estate as something they helped create. Results from a post-occupancy survey were exceptionally positive: over 96% said they were satisfied with the design and provision of facilities within the estate.

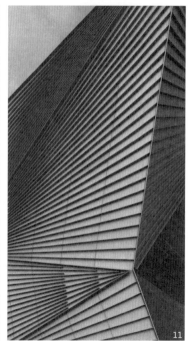

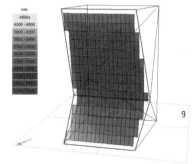

2008 Ningbo,
People's Republic of China

Centre for Sustainable Energy Technologies
Culture meets science

This is one of a rare breed of Green buildings that speaks to both the layperson and the building professional. Standing 22 m tall, the facades of the Centre for Sustainable Energy Technologies (CSET) *fold* to form dynamic shapes, reminiscent of traditional Chinese paper lanterns. Behind the culturally inspired exterior is a measure of scientific rigour that is all about managing energy flows through this 1,200 m² building. Spaces inside have been configured to support a number of different heating, cooling and ventilation strategies. The double-skin envelope – with its screen-printed patterns on the glass evoking historical buildings of the area – functions as a thermal barrier in summer and a ventilation cavity in winter. Renewable technologies such as solar thermal collectors (linked to a vapour absorption cooling system) and a ground-source heat pump (linked to heating/cooling coils within the floor slabs) satisfy the residual heating and cooling demand. Energy for power and artificial lighting requirements is met by photovoltaic arrays. These are integrated into the landscape and visible to the public at large. The centre accommodates laboratories and classrooms for postgraduate courses. And while the building gets on with the business at hand, it offers up a vision of culture-meets-science to visitors who are free to wander about the grounds and exhibition space. The latter provides real-time information on how the building, its systems and strategies are performing.

2011　　Tainan City,
　　　　Taiwan

Magic School of Green Technology, National Cheng Kung University
Signals and symbols

The project's moniker – *Magic School of Green Technology* – is as fantastical as the building's appearance. Its design speaks in several ways. The leaf-shaped solar panel on the roof (complete with make-believe ladybird) generates electrical power. Several solar chimneys nearby draw air through the building, reducing the need for air conditioning. A terraced roof garden is linked to ground-level ponds that capture rainwater and cool the building's exterior. And in case the allegorical reference to Noah's Ark is missed, there is a ship's

wheel on the front lawn that is used to rotate the solar panels. As visitors walk through the building's interior, they can point to its palette of Green materials. Carpets are made of corn. The concrete has a chemical composition that is said to improve air quality. Perhaps the most striking part of the school's accomplishment is how it was built. The three-storey 4,800 m² building is an instructive tale of industry partnership. Faced with a lack of government support, the developer – Taiwan's National Cheng Kung University – sought out

private funding. The project is now touted as a symbol of corporate involvement, the how-to of Greening in a world of limited financing. None of this would have any significance if its performance wasn't up to scratch. The building needs only 43 kWh of electrical power per m² floor area per year – about 65% less than similar office buildings in Taiwan. It is made with 100% Green materials. Carbon offsetting (off-site reforestation) makes this Taiwan's first carbon neutral building.

INTEGRATION

ALIGNING PROCESS TOWARDS PERFORMANCE

The design process gets little attention in Asia despite evidence that the sequence of decisions made on the drawing board and multi-stakeholder collaboration can profoundly affect outcome. Process has often been argued to be one of the most important considerations in the pursuit of sustainable goals in the building sector.[97]

The Integrated Design Process (IDP) is regarded as a methodological framework for correcting the prevailing culture of short-termism

---

97_ United Nations Environment Programme.
(2007)

and fragmentation.[98] It does this by encouraging "collaborative exchange at the drawing board and actively blurring traditional disciplinary knowledge boundaries".[99]

Some projects in Asia are starting to seek out a higher order of integration by applying IDP, looking for synergies, closed loops and multiplier effects. The water loop at the Evason Resort,[100] for instance, recycles wastewater via open ponds that create a cooler microclimate *and* offer guests an attractive landscape. These ponds also recharge the water table and support plant and bird life. A single intervention that started out as a means of wastewater management offers dividends on wellness, embeddedness and ecology.

Elsewhere the quest for integration is increasingly supported by performance modelling software. There is a proliferation of computing tools offering visualisation and diagnostics that aid a designer's intuition. These tools permit a discussion of performance earlier in the design process, making performance itself more accessible and better understood. Building Information Modelling (BIM) is an example of a tool that permits different stakeholders to work within a single virtual platform. A BIM model allows performance to be understood in a number of new ways, streamlining tedious calculations that are needed to estimate outcome.[101]

For an alignment of process towards integration, three shifts are necessary:

1. Performance must be seen as something that continues long after the project is completed. The boundary of time should be no less than the predicted life of the building.

2. Performance must be described as something more than economic return; it must embrace social and ecological agenda that are peculiar to a place and linked to the principles of

---

98_ "Integrated design is a procedure considering and optimising the building as an entire system including its technical equipment and surroundings and for the whole lifespan. This can be reached when all actors of the project cooperate across disciplines and agree to far-reaching decisions jointly from the beginning. The integrated design process emphasises the iteration of design concepts early in the process by a coordinated team of specialists." | Lohnert, G., Dalkowski, A. & Sutter, W. (2003)

99_ Cole, R.J. (2012b)

100_ See section on Efficacy, pp. 64–69

101_ "Digital information can be used inferentially to analyse and optimise the design itself, derive detailed mathematical models of building performance for energy consumption or heating/lighting performance, extract control instructions for fabrication of building components, coordinate the interaction of enclosure, structure and mechanical systems, or form the basis of a construction sequencing strategy for the contractor. As the building industry struggled in the first decade of the 21st century for improved efficiency, profitability and environmental responsibility, it increasingly turned to building information modeler (BIM) tools

to address these needs in support of an improved design agenda." | Bernstein, P.G. (2010)

wellness, embeddedness and ecology. In some instances, these can be assigned a monetary value.[102] But value must be broadly defined as something meaningful to a building's users and the community at large. It is important to explicitly articulate these less tangible, nonetheless important, goals on the drawing board.

3. A *dashboard of metrics* should be relied upon to describe both quantitative and qualitative indicators of performance. A target for energy-efficient lighting might, for instance, be set alongside one for occupant satisfaction with the indoor environment. This juxtaposition permits the design process to become an act of calibration where the demands on one metric are balanced with another. The metrics suited to a project will depend on where it is and what purpose it serves over its lifetime.

102_ Value can, for instance, be assessed in terms of the added appeal to a potential buyer, the perceived impact on a tenant's corporate brand or the predicted increase in occupant productivity.

THE INTEGRATED DESIGN PROCESS IS REGARDED
AS A METHODOLOGICAL FRAMEWORK FOR
CORRECTING THE PREVAILING CULTURE OF
SHORT-TERMISM AND FRAGMENTATION. IT
DOES THIS BY ENCOURAGING "COLLABORATIVE
EXCHANGE AT THE DRAWING BOARD AND ACTIVELY
BLURRING TRADITIONAL DISCIPLINARY KNOWLEDGE
BOUNDARIES".

1 Skylight glazing doubles up to generate electrical power
2 Daylight ingress is enhanced with light shelves
3 Atrium interior
4 Concrete slabs above work-spaces are cooled to reduce reliance on conventional ducted air conditioning

2007   Bangi,
        Malaysia

Green Energy Office Building
Crossing disciplinary boundaries

The Green Energy Office (GEO) building followed in the footsteps of the Low Energy Office (LEO) building, an earlier project that sought to encourage the adoption of energy-efficient practices in buildings in Malaysia. The latter was the first to consume less than 100 kWh/m²/year, a significant threshold for air-conditioned office buildings. To improve on this, GEO's design process was rethought. All consultants and stakeholders were engaged before the commencement of sketch design phase. The form of the building – its early considerations of geometry and orientation – was seen to be the most effective strategy for reducing energy demand. The stepped profile of the building was conceived in direct response to sun angles in Malaysia. This lead to the design of facades that are perpetually shaded. With solar heat under control, an innovative cooling system was devised for the interior. The structural slabs are cooled with chilled water. The resulting *radiant* cooling is combined with conventional space cooling to deliver thermal comfort at a much lower energy cost. The risk with this system was condensation forming on the chilled slabs. Success meant getting the structural engineer (responsible for slabs), mechanical engineer (responsible for cooling technologies) and architect (responsible for air-tightness of the envelope) to work in an integrative manner eliminating the risk of failure. The building clocked a consumption index of 64 kWh/m²/year, one of the lowest for a fully air-conditioned building in Southeast Asia.

5 Architectural model showing exterior view
6 Performance modelling showing daylight distribution on lower floor
7 Performance modelling showing solar exposure of building envelope
8 Integration of landscaping, water and building

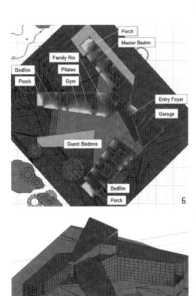

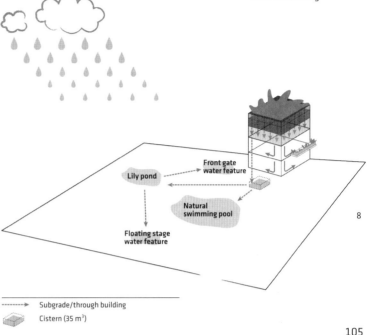

Subgrade/through building

Cistern (35 m³)

105

2012   Singapore

Two Astrid Hill
Resource loops and systems

The owner of this residential development sought to define ethical living for her family through this new multi-generational home built to last several generations. Greening began with the formulation of a *performance brief* that sought, first, to translate her vision to specific targets for the new home and, second, to examine opportunities of site and context. Benchmarks for consumption patterns in Singapore were assembled; microclimate of the site was logged. Early sketches focused on the potential for passive comfort and tapping available energy, water and materials on-site. The design-construction process that followed was punctuated by a series of design *charrettes* in which the entire project team met to review strategies and targets. Integration was central to these discussions. This meant seeking synergy between architecture, mechanical systems and landscaping. Rainwater, for instance, would be collected to satisfy water demands arising from landscape irrigation, swimming pool top-up and toilet flushing. This water retention system consisted of several water features that form an ecosystem in which new and existing flora would attract butterflies and birds. The landscaping, extending onto building facades and roofs, was expected to improve microclimate by making the site cooler, less heat retentive, allowing the building to open up to breezes and daylight. To assess these outcomes, the design team relied on performance modelling tools.

9

10

11

106

| 2014 | Shanghai, |
| | People's Republic of China |

Shanghai Tower
Building information modelling

Shanghai Tower is one of a new breed of tall buildings that presents its complex, hypertall form as an explicit response to climate and energy. The spiraling geometry of the tower is expected to reduce wind load by 24% and aid rainwater harvesting. Vertical axes turbines located near the top of the tower will generate some 350,000 kWh of energy per year. The importance of wind load and potential for wind energy are tied in with the height and size of the building: some 632 m tall, consisting of 128 storeys with a total floor area of 380,000 m². To break down this massive scale, the tower was conceived as nine vertically stacked cylindrical buildings, wrapped in a double-skin facade. Each segment of the tower has its own atrium with sky gardens that offer community and commercial spaces. To make the process faster and less costly, BIM software was used. The building's response to wind, for instance, could be readily understood in terms of material savings: 25% less structural steel and 14% less glass than a conventional square building of the same area. The tool offered an estimate on energy yields from renewable technologies so that the team could work towards integrating solutions and meeting specific targets. By enabling the reduction of the number of customised parts needed, BIM in effect lowered cost and carbon footprint. Lastly, with the BIM link to LEED credit structure, the team – consisting of many experts across continents – could simultaneously track its ambition for certification.

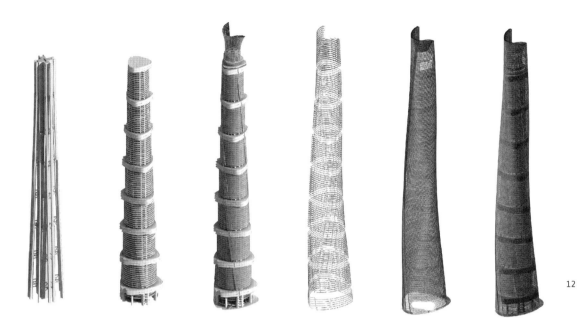

FROM GREEN
TO SUSTAINABLE
MINDING
THE GAPS

The question asked here – how Green might transition to *sustainable* – started with subquestions about Greening in Asia leading to a discussion on system boundaries. It was found that Greening, as it stands, does not challenge boundaries of *Space*, *Time* and *Exchange* that frame how buildings are designed and valued by the building sector. This results in a pace of change that is slower than necessary or meaningful to Asia. The current framework, represented by assessment tools, is not enough to address the diversity of the region, its variations of climate, wealth, culture and ecology.

Six principles of sustainable design were extracted from recent developments that are stepping out of the shadow of assessment tools. Unlike the nomenclature of assessment tools, these principles – and the words that describe them – are inclusive and do not compartmentalise knowledge. They pose questions on the drawing board that can be put to any development in Asia. Efficacy as a goal, for instance, can be applied to buildings with low technological dependency as well as those that have high reliance on electro-mechanical systems. Wellness applies to building occupants who are affluent as well as to those who are not. Embeddedness and ecology matter in both urban and rural settings. Advocacy and integration prescribe rules of engagement that hold true for all building types, anywhere in Asia.

In the principles put forth, Green and sustainable are found to be different in three ways:

Parts versus whole
A Green building is an aggregate of technologies and strategies that reduce environmental impact through systemic and incremental improvements of performance, mostly within the physical limits of site and shell. To design sustainably is to see the building embedded within a wider system of exchanges at the scale of neighbourhood and city that includes social and ecological considerations of place. In taking on these exchanges, sustainable design sets out to close loops and restore flows, create synergies and bring about multiplier effects.

Certainty versus risk
Greening seeks certainty of outcome and calculable risks for short-term gains. This creates a bias for solutions that are technological and quantifiable. Sustainability is a long-term perspective; while short-term concerns may be addressed en route, it seeks ultimately to address both the uncertain and the qualitative. In mapping exchanges over the life of a building – however imprecise these might be – the design team begins to ask different questions.

Design becomes a way of formulating strategies that make a building more resilient and better able to adapt.

Needs versus wants

Greening concerns itself with the efficiency of systems that deliver what occupants are assumed to need or want for their well-being. Sustainable design sees the occupant as an active agent in the building-user exchange whose needs and wants are negotiated. The goal here is wellness which embraces the physiological, psychological and emotional responses of users. Sustainable design creates opportunities for its occupants to connect with community and nature, and to adopt sustainable patterns of living.

What will a sustainable building in Asia be like? There isn't a definitive answer yet. This may be because the realignment from Green to sustainable has just begun. Some projects presented in this book do some things well, none do them all. There are also, within this sampling, two seemingly diverging constructs of what it means to be sustainable: *ecological* and *technological*.[103]

Ecological sustainability is a biocentric perspective in which a development is seen in relation to the natural world, the dynamic but finite ecologies that are in a state of balance. It translates into careful deliberation of how a project is integrated into the wider system that it inhabits, what and how much it consumes, and at what cost to human beings and nature.

Technological sustainability makes the case that buildings should be designed to work smarter and harder. Technology needs to catch up or, as the case might be, we need to catch up with what is available. Current solar technologies, for instance, could meet Earth's energy needs many times over. The leaders in adoption, such as Germany, are not necessarily the ones with the most sunshine or more advanced systems. Rather, they are the ones with political will and fiscal foresight.[104]

110

103_ Orr, D.W. (1992)
104_ National Geographic Society. (2009, September)

This approach to sustainable design implicitly takes the view that if technology were properly harnessed we may not need to alter our lifestyles or compromise comfort.

Both approaches appear to be taking root in Asia, with some projects subscribing to one more than the other. The developments featured in the pages ahead present this ecological-technological dichotomy in action.

As an example of the technological viewpoint, the Headquarters of Energy Commission of Malaysia reports an energy efficiency index of 58 kWh/m^2/year. What is noteworthy here is that this building is 80% mechanically cooled, no different from conventional office buildings in Malaysia that consume four times the energy. The Energy Commission's smarter use of resources is made possible with technological innovation.

The Green School in Indonesia takes the opposite view. Its bamboo structures, set in the landscape of Bali, challenge the way its users see themselves in relation to nature. Technology is a bit player in this dialectic. By engaging site and climate productively, it asks how we should conduct our lives. This project is exemplary of the ecological paradigm.

There are others that straddle the fence. The Met in Bangkok, Thailand, for instance, offers every one of its resident the option to switch on air conditioning. The architects also took pains to design the building for natural ventilation. About half its residents say they are dependent on air conditioning, the rest say they enjoy the free cooling. This is significantly better than other equivalent residential towers in Bangkok, many of which are wholly reliant on air conditioning most of the time. How The Met's residents behave in the future will depend on the economic and ecological challenges they will face. The building, for its part, allows them the option to adapt.

In the decades to come, both strands of sustainable thinking will matter profoundly. As Asia urbanises, there will be greater need for technological innovation and efficacy. As its cities densify and expand, there will be calls for an ecological approach that can repair and restore natural systems. As the effects of climate change are felt, it will become critical that buildings are designed for resilience and adaptation.

The worst that can happen now is for buildings to continue to be designed in ways that pretend not to see what's coming.

ALILA VILLAS ULUWATU

BALI,
INDONESIA

Bali, Indonesia ◉

◉ Alila Villas Uluwatu

Jalan Belimbing Sari
Banjar Tambiyak
Desa Pecatu 80364
Bali, Indonesia

Location
8.84593° S
115.15167° E

Completion
June 2009

Cost
US$60,000,000

Size
Up to 2 levels

Gross floor area
26,595 m²

Built-up area[1]
58,635 m²

Site area
144,642 m²

Site coverage
40.5%

Type
Hospitality

Programme
50 suites
35 residential villas
2 restaurants
Spa
Gym
Yoga pavilion

Occupancy
138 guests
277 staff

Operational hours
8,760/year

115

1_ Including walls, gardens, walkways, circulation, pool decks and paved areas

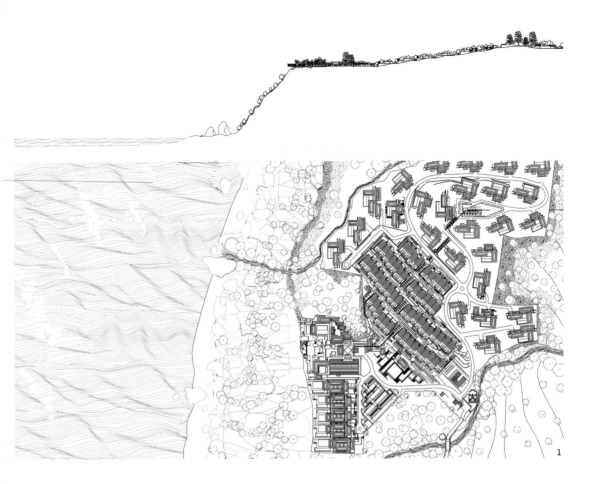

1   Site plan and section
2–3   Uninterrupted view of sea
       over villa rooftops
4–5   Flat roofs of villas with
       lava rock insulation

Alila Villas Uluwatu (AVU) is situated on the southern coastline of Bali against a landscape of rocky limestone cliffs. Its competitors on the island are typically lush year round with vernacular affectations known as the *Bali style*, popularised in the 1980s. These conventions of style and landscaping would have been costly in a semi-arid setting like Uluwatu where a lot of water would be needed to keep up appearances. Breaking with these norms might have been costly too. At stake were the expectations of travellers who come to Bali for its particular mix of design and lifestyle.

The rethink of what is tropical began on the drawing board with a site-specific response to climate and topography. The resort's flat roofs and orthogonal volumes create pathways for wind, light and views. Its heavy walls offer insulation and shade. In a conventional resort, when guests switch on the air conditioning, the lightweight timber walls and thatched roofs are unable to hold in the *coolth*. At AVU the interface between inside and out is calibrated with mass, permeability and air-tightness. Its villas work equally well when naturally ventilated or air-conditioned.

The resort also takes the idea of the Balinese garden forward, marrying the formal aesthetics of landscaping with concerns for ecology. The design process started with a mapping of existing flora and fauna, geographical contours and storm water flows, all of which influenced the final site layout.

There are two assumptions about resort architecture that AVU has challenged. First, that resorts must conform to a style mantra. Second, that a resort should always look the way it did when it first opened: in a frozen state of perfection. Several years into operation there is an emerging patina of weathering on its walls. Some guests do not *get* this seeming oversight but many more

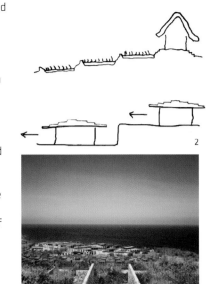

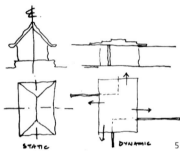

reportedly come back for a second and third visit. And when enough come back, it becomes proof of an emerging brand loyalty. This linking of ethics on the drawing board to profits *tomorrow* is what makes AVU something of a game changer. Since its opening, AVU has been lauded by the design profession and international media, all of which speak of the adoption and integration of ecological strategies that set it apart. The gamble to be different yet responsible seems to be paying off.

120

Wellness
Architecture and nature

The palette of materials consists of sandstone, limestone, lava stone, bamboo and iron wood, all of which allude to a link to nature and locale. This continues outdoors with rubble and stone walls, stone-filled water channels and ponds, and greenery that extend onto roofs and vertical surfaces. The persistence of things natural is central to how wellness is grounded here.

The pursuit of wellness is also evident in the play of shadow and natural light. The building skin is a climatic filter with deep overhanging roofs and perforated facades. Circulation linkways are ventilated arcades that are connected to open-to-sky courtyards. Light coloured walls amplify daylight. Shadow patterns are everywhere – lobbies, cabanas, restaurant interiors – resulting from a number of cleverly designed sunscreens that continuously emphasise the link between inside and outside.

11

121

10

12

13

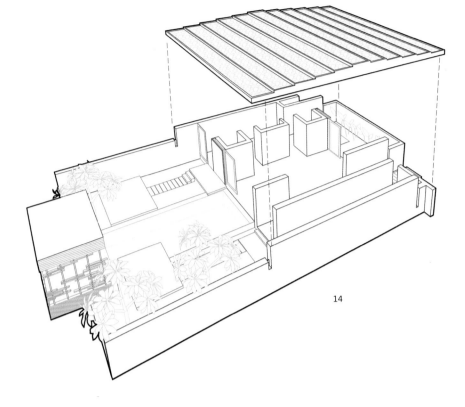

14

Wellness
Climate and comfort

A guest villa at AVU is designed as a mix of indoor and outdoor spaces. Its front courtyard faces the sea and is separated from the rear court by several layers of living spaces. This makes the villa, volumetrically, a conduit for air and light. When partitions slide into place, they permit the living spaces to be air-conditioned. When partitions are left open, air moves from front to back with little interruption or turbulence.

Both front and back courts have water and plants that temper ambient temperatures. This arrangement of space and skin results in indoor conditions that are up to 2°C cooler than air temperatures in the front courtyard.[2] Air speeds inside can reach up to 0.5 m/s. There is an equitable distribution of light with an average daylight factor of 0.5.

The villa relies on the thermal mass of its envelope – block work and concrete slabs – to create an added buffer to the tropical heat. Roofs are covered in lava rock that act as insulation and a growing medium for plants, reducing heat build-up and thermal transmission. Internal surface temperatures of wall and ceiling rarely rise above 28°C regardless of outdoor fluctuations, proof that thermal lag and insulation work well. The difference between surface and air temperatures results in a measure of radiant cooling that is equivalent to a modest drop in operative temperature.

2_ Sze, T.Y. (2011)

15

16

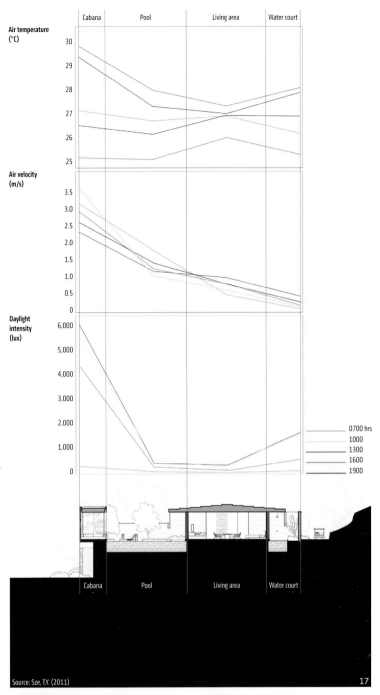

Air temperature (°C)

30
29
28
27
26
25

Air velocity (m/s)

3.5
3.0
2.5
2.0
1.5
1.0
0.5
0

Daylight intensity (lux)

6,000
5,000
4,000
3,000
2,000
1,000
0

| Cabana | Pool | Living area | Water court |

0700 hrs
1000
1300
1600
1900

| Cabana | Pool | Living area | Water court |

Source: Sze, T.Y. (2011)

17

Guest acceptance of passive modes is reportedly high. The lower-than-average consumption at AVU reflects, in part, a low reliance on electro-mechanical systems. At 179.5 kWh/guest night, AVU is 28% more energy efficient than equivalent properties in a similar climate.[3]

18

19

20

3_ EarthCheck. (2010)

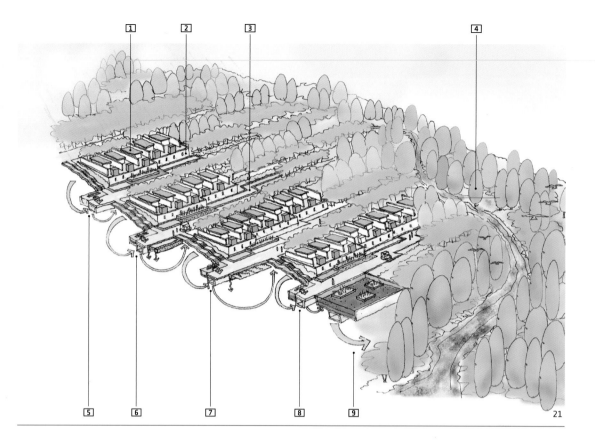

1 Green roofs absorb rainwater
2 Spouts relieve water pressure from retaining walls and drain water out to soakaways and rain gardens
3 Lava rock-filled soakaways intercept surface run-off through the site
4 Preservation of the wildlife ecosystem around the site through protection and conservation of biodiversity belts

5 Collected storm and grey water are aerated through the lava rock cascades running alongside the grand stairway, forming the key access feature and backbone of the development
6 The entire landscape surface functions as infrastructure for infiltration and collection of rainwater through soakaway drains and rain gardens
7 Underground collection tanks provide water for irrigation

8 Aerated water will be further cleaned by biofiltration in ecological ponds
9 Delayed discharge of excess filtered water to the river to prevent erosion of the ridge and disturbance of its rich flora and fauna

100%

OF ALL WATER USED FOR IRRIGATION AND LANDSCAPE FEATURES COMES FROM RECYCLED SOURCES

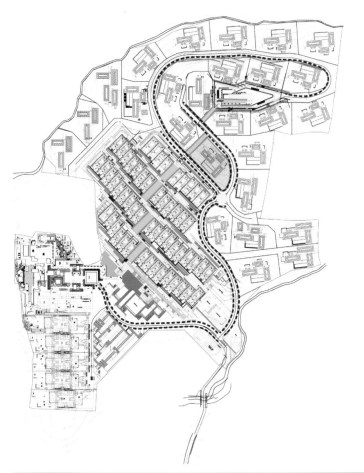

39%

OF ALL WATER NEEDED IS SOURCED
FROM RAINWATER COLLECTION OR
GREY WATER RECYCLING

AN ADDITIONAL

20%

IS SOURCED ON-SITE FROM
DEEP WELLS

Water cascading to aerate grey water

Ecological retention pond A (allowed to recede during dry season)

Ecological retention pond B (kept in operation with grey water during dry season)

Collection tanks

Seepage garden with lush planting and birdbath/rain garden water feature

Sponge wall/living fence

Swale along road with interval soakaway

25

Efficacy
Site hydrology and water reuse

Water as a resource was considered early in the design process. The team, conscious of the potential for capture and reuse, also sought to retain links with ecology. Aquifer recharge, for instance, takes place through soakaways, swales and rain gardens. Only plants that are indigenous to dry climates are used so as to reduce demand for irrigation. Swimming pools are fed with saltwater; none rely on chlorine.

On-site flows of rain and grey water are integrated into a formal arrangement of water features. A network of channels and retention ponds runs from high to low points of the site, running alongside pathways that link the villas to the resort's hub of amenities. The co-location of hydrological flows and movement corridors was seen as a way of peaking guest awareness. The surface network for rainwater capture, cleansing and retention is linked to a below ground system of filtration equipment and storage tanks where all wastewater from guest showers and washbasins ends up for recycling. Sewerage is likewise treated on-site; all water from this is added to the grey water system. Treated wastewater is used for site irrigation and toilet flushing.

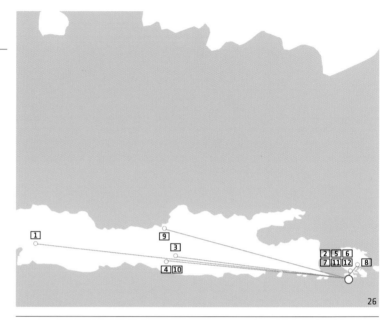

CONSTRUCTION WASTE SENT TO
LANDFILL WAS

22.4%

BETTER THAN THE INDUSTRY
AVERAGE

26

Embeddedness
Materials

Materials in tropical resorts often express place and craftsmanship. The design team at AVU added to this the criterion of environmental impact. The material palette here is a juxtaposition of the rough and refined, almost all sourced from the project site, Bali and the nearby island of Java. External wall cladding, for instance, is limestone that was left behind by site excavation. This is paired in places with sandstone from Java. Balinese lava rock is laid onto roofs and within hydrological channels because of its porous quality and lightness. Rescued telegraph poles and railway sleepers from various parts of Indonesia provide the Ulin ironwood that is used in doors and cabana screens, furniture and cabinets. Disused batik stamps from Indonesia's textile industry become the sunscreens in one of AVU's restaurants. Bamboo and plantation teak are used throughout as interior finishes. During construction, care was taken to separate waste and recycle it on-site. No chemicals were used for termite treatment and, across all instances of wood application, non-toxic preservatives were sourced.

62%
OF ALL SOLID WASTE GENERATED
DURING OPERATION IS RECYCLED,
REUSED OR COMPOSTED

127

Ravine forest

Fingers of ravine forest

Extended reinforcement of native shrubland vegetation

Speciment stands of ravine forest

Indigenous stands of evergreen

Single indigenous stands (*Ceiba Pentandra*)

Single indigenous stands (*Plumeria* 'Bali' Yellow)

Living fence

Roof garden

Single indigenous stands (*Corypha Utan*)

34

Ecology
Site and landscape

Large trees on-site were identified and retained; those that could not be kept were transplanted. Cut-and-fill of contours was minimised; existing gradients determined the eventual terracing of villas. Only indigenous plants were selected. To get this right, vegetation was surveyed and documented; specimens were sent to Royal Botanic Gardens, Kew, United Kingdom (UK), for identification. This meant that the site would continue to attract local animals and birds. The repopulation of the site, following the end of construction, has been rapid. There are enough sightings at AVU of nesting birds and dragonflies to suggest that there is a thriving ecosystem, extending from primary to tertiary consumers.

Reliance on native vegetative species has resulted in a temporal, cyclical effect on the landscape. Plants that are dormant in the dry season begin to flower when it rains. The rocky roofscapes of the villas are then transformed into verdant terraces. This rhythmic bloom-and-recede cycle in landscaping is almost never seen in other Balinese resorts which are known for year-round lushness.

34   Landscape diagram
35–37   Local flora and fauna

PROJECT TEAM

Developer
Franky Tjahyadikarta,
PT Bukit Uluwatu Villa

Architect
WOHA

Mechanical and electrical engineer
PT Makesthi Enggal
Engineering

Civil and structural engineers
| Worley Parsons Pte Ltd
| PT Atelier Enam Struktur

Ecologically sustainable design consultant
Sustainable Built
Environments

Lighting consultant
Lighting Planners Associates

Quantity surveyors
PT Kosprima Sarana
Kuantitama

Landscape consultant
Cicada Pte Ltd

Contractor
PT Hutama Karya

Operator
Alila Hotels and Resorts

SUPPLIERS

Steel columns
PT Ronasarana

Stone
| Jogja stone
  Yogya Lestari

| Batu Candi
  UD Citra Candi
| Batu Suka Bumi
  CV Alam Fajar
| Lava rocks
  UD Pada Dadi

Recycled wood (Ulin)
CV Hijo Mas

Recycled glass blocks
Deddy Shop

Bamboo ceiling
| PT Hakersen Indonesia
| CV Pande Kreasi
| CV Zuma

Recycled/plantation teak
CV Bhmi Cipta Mandiri

Low-VOC paint
Nippon Paint

Polished cement tiles
CV Limas Jaya Nusantara

In situ white terrazzo
CV Limas Jaya Nusantara

Batik stamps
Vendors in Pekalongan, Solo,
and Yogjakarta

Energy-saving heat pumps for water heating
PT Dewata Vulcannindo

Local electricity supplier
PT Medco Power Indonesia

Local water supplier
Perusahaan Daerah Air
Minum (PDAM)

AWARDS

2011
| Winner, *International Architecture Award*, Chicago Athenaeum: Museum of Architecture and Design and the European Centre for Architecture, Art, Design and Urban Studies
| Winner, *RIBA International Awards*, Royal Institute of British Architects
| Finalist, *ULI Awards for Excellence, Asia-Pacific* Urban Land Institute

2010
| Winner, *Good Design Award*, Chicago Athenaeum: Museum of Architecture and Design and the European Centre for Architecture, Art, Design and Urban Studies
| Bronze Award, *Design for Asia Award*, Hong Kong Design Centre
| Bronze Winner, *Asia Pacific Interior Design Awards*, hotel space category, Hong Kong Interior Design Association
| Winner, *Gold Key Award for Excellence in Hospitality Design*, best hotel design category, International

Hotel/Motel & Restaurant
Show
| Winner, *World Holiday Building of the Year*, holiday category, World Architecture Festival
| National Commendation for International Architecture, Australian Institute of Architects
| Winner, *Best Aesthetics Conception Award*, Asia-Pacific Interior Design Biennial Awards, Asia Pacific Federation of Architects/Interior Designers
| Winner, *Best Design Client Award*, Asia-Pacific Interior Design Biennial Awards, Asia Pacific Federation of Architects/Interior Designers
| Winner, *Outstanding Design Award*, Asia-Pacific Interior Design Biennial Awards, Asia Pacific Federation of Architects/Interior Designers
| Honourable Mention, 10th SIA Architectural Design Awards, commercial projects category, Singapore Institute of Architects

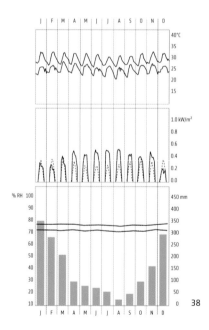

38

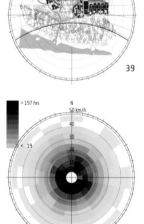

39

40

Honourable Mention, 10th SIA Architectural Design Awards, interior architecture category, Singapore Institute of Architects

Winner, BCI Green Leadership Award, commercial category, BCI Asia Construction Information Pte Ltd

Finalist, ULI Awards for Excellence, Asia-Pacific Urban Land Institute

Finalist, 6th Annual Hospitality Design Awards, resort category, Hospitality Design Magazine

First Place Winner, Earth-Minded Awards, hospitality projects, Hospitality Design Magazine and the American Society of Interior Designers

2009

Winner, Best of Year Awards, Hospitality, hotel-resort category, Interior Design Magazine

Gold Winner, 3rd LIAS Awards for Excellence, Landscape Industry Association (Singapore)

Winner, Green Good Design Award, Chicago, Athenaeum: Museum of Architecture and Design and the European Centre for Architecture, Art, Design and Urban Studies

2007

Commended, MIPIM Architectural Review Future Project Awards, retail and leisure category, The Architectural Review

---

PERFORMANCE[4]

Annual energy consumption
3,141 MWh

On-site energy sourcing (% of total consumed)
Diesel generator: 35.4%

Greenhouse gas emissions
| 1,233 tonnes CO_2e/year
| 161.6 kg CO_2e/guest night

Energy intensity
| 118 kWh/m²/year
| 179.5 kWh/guest night (28% lower than EarthCheck[5] baseline)

Annual water consumption[6]
150,772.6 m³

Water intensity
5.49 m³/guest night (12% lower than EarthCheck baseline)

On-site water sourcing (% of total consumed)
| Rainwater collection: 18%
| Grey water recycling: 21%
| Deep well: 30%

Materials (construction)
| 954 m³ recycled Ulin timber
| 3,100 m³ locally sourced lava rock
| 54 m³ bamboo
| Artwork consists of naturally sourced elements and indigenous craft from within Indonesia

Materials (operations)
| 62% of waste is recycled, reused or composted
| 100% of water used for irrigation and in landscape features is from a recycled source
| 52% of paper used is eco-label paper
| Most cleaning products are environmentally friendly (Ecolab)
| All swimming pools are treated with salt (in place of chlorine)

100% of hot water is produced with a heat pump with a coefficient of performance of 4.8

Waste sent to landfill is 0.005 m³/guest night (22.4% lower than EarthCheck baseline)

Comfort modes[7]

Thermal comfort
| Passive (natural ventilation): 75%
| Active (air conditioning): 25%

Visual comfort
| Passive (daylight): 89%
| Active (electrical light): 11%

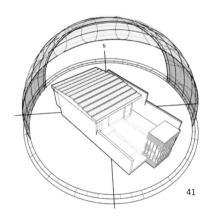

41

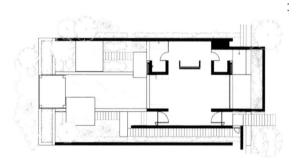

42

4_ Energy and water consumption figures are for the period November 1st 2009 to October 31st 2010.

5_ EarthCheck is a benchmarking, certification and environmental management programme used by the travel and tourism industry. | EarthCheck. www. earthcheck.org

6_ Subsequent water management (in early 2011) brought the figures down from 500 m³ a day to 250, about half to one third of other equivalent resorts in Bali. This was achieved through monitoring of consumption, including leak and waste detection.

7_ Percentage of gross floor area that is designed to be primarily reliant on passive strategies or active systems

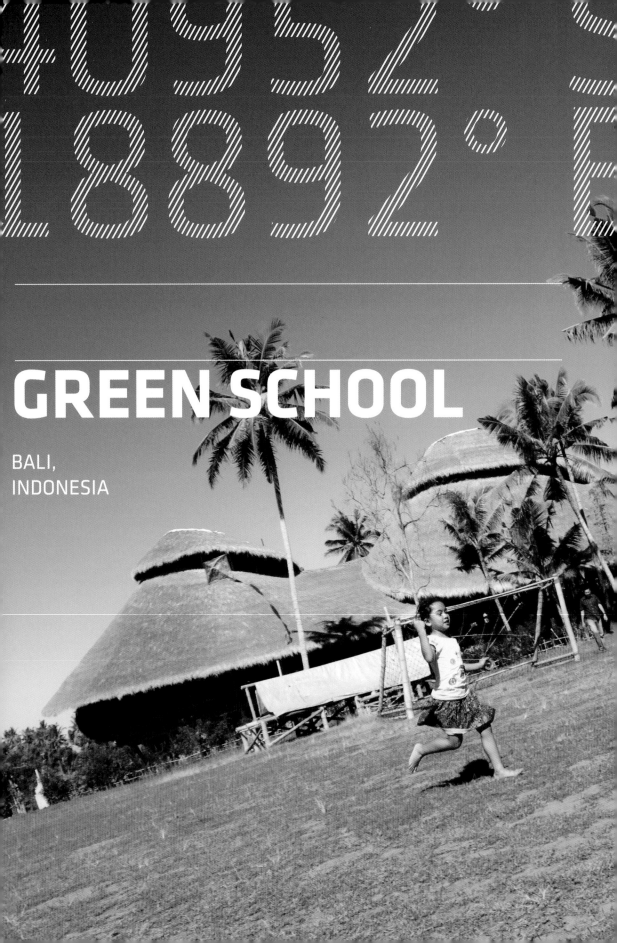

GREEN SCHOOL

BALI,
INDONESIA

Jalan Raya Sibang Kaja
Banjar Saren, Abiansemal
Badung
Bali 80352, Indonesia

Location
8.40952° S
115.18892° E

Completion
December 2007

Cost
US$3,116,318

Size
Up to 3 levels

Gross floor area
7,542 m²

Built-up area[1]
15,000 m²

Site area
103,142 m²

Site coverage
7%

Type
Education

Programme
Classrooms
Gymnasium
Heart of School
Sports field
Assembly hall
Staff housing
Medical clinic
Science laboratory
Library
Kitchen

Occupancy
200 students
160 staff

Operational hours
1,820/year

133

1_ Including walls, gardens, walkways, circulation and outdoor paved areas

The Green School (GS) campus is a cluster of bamboo buildings on a site southwest of the tourism hub of Ubud. Situated amidst rice terraces and modest village homes, the buildings of GS make a powerful first impression. The most iconic of these – the *Heart of School* – is the nexus of the campus. Its tent-like appearance reveals itself, on the inside, to be an architecture of struts and sweeping roofs. Structural supports – made of large, intertwined bundles of bamboo poles – rise through several shell-shaped floor plates, drawing the eye up to skylights. The theatricality of the space, its spatial and structural boldness, underscores the fact that this is home to a unique institution in Asia.

The School is the brainchild of John and Cynthia Hardy, a North American couple who settled in Bali in 1975 to set up a jewellery company. In public talks John tells the story of how the 2006 Al Gore film[2] proved to be something of an inconvenience. On the brink of retirement, having just sold his company, John and wife Cynthia felt compelled to start something new to change the course of their (and other) lives. Thus was born GS, a simultaneous critique of the state of the world and the role of education.

Known for its environment-based curriculum and innovative use of bamboo, the School enjoys a high profile in Asia. It advocates change on two fronts. First, it explicitly teaches environmental stewardship; second, the campus itself is a working model of embeddedness in site and community.

The success of GS as an educational enterprise has raised the profile of bamboo as a building material with an ecological advantage. Bamboo is regarded as being inferior to tropical hardwoods and is rarely used for structure or envelope unless it is in a resort where the vernacular styling serves to make a point. Like several other projects in Southeast Asia,[3] GS has changed that perception, raising the stature of bamboo to a material that can be used to create buildings that are contemporary and complex.

Just about everything in GS is made with bamboo – structure, floors, furniture, fences – grown on the island, processed and assembled by local craftsmen. Two sister concerns of GS, PT Bamboo Pure and Merangi Foundation, harvest and process the material. In 2011 PT Bamboo Pure announced the sale of Green Village, a cluster of eco-friendly residential villas near the GS campus.[4] This overlap of ethical and commercial interests, represented by the School and its affiliates, is noteworthy in Asia where the two are rarely seen to converge.

139

1–2   Interior of Mepantigan amphitheatre
3   Exterior perspective of Heart of School

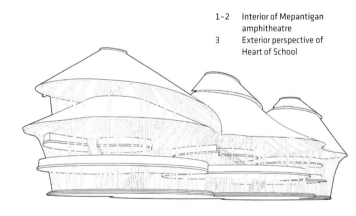

3

2_ Guggenheim, D. (Director) & Bender, L. (Producer). (2006)
3_ Le, V.C. & Lee, B.L. (2010) and Lim, C. & Lee, B.L. (2011b)
4_ Lim, C. & Lee, B.L. (2011a)

Advocacy
Teaching environmental stewardship

4-6   Curriculum built around learning from the environment

7   Donor names etched onto bamboo in Heart of School

8   Exploded axonometric of Heart of School

The most visible evidence of advocacy at work is the list of sponsors at the Heart of School where names are etched onto bamboo struts in recognition of contributions made by individuals to the School's scholarship fund. At last count there were 420, including celebrities like illusionist David Copperfield and fashion designer Donna Karan. Many lend support to the GS enterprise – its curriculum and the values that it imparts – and to its promise to shape a generation of environmental leaders.

The GS curriculum caters to learning from nursery to secondary level, mixing core subjects (English, Mathematics and Science) with Green Studies and Creative Arts encompassing craft, music and drama.[5] All GS students also have an opportunity to plant, cultivate and harvest their own bamboo and eventually use it to build something. What is imparted here is an appreciation for the living environment and its value to everyday life. News of this approach to learning has resonated internationally; some couples have reportedly moved to Bali so that their children can enrol in GS.

5_ "This is an approach of hands-on, mud-between-your-toes learning... a progression from nature study to ecological studies to environment studies to sustainability studies... It's in the planting, it's in bamboo design technology, it's in looking after animals, it's permaculture as a way of life." | Hardy, J. & Stones, R. (2010)

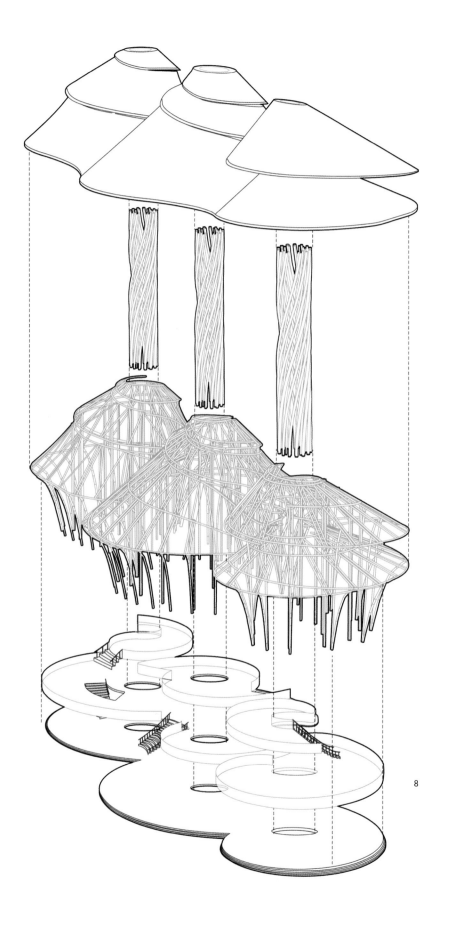

8

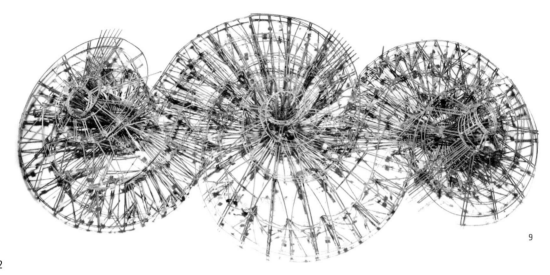

9

Embeddedness
Materials

The bamboo used to construct GS was planted by the School, harvested by local farmers and processed on-site. In the Heart of School, for instance, a total of 32,000 m of bamboo was used. It was soaked with a natural pest-resisting agent and assembled without heavy machinery. The task of assembly was carried out almost entirely by local craftsmen who already knew how to make floors from bamboo splints, held together by bamboo pins (hand-made dowelling), then planed to a smooth finish. However, the building was bigger and far more complex than anything they had worked on before. The roof, for instance, has 20,000 pieces of *alang-alang* thatching – a traditional roofing finish – significantly more than is used in a Balinese home. To make these tall and wide-span structures safe, these craftsmen worked with international experts and building professionals. This partnership – the mix of local know-how and global expertise – is what makes the buildings of GS seem familiar, and yet on another level, radically different from anything else in Bali.

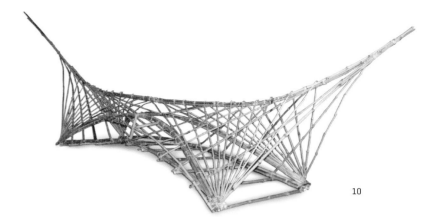

10

11

12

13

14

15

1 In every classroom:
kale, long bean, cucumber,
tomato, carrot, mint, peanut,
oregano, tarrangon, turmeric,
ginger

2 Heart of School area:
carrot, cabbage, tomato, cucumber,
peanut, long bean, mint, oregano,
celery, parsley, coriander, basil,
spinach, water spinach

3 Teachers' residential area:
mint, oregano, papaya, long bean,
eggplant, cabbage, red lettuce,
pok choy, paprika, bean, kailan

Embeddedness
Food

Some 2–4 kg of produce is generated per month per 100 m² patch of land. Aggregated across the GS campus, its 10,000 m² of arable land yields some 400 kg of vegetables which satisfies some 40% of on-site needs. This is in the process of being ramped up. With new biointensive farming methods on the way, this figure is expected to increase to 50–100 kg per 100 m² patch, over some 50,000 m² of arable land. A fifth of this will be set aside for leafy vegetables, the rest for carbohydrates such as root crops. By the time this is in place, GS will be 80% self-sufficient.

Wellness
Community

The GS vision is tied in with explicit
goals for community engagement.
Its bamboo operations, led by
PT Bamboo Pure and the Merangi
Foundation, employ some 30 craftsmen. The Foundation claims to have
planted 15,000 seedlings of bamboo
with 1,500 Balinese families. This
bamboo is expected to supplement
their living when harvested. It is
predicted that the artisan roofs of
the GS campus – which require routine
upkeep and replacement – will keep
many Balinese thatchers in business
in the years to come. For its day-to-
day operations, GS employs 50 locals
as teachers and administrators.
Ten per cent of student enrolment
is reserved for Balinese children.

16   Food map of GS campus
17–18   Vegetable gardens on
        campus
19–22   Local skills and labour in
        GS and PT Bamboo Pure

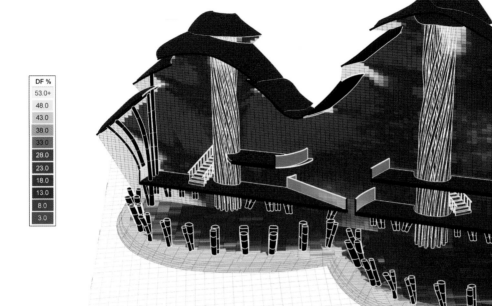

DF %
53.0+
48.0
43.0
38.0
33.0
28.0
23.0
18.0
13.0
8.0
3.0

146

23–27 All buildings on campus are predominantly reliant on daylight and natural ventilation

28 Computer simulation of daylight entry into Heart of School

Wellness
Climate and comfort

Deep overhangs and steep pitches protect interiors from sun and rain; wide openings make possible cross ventilation and daylight ingress; lightweight materials retain little of the daytime heat; dense landscaping creates a cool microclimate. The Heart of School draws air up and through its volume, thermal buoyancy generating air flow.

There are, on closer examination, subtle innovations to the tropical idiom, some as ad hoc adaptation of completed buildings. Skylights of all shapes and sizes are inserted into the bamboo structures, some in response to occupant feedback. One classroom, deemed too dark, had roof-lights cut into its thatching. The openings were sealed with polycarbonate to keep the rain out. In another, an inflatable structure – made from organic cotton and natural rubber – balloons up when needed to offer a different kind of learning space. Teaching inside this space comes with privacy and thermal comfort on hot days. This is one of few mechanically ventilated rooms on the GS campus.

Across the board, buildings moderate the climate, free of climate-control technologies. Reportedly, GS consumes less than 10 kWh/m^2/year.

PROJECT TEAM

Developer
Yayasan Kul-Kul

Architects
| Elora Hardy
| Cheong Yew Kuan, Areas Design
| Effan Adhiwira, PT Bambu-Bambu
| Miya Buxton
| Hanno Burtscher
| Philip Beck, Beck Studio

Engineers
| Prof Ir Morisco, PhD
| Ashar Saputra, PhD
| Inggar S. Irawati, ST, MT

Bamboo consultants
| Jorg Stamm
| Iskandar Halim

Environment power consultant
Rinaldo S. Brutoco

Author and environment consultant
Thomas L. Friedman

Main contractor
PT Bambu-Bambu

Contractors
| Ketut Indra Saputra
| I Ketut Sudarma

Master craftsmen
| Sutanaya, I Gede
| I Made Kura
| I Wayan Murdita
| I Ketut Sumerta
| Budiarta, I Made

| Dama, I Wayan
| Agustina

Facility manager
Nina Tresia

SUPPLIERS

Bamboo
PT Bambu-Bambu

Local electricity supplier
Perusahaan Listrik Negara (PLN)

ACCREDITATION/AWARDS
Member, Council of International Schools

2011
Finalist nominee, Design to Improve Life Award, INDEX

2010
| *Finalist nominee, Aga Khan Award for Architecture*, Aga Khan Foundation
| *Grand Award, Special Award for Sustainability, Design for Asia Award*, Hong Kong Design Centre

2009
Nominee, World Architecture Festival, Barcelona, learning building and structural design categories

---

PERFORMANCE[6]

Annual energy consumption
68.66 MWh

On-site energy sourcing (% of total consumed)
| Diesel generators: 27%
| Photovoltaic panel: 0.7%

Greenhouse gas emissions
Not available

Energy intensity
9.1 kWh/m^2/year

Annual water consumption
8,640 m^3

Water intensity
Not available[7]

On-site water sourcing (as % of total consumed)
Spring water from well: 100%

Materials (operations)
Organic
| Horticultural waste is used as a fertiliser
| Food waste is fed to pigs
| Cow dung is used to generate biogas for kitchen

Non organic
Glass, metal, plastic and paper are recycled off-site

On-site food sourcing (as % of total consumed)
40%
| Vegetables (water spinach, spinach, cabbage, lettuce)

| Fruits (eggplant, tomato, cucumber, sweet corn, okra, chilli)
| Roots (radish, carrot, cassava, peanut)
| Beans (long bean, red bean)
| Herbs (oregano, mint, basil, celery, parsley, turmeric, ginger, lemongrass)

Comfort modes[8]
Thermal comfort
| Passive (natural ventilation): 100%
| Active (air conditioning): Nil

Visual comfort
| Passive (daylight): 95%
| Active (electrical light): 5%

148

29–31 Weather for Bali, Indonesia
32 Sun path over GS
33 Mepantigan amphitheatre
34 Kul-Kul bridge

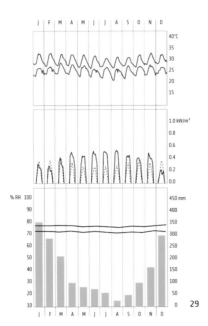

29

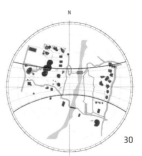

30

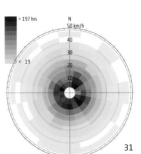

31

6_ Energy and water consumption figures are for 2011.

7_ Water consumed by GS includes water supplied to nearby village. The total number of consumers is not known.

8_ Percentage of gross floor area that is designed to be primarily reliant on passive strategies or active systems

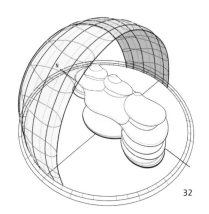

32

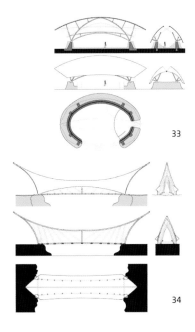

33

34

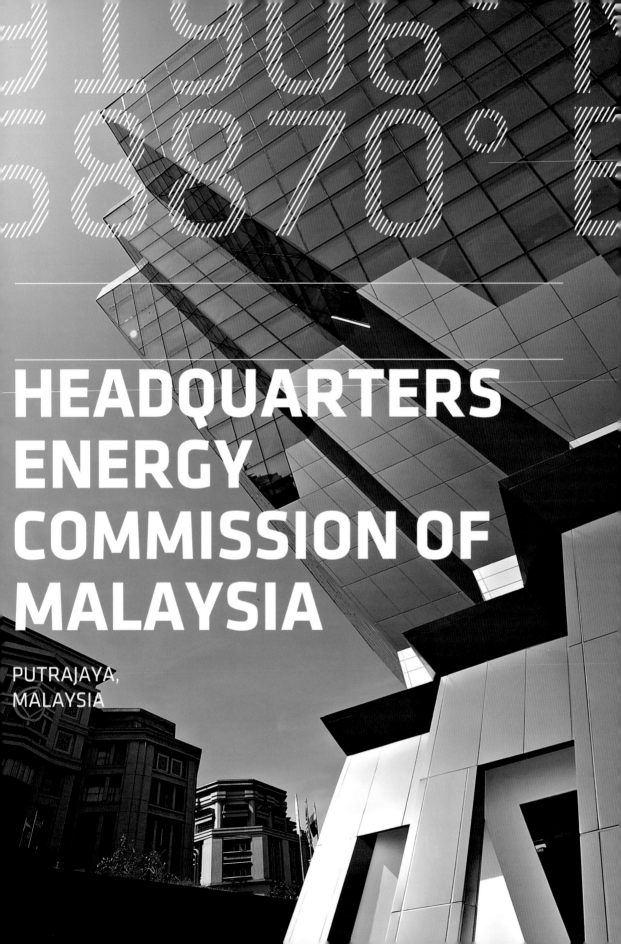

HEADQUARTERS ENERGY COMMISSION OF MALAYSIA

PUTRAJAYA,
MALAYSIA

Headquarters
Energy Commission
of Malaysia

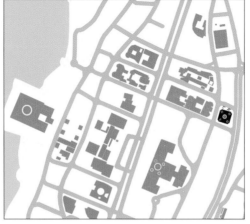

12, Jalan Tun Hussein
Precinct 2, 62100
Putrajaya, Malaysia

Location
2.91906° N
101.68870° E

Completion
June 2010

Cost[1]
US$21,982,000

Size
10 levels (including 2 basements)

Gross floor area
14,621 m²

Total built-up area[2]
23,215 m²

Site area
4,000 m²

Site coverage
58%

Type
Workplace

Programme
Offices (72% of gross floor area)

Occupancy[3]
145 staff

Operational hours
2,700/year

1_ Seventy-two point one million Malaysian
Ringgit in US dollar equivalent based on
international exchange rates on June 1st
2010 | International Monetary Fund. www.
imf.org
2_ Including covered and uncovered carparks,
walls, gardens, walkways, circulation, pool
decks and paved areas
3_ Number of occupants in 2012. The maximum capacity is 300.

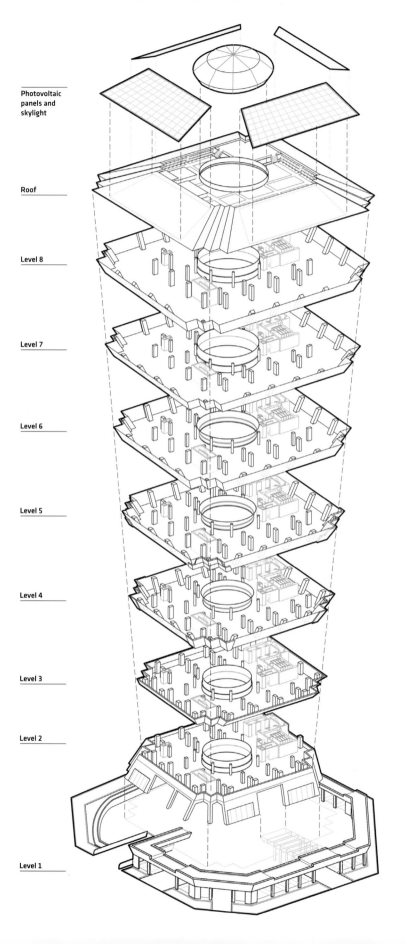

Photovoltaic
panels and
skylight

Roof

Level 8

Level 7

Level 6

Level 5

Level 4

Level 3

Level 2

Level 1

1

Putrajaya is the administrative centre of Malaysia, 25 km south of the nation's capital. Many buildings here depict identity with styles that are culturally derived. In this milieu, the Headquarters for the Energy Commission of Malaysia[4] (EC) stands out. Its crisp form – an inverted pyramid, precisely engineered – speaks of a different aspiration, of how buildings might be designed in an age of environmental concerns.

The energy index of EC says something of why it matters. It consumes 69 kWh/m^2/year; an average office building in Malaysia with similar cooling, occupancy and operations will consume three to four times as much. Two earlier buildings had paved the way for this interest in super-efficient government buildings. The Low Energy Office building (LEO) and Green Energy Office building (GEO), like EC, are home to agencies that sought to make a case for energy efficiency. Whereas LEO and GEO were products of a 1990s approach to efficiency, EC speaks of the Green movement that took off in Malaysia post 2005. By then other factors besides energy had begun to matter. The consumption of water and materials, the state of occupant well-being and environmental health of the site were prescribed by assessment tools. Its ambition to be platinum-certified with the Singapore and Malaysia tools had a profound impact on the design process. But this does not fully explain its architectural form.

Form as a precondition for performance was first explored in the GEO building that sought to minimise solar heat gain and maximise daylight. The trek from intent

to execution however resulted in a somewhat utilitarian object. With EC, form as a *communicator* of performance set out to be more accessible. The smooth, sloping and reflective skin has made it an instant landmark. Each floor is visibly bigger than the one below, making the building loom large. The skin mirrors activity on the street; the building reaches up in a skyward gesture. The skylight, rainwater collection system and photovoltaic arrays on the roof are its interface with climate. The atrium feels like a set piece. It links spaces with lines-of-sight, disseminating daylight equitably to all that sit around it. Seen from all corners, the atrium is an orienteering device that defines relationships indoors while connecting occupants to conditions outdoors. The atria of LEO and GEO were never quite this dramatic.

The sensorial experience that EC offers, coupled with its roots in performance, is made explicit. Trade-offs were expected and accepted from the outset. The pyramid shape, for instance, is only partly effective in self-shading (its east and west facades continue to get low-angle solar exposure). The explanation offered here – that this suboptimal outcome is nonetheless 41% better than a non-sloping facade – suggests a reconciliation between quantitative and qualitative aspirations.

In the final analysis GEO is only marginally better than EC in terms of energy use. However, EC speaks volumes more to its users and visitors. Since its opening EC has captured media attention and earned the moniker *ST Diamond*, becoming an emblem of Green design in Southeast Asia.

157

1	Exploded axonometric
2	Photovoltaic panels on roof
3	Sloping facades that self-shade
4	Atrium
5	Table 1: Comparison of three high performance buildings in Malaysia

	Year	Gross floor area (m^2)	Energy index (without photovoltaics)	Energy index (with photovoltaics)
Low Energy Office building	2004	20,000	100	Not applicable
Green Energy Office building	2007	4,000	64	30
Headquarters Energy Commission of Malaysia	2010	14,621	69*	63

* 85 with full occupancy

4_ The Energy Commission regulates and promotes all energy matters in Malaysia, relating to the electricity and gas supply industry.

44%
OF ALL WATER NEEDED COMES
FROM RAINWATER HARVESTING

44%
OF ALL WATER NEEDED COMES
FROM GREY WATER RECYCLING

9%
OF ALL ENERGY CONSUMED
COMES FROM PHOTOVOLTAIC
PANELS

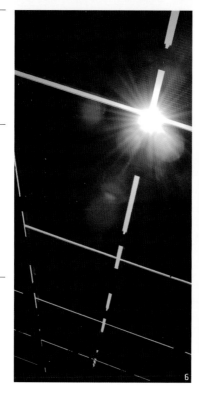

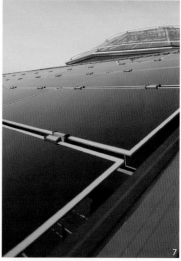

158

6–7	Photovoltaic arrays
8	Rainwater storage tanks
9	Chilled water pipes
10	Ceiling-mounted ducts
11–12	Heat recovery system link-ing outgoing and incoming water in sanitary plumbing
13	Dual cooling system: chilled water pipes in structural slab for radiant cooling and ducted air for space cooling

Efficacy and Embeddedness
Energy and water

The most visible on-site sourcing is the array of photovoltaic panels on the roof. An installation of 71.4 kWp thin films produces some 102 MWh each year, some 9% of EC's total energy demand. From the same roof, rainwater is harvested into four tanks, each with a capacity of 12 m³. Closer to the ground, grey water from the sinks and floor traps is piped separately through a sand filter to a collection tank from where it is used to irrigate a patch of mini-wetlands. A heat recovery system attached to plumbing means that incoming water is pre-heated by outgoing warm shower water. About 30–40% of the heat energy is recovered this way.

Indoor thermal comfort is delivered with a two-tiered cooling system. Cool air, supplied via ducts, is augmented with radiant cooling from the building's structure. At night water at 18°C is circulated in the slabs cooling them down to 21°C. During the day the system shuts down and the floor passively absorbs internal heat loads and solar gains. Forty per cent of cooling is delivered by radiant slabs, the rest by conven-tional space cooling. This results in a 64% drop in energy needed to move the cooling agent (water in place of air) and a 30% downsizing of air handling units. It also allows for high set points of air temperature which reduces overall demand for chilled water. Less ducted air also means the building is quieter.

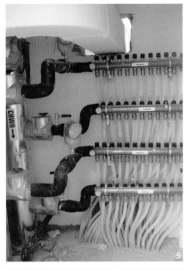

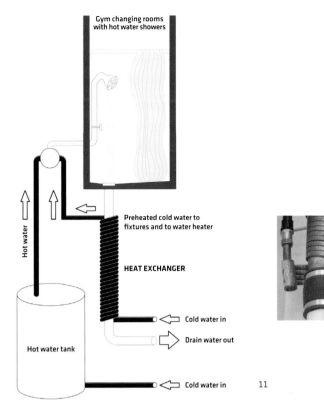

Gym changing rooms
with hot water showers

Hot water

Preheated cold water to
fixtures and to water heater

HEAT EXCHANGER

Cold water in

Drain water out

Hot water tank

Cold water in

9

10

11

12

1   Radiant cooling from floor slab
2   Cool air supply

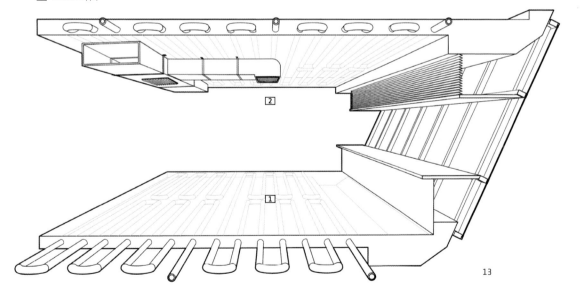

2

1

13

20%
OF THE GROSS FLOOR AREA IS
DAYLIT BY THE ATRIUM

30%
OF THE GROSS FLOOR AREA IS
DAYLIT BY OUTER ENVELOPE

14

15

14–15 Settings for atrium blinds
respond to degrees of
solar exposure
16 Solar ingress and shading
17–19 Daylight ingress into
atrium

Wellness
Daylight and shade

On plan the building is shaped like a square doughnut. This configuration, with a central void acting as atrium, means that no occupant is more than 11 m from a window. The building is 50% daylit: the atrium provides daylight to 20% of the GFA while the building facade lights up another 30%.

The slope of the external envelope – a precise 25° tilt – means that sunlight never makes it in through the north and south facades. Entry through east and west facades is partial. All outer windows are two-tiered, with a mirrored light shelf and white-painted sill. These surfaces bounce daylight onto the soffit, pushing it in by as much as 5 m from the facade. There is no ceiling as this would have interfered with radiant cooling and daylight entry. The resulting headroom – 3.7 m from floor to soffit – is substantially higher than in conventional office spaces.

The atrium brings light to the building's core, illuminating up to 2 m of office space around it. Windows are sized bigger on the lower floors to compensate for diminishing levels of light. A series of reflectors on the fourth and fifth floors reflect about 85% of incident light to the lower levels. Automated blinds over atrium skylight have six settings, corresponding to the sun's position. This reduces solar heat gain by over 40%.

January/
December

February/
November

March/
October

April/
September

May/
August

June/
July

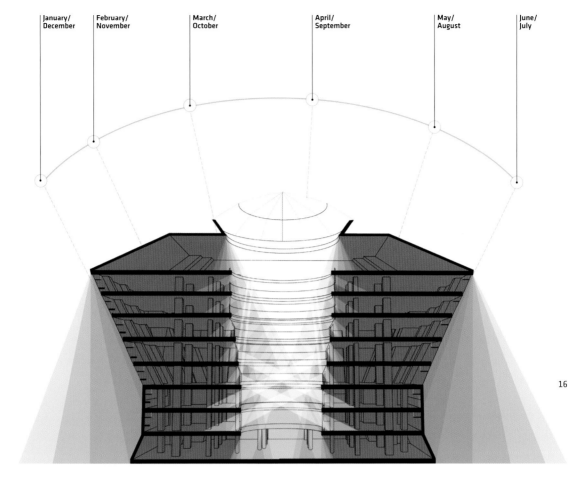

16

NO OCCUPANT IS MORE THAN

11 m

FROM A WINDOW

17

18

19

20

21

22

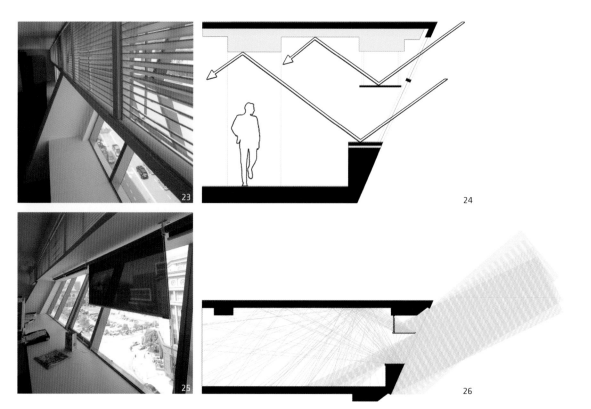

23

24

25

26

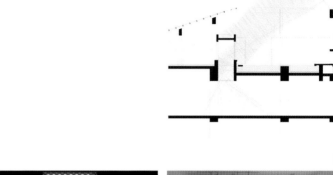

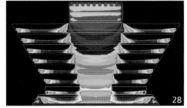

27

28

30

Integration
Performance prediction and validation

It was decided early in the design process that this would be a landmark development. This had two implications. First, it meant that EC had to be engineered to performance standards deemed high in the Malaysian building sector. Second, its architectural design had to set it apart from others of its kind. The design process began with a series of *charrettes* in which team members brainstormed ideas and discussed what *landmark* meant. The team then moved onto design development phase during which many performance issues were explored, often with the aid of computer simulations. Virtual models for energy use, daylight access, solar exposure, thermal comfort and rainwater collection were created, some with in-house software designed by environmental specialists. Several life-sized prototypes of daylight systems and floor cooling slabs were constructed. Guidelines for procurement of office equipment were issued to occupants as these would affect the energy load. Shortly after the building was completed, an occupant survey was carried out. The results from this were used to further tweak the occupant-building interface. Remedial measures were taken to improve acoustics and lighting levels which had the lowest satisfaction rating.

20–22	Conditions of shade and transparency along the building envelope
23–25	Light shelf and window sill as daylight reflectors
26	Ray trace simulation of light path through outer window
27	Visitors to EC
28	Computer simulation of daylight ingress and distribution
29	Ray trace simulation of light path through skylight
30	Effectiveness of skylight

PROJECT TEAM

Developer
Energy Commission of Malaysia, Senandung Budiman Sdn Bhd

Principal architect
Dr. Soontorn Boonyatikarn, Thailand

Architect and interior designer
NR Architect

Energy efficiency and sustainability consultant
IEN Consultants Sdn Bhd

Mechanical and electrical engineer
Primetech Engineers Sdn Bhd

Civil and structural engineer
Perunding SM Cekap

Lighting consultant
Megaman, Arcimedia Sdn Bhd

Quantity surveyor
ARH Jurukur Bahan Sdn Bhd

Landscape architect
KRB Enviro Design Sdn Bhd

Commissioning specialist
Pureaire Sdn Bhd

Main contractor
Putra Perdana Construction Sdn Bhd

Building operator
Energy Commission of Malaysia

Facility manager
Energy Commission of Malaysia, Putra Perdana Construction Sdn Bhd

SUPPLIERS

Energy-efficient lighting and task lights
Megaman

Floor slab cooling
George Fisher

Energy-efficient ventilation
AHUs with air-foil fans
Durnham Bush

Controls and sensors
Enctech Sdn Bhd

Low-e glazing
Ajiya

Insulation
Roxul, Dongji (M) Sdn Bhd

Low-VOC materials
Dulux, Shaw

Grey water recycling
Heng Jhoe Construct Sdn Bhd

Green roof
KRB Enviro Design Sdn Bhd

Solar photovoltaics
Solamas Sdn Bhd

CERTIFICATION/AWARDS

2011
| *Certified, Green Mark Platinum, new building category*, Building Construction Authority, Singapore

| *Certified, Green Building Index Platinum*, Greenbuildingindex Sdn Bhd

2010
Winner, Malaysian Construction Industry Excellence Award for Innovation, Construction Industry Development Board of Malaysia

___

PERFORMANCE[5]

Annual energy consumption
12,000 MWh

On-site energy sourcing
8.7% (71.4 kWp thin-film roof integrated photovoltaic panels)

Energy intensity
| 69 kWh/m²/year (without photovoltaics)[6]
| 63 kWh/m²/year (with photovoltaics)

Annual water consumption
5,700 m³

Water intensity
40 m³/resident/year (67% better than the Malaysian average)

On-site water sourcing (as % of total water consumption)
| Rainwater harvesting: 44%

| Grey water recycling: 44%

Materials (construction)
75% waste reduction

Wellness (occupant response)
| Thermal comfort: 86% satisfaction
| Acoustics: 68% satisfaction
| Indoor air quality: 89% satisfaction
| Lighting levels: 70% satisfaction
| Cleanliness: 95% satisfaction

Comfort modes[7]
Thermal comfort
| Passive (natural ventilation): 20%
| Active (air conditioning): 80%
Visual comfort
| Passive (daylight): 50%
| Active (electrical light): 50%

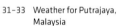
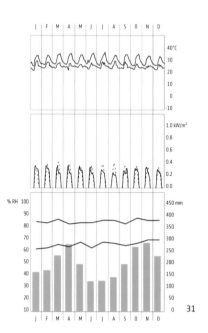

31

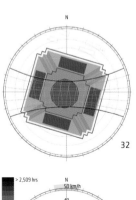

32

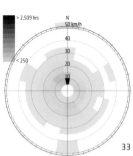

33

___

5_ Energy and water consumption figures are the *predicted* 12-month total based on data from October 2010 to January 2011.

6_ When full occupancy is reached the energy index without photovoltaics is predicted to rise to 85 kWh/m²/year.

7_ Percentage of gross floor area – excluding car park – that is designed to be predominantly reliant on passive or active design

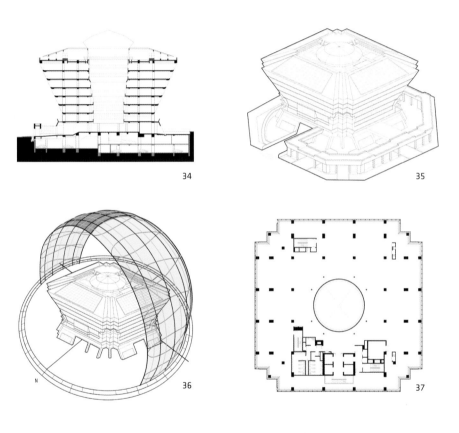

34

35

36

37

KHOO TECK PUAT HOSPITAL

SINGAPORE

90 Yishun Central
Singapore 768828

Location
1.42432° N
103.83859° E

Completion
June 2010

Cost[1]
US$499,000,000 approximately

Size
12 levels (including 2 basements)

Gross floor area
108,600 m²

Built-up area
138,986 m²

Site area
34,000 m²

Site coverage
47.54%

Type
Healthcare

Programme
550 beds
19 wards
17 specialist clinics
160 consultation rooms
8 operating theatres
6 operating rooms
4 endoscopy suites
Training centre (auditorium, lecture
hall, seminar rooms, learning labs)
Staff facilities (library, childcare
centre, game room, TV rooms)
Food court, café and retail

Occupancy[2]
271,682 outpatient clinic attendances
26,169 inpatient admissions

Operational hours
8,760/year

1_ Seven hundred million Singapore dollars
in US dollar equivalent based on international exchange rates on June 1st 2010
| International Monetary Fund. www.
imf.org
2_ For the year 2011

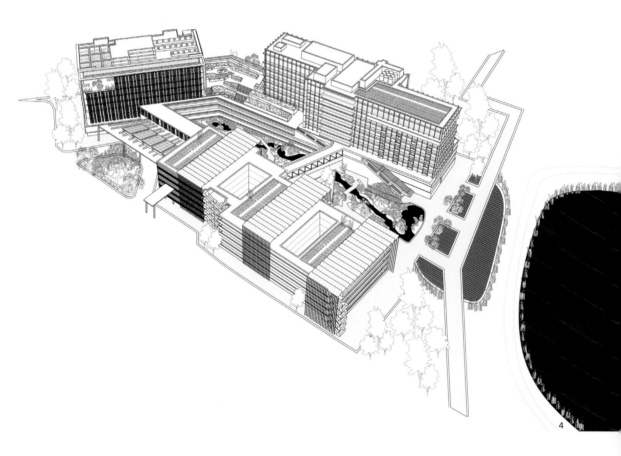

Hospitals aim to be efficient and (sometimes literally) clinical. Rarely is a hospital, particularly one built with tax dollars, designed for something other than operational ease-of-use. The underlying message – that healthcare is serious business with no unnecessary frills – results in a conservatism that creates obstacles to thinking of the built environment holistically, as part of a wider strategy to improve occupant well-being. With few precedents at hand, Khoo Teck Puat Hospital (KTPH) set out to be a game changer. It widened the question of healthcare delivery to that of *healing spaces* in which the physical setting actively contributes to wellness.

The KTPH brief – for the design tender in 2006 – spoke explicitly of a patient-centric approach. Several stipulations hinted at what this would mean.[3] Patients had to have access to daylight, good ventilation and views. The hospital should be easily navigable by all users, including first-time visitors. Everyone should have access to gardens and nature. The winning scheme responded to all three with a single stroke. The hospital would be built around a central court with criss-crossing lines-of-sight. This space would open up to an off-site pond from which it could tap vistas and breezes. The buildings themselves would be permeable, their facades designed to let in light and air.

In the transition from early ideas to final form, the idea of wellness found fuller expression in the way that greenery assumed importance. The *biophilic* experience of the central court is reminiscent of KTPH's predecessor – Alexandra Hospital – the grounds of which had been transformed into a butterfly park by the same management team.

Engagement of the community-at-large became more important. Residents of the neighbouring estate make up a large proportion of casual visitors. Many drop by to use the landscaped decks and food outlets; some volunteer, tending to KTPH's rooftop farm.

Conceptual sketches of *bioclimatic* facades led to technically and aesthetically articulated envelopes that would be calibrated to Singapore's climate. The design of these fixed and operable weather-responsive elements relied greatly on performance modelling tools and full scale mock-ups.

Through the design process, the KTPH team overlaid healthcare concerns with the question of how public buildings contribute to the common good. The overlap between public use and private domain, the coexistence of people and nature, the circumspect view of consumption and waste, all point to an act of Greening that goes far beyond industry norms at the time when KTPH was on the drawing board.

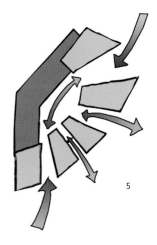

5

173

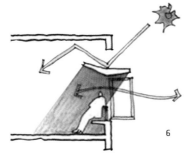

6

1–3   Exterior views
4   Exterior perspective
5–8   Early conceptual sketches establishing permeability of form and envelope

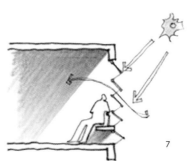

7

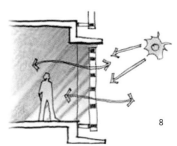

8

3_ Tan, S.Y. (2012)

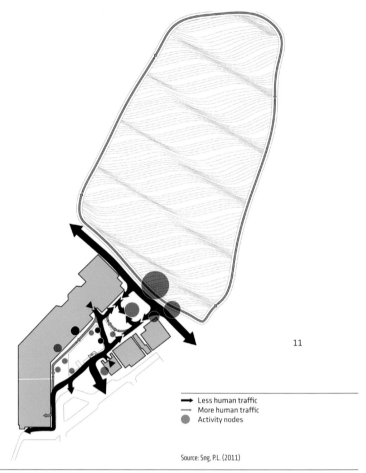

11

➤ Less human traffic
— More human traffic
● Activity nodes

Source: Sng, P.L. (2011)

Wellness
Community and greenery

The central court at KTPH is the *Heart of the Hospital*, a moniker that alludes to both its role as a spatial focus and the gesture of welcome it represents. Alongside patients, who spill out from the wards, visitors come from the nearby public housing estate. The familiarity that this latter group feels has something to do with how the building opens up to the community. In the course of a day, many will have walked past the front of the court, the open end of its Y-shaped configuration, along the boundary between hospital and pond. The hospital *adopted* this adjacent storm water pond in 2005 with the intention of creating a wider network of shared spaces, connecting its own court with a walking and jogging track around the pond. In these spaces hospital staff oversee *taichi* sessions and jogging groups.

The landscaping in the court cascades up to the upper levels and down into the basements, creating the impression of a building deeply enmeshed with nature. The green plot ratio of KTPH is 6.18, which is to say that the surface area of greenery is more than six times the size of the land on which it sits. A post-occupancy survey of visitors confirms the impact of this effort; greenery is the foremost element linked with perceived wellness, followed by the presence of community activity.[4]

An added outlet for community engagement is the rooftop vegetable and fruit gardens. About 20 volunteers,

4_ Sng, P.L. (2011)

■ Greenery and community spaces

Source: Sng, P.L. (2011)

mostly retirees who live nearby,
tend to these alongside the hospital's
own gardeners. Some of the produce
grown is used by the hospital kitchen;
all organic waste is composted and
returned to the gardens.

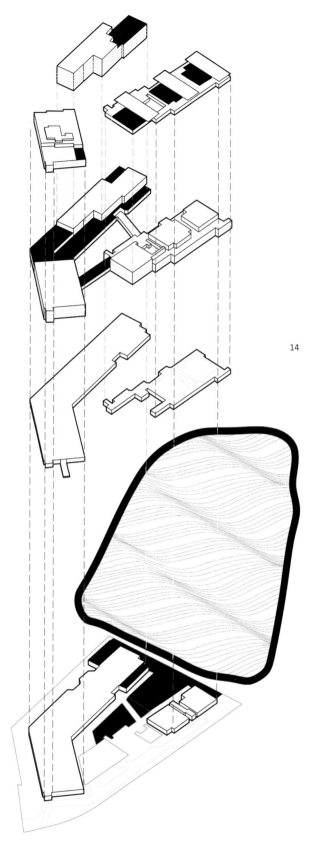

14

15

15–16   Exterior view of naturally
         ventilated wards
17–18   Envelope system for natu-
         rally ventilated wards

Wellness
Climate and comfort

The facade and interior are designed to enhance daylight entry and maximise natural ventilation. In subsidised wards, which must be naturally ventilated, this is especially critical. The facades of this block are grids of horizontal and vertical fins that deflect heat but admit air. Light shelves here push daylight deeper into the interior and reduce glare. As a result reliance on electrical lighting is estimated to be reduced by 30%.

Also found here is a system of *jalousies*. These operable louvres can be angled for airflow even when there is heavy rainfall. Ceiling fans in the wards pick up the slack when wind speeds are low.

In the private wards that are air-conditioned, fixed external fins temper the entry of sunlight. Here too there are operable windows so patients can switch to natural ventilation. A dual switch cuts off air conditioning when windows are opened. All private single-bedded wards are installed with ceiling fans.

A post-occupancy survey of patients and staff found that thermal comfort at KTPH was better than at another older hospital in Singapore.[5] Managing the changing conditions of rain and wind, light and shade has meant that staff and patients are expected to routinely interact with the building.

5_ Wu, Z. (2011)

16

Section

Elevation

17

Plan

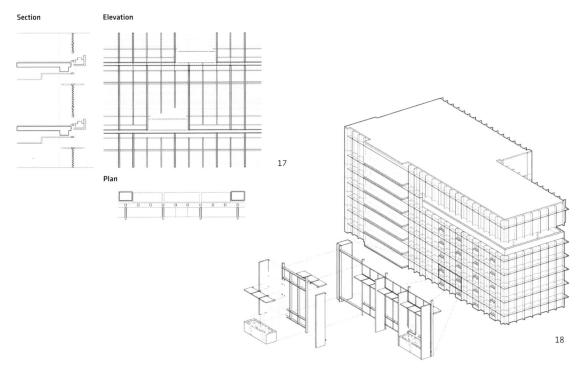

18

150 MWh

OF ELECTRICAL POWER
IS PRODUCED EACH YEAR
BY PHOTOVOLTAIC PANELS

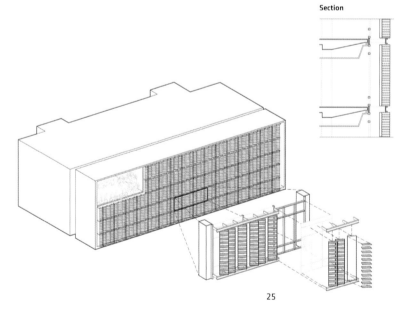

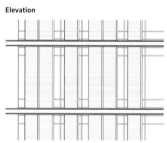

Section

Elevation

Plan

24

25

284.7 MWh

LESS ELECTRICAL POWER
IS NEEDED EACH YEAR AS A RESULT
OF SOLAR HOT WATER SYSTEMS
AND HEAT PUMPS

13,140 m³

OF WATER IS SOURCED ON-SITE
EACH YEAR

Efficacy and Embeddedness
Energy and water

Design for efficacy started with the question of energy and water use. The biggest consumer of energy, KTPH's air conditioning system, has strong performance indicators across all its components. Its chillers, for instance, are 18% more efficient than the average, chilled water pumps 33%, cooling tower 29%. The system as a whole operates at 0.689 kW/Ton, one of the most efficient in Singapore.

Its electro-mechanical systems are augmented with waste detection and recovery devices. Motion sensors, for instance, switch off lights in transient spaces like toilets and stair cores. Heat exchange pipes are installed at air handling units serving operating theatres which recoup *coolth* from exhausted air. Condensate water discharged by all air handling units is looped back into the cooling towers, reducing water demand.

There is thought put into on-site sourcing. Rainwater from the nearby pond is used for irrigation. Solar vacuum tubes are used to generate hot water. The solar thermal system and heat pumps produce all hot water needed (some 21,000 litres daily) which saves 780 kWh of electrical power each day. Photovoltaic arrays with a capacity of 137 kWp are installed on the roof, producing up to 150 MWh of electrical power each year.

19	Gym interior
20	Facade close-up with light shelf and *jalousies*
21	Wind-wing walls to improve natural ventilation
22	Interior of ward
23	Envelope of air-conditioned wards
24–25	Envelope system for air-conditioned wards
26	Roof-mounted photovoltaic arrays
27	Roof-mounted solar hot water system

28

29

30

Ecology
Flora and fauna

The sheer volume of new landscaping has turned KTPH into a natural oasis. By linking itself spatially and ecologically with the nearby pond, the hospital has more than doubled the area of connected greenery and water. Since its opening there have been several surveys of insect and bird populations. In one such survey over 35 species of butterflies and ten species of dragonflies were counted. There have also been repeat sightings of migratory birds.

32

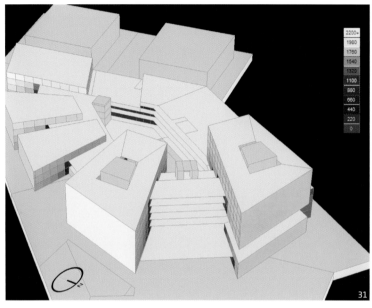

31

33

Integration
Users becoming stakeholders

The design brief was the most powerful tool of integration. It made explicit references to targets and outcomes that compelled cross-disciplinary collaboration. The team adopted an evidence-based approach – design intuitions were routinely tested with performance tools. In designing natural ventilation for a particular ward, for instance, both computation fluid dynamics modelling and wind tunnel tests were carried out.

At the onset of the project, the hospital had set up a planning committee that was actively involved in the design process from brief formulation to construction. Work groups comprising clinician nurses and hospital administrators from all departments would meet to discuss specific areas of interest such as toilets, signage and landscaping. Focus groups were set up to understand the needs of patients. Feedback from these was passed to the design team.

This flow of information – from design brief to user-group consultations – created a multiparty, multidisciplinary approach that ensured that by the time KTPH was completed, almost everyone affected by it had had a say.

PROJECT TEAM

Developer
Ministry of Health, Singapore

Operator
Alexandra Health Pte Ltd

Architect, mechanical and electrical engineer, civil and structural engineer, quantity surveyor
CPG Consultants Pte Ltd

Design consultant and medical planner
RMJM Hillier

Landscape consultant
Peridian Asia Pte Ltd

Project manager
PM Link Pte Ltd

Green consultant
Total Building Performance Team

Interior design consultant
Bent Severin & Associates Pte Ltd

Facade consultant
Aurecon Singapore Pte Ltd

Signage consultant
Design Objectives Pte Ltd

Main contractor
Hyundai Engineering & Construction Co Ltd

SUPPLIERS[6]

Curtain wall/cladding fabricator and installer
LHL International Pte Ltd

Floor
| Prefabricated hollow core slab
Eastern Pretech Pte Ltd
| Bondek
BlueScope Lysaght Pte Ltd

Floor coverings
| Vinyl
NSK, Gerflor
| Carpet
Milliken

Paints/coatings/finishes
| Internal
Nippon
| External
SKK
| Car park flooring
Remmers

Insulation
Rock wool insulation
Roxul

Lifts/escalators
Fujitec

Sealants/adhesives
| GE Sealant
| Tile adhesive
Laticrete

Ceiling/partitions/building boards
Boral, USG

Doors/window/glazing hardware
| Internal doors
Yi Lin Timber
| Windows
LHL International Pte Ltd

Security
STE

Fire products
Chubb

Fittings
| Bathroom and sanitary ware
Toto
| Kitchen ware
Fabristeel

Lighting/electrical equipment
| Eye Lighting
| ABB
| Areva
| Sunlight

Air conditioning
| Chiller R123
Trane
| Air handling units, fan coil units
Carrier

Solar technology
| Building integrated photovoltaics
Sunseap
| Solar photovoltaics
Showa Shell, Sunset
| Solar thermal
Seido, Beasley

Greenery
Tropical Environment Pte Ltd

Building maintenance system
IES

AWARDS/CERTIFICATION
2011
| Winner, President's Design Award, DesignSingapore Council and Urban Redevelopment Authority, Singapore
| Winner, Gold Award, BCA Universal Design Awards for the Built Environment, Building and Construction Authority, Singapore
| Winner, FuturArc Green Leadership Award, institutional category, BCI Asia Construction Information Pte Ltd
| Winner, Design Award, 11th SIA Architectural Design Awards, institutional category, Healthcare Buildings, Singapore Institute of Architects
| Winner, Building of the Year Award, 11th SIA Architectural Design Awards, Singapore Institute of Architects
| Winner, Design & Health International Academy Awards, category of international health project over 40,000 m², International Academy for Design & Health

182

34–36   Weather for Singapore
37   Sun path over KTPH
38   Section through site

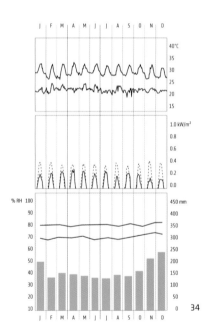

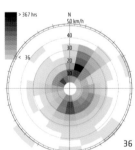

6_ This is a shortlist of suppliers. Others, not mentioned here, would have contributed in one way or another to the Greening of Khoo Teck Puat Hospital.

| Winner, *Design & Health International Academy Awards*, category of *sustainable design*, International Academy for Design & Health
| Winner, *Gold Award, Landscape Industry Association Singapore Awards*, Landscape Industry Association, Singapore

2010

| Winner, *Emerson Cup (India and Southeast Asia) Special Appreciation Award*, Emerson Climate Technologies
| Winner, *First Prize, Skyrise Greenery Awards*, Singapore Institute of Architects & Singapore National Parks

2009

Certified, Green Mark Platinum, new building category, Building and Construction Authority, Singapore

---

PERFORMANCE[7]

Annual energy consumption
30,000 MWh approximately

On-site energy sourcing (% of total consumed)
Photovoltaic panels:
0.5% (137 kWp)

Greenhouse gas emissions
Not available

Energy intensity
| 325 kWh/m²/year
| 5,464 kWh/bed/month

Annual water consumption
73,484 m³

Water intensity
Not available

On-site water sourcing (% of total consumed)
Yishun Pond:
17.9%

Wellness (design)
6.18 green plot ratio
(497 trees, 71 palms,
5,900 m² of shrubs and
2,315 m² of grass)

Comfort modes[8]

Thermal comfort
| Passive (natural and mechanical ventilation): 36%
| Active (air conditioning): 64%

Visual comfort
| Passive (daylight): 22–30%
| Active (electrical light): 78–70%

183

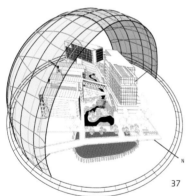

37

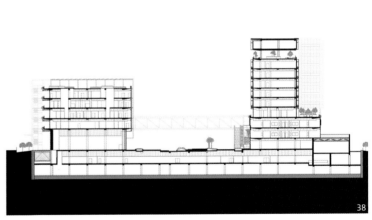

38

7_ Energy and water consumption figures are for the period July 2010 to June 2011.

8_ Percentage of gross floor area that is designed to be primarily reliant on passive strategies or active systems

PEARL ACADEMY
OF FASHION

JAIPUR,
INDIA

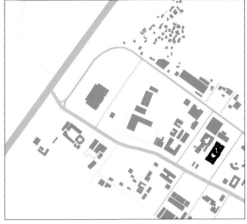

SP-38A, RIICO Industrial Area,
Delhi Road, Kukas,
Jaipur 302028, India

Location
27.03076° N
75.89667° E

Completion
June 2008

Cost
US$3,800,000

Size
3 levels (including a sub-basement)

Gross floor area
11,745 m²

Site area
12,250 m²

Site coverage
30%

Type
Education

Programme
4 classrooms
24 studios/workshops
18 offices
Library (55 persons)
Auditorium (195 persons)

Capacity
600 students
100 staff

Operational hours
1,100/year

185

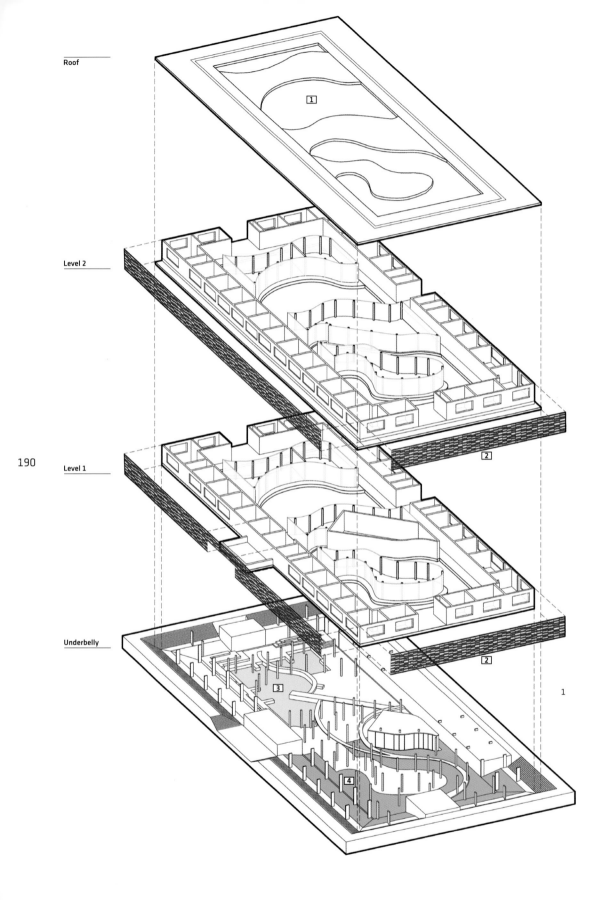

Roof

Level 2

190

Level 1

Underbelly

The Pearl Academy of Fashion (PAF) is some 20 km from the city centre of Jaipur, off the Jaipur-New Delhi highway. To be appealing as a school for the creative arts, the architecture of PAF had to be visually arresting and somehow connected to the *genus loci*, the culture and history of the state of Rajasthan. The project site – set in a characterless industrial estate – and a low construction budget were two constraints that had to be overcome.

Tackling locus and cost simultaneously, PAF's architecture adapts principles of passive design from antecedents in history. Rajasthan-inspired elements, such as *jaali* and stepwells,[1] offered a point of reference that speaks of where the building is culturally and how it might operate climatically. These strategies, central to its approach to wellness, are integrated into the building as spatial layers. Each layer is in effect a thermal zone that separates the inside from the outside. The lowest floor of the building, the *underbelly*, is one such layer, moderating ambient temperatures with water, shade and plants. Another is the 1.2 m-wide swath of space between the two outer skins of the teaching block. This cuts down solar heat gain without curtailing airflow or daylight.

The Academy does not make a virtue out of necessity; there is some installed capacity for air conditioning for periods when the summer heat can be intolerable. There is also a deliberate focus on crafting delight. The full height glass panels on its inner facade, for instance, create a lively *mise-en-scène*, offering lines-of-sight criss-crossing teaching studios, movement corridors and voids.

1	Light air wells
2	*Jaali* window screens
3	Water feature
4	Green lawn

To balance experience and comfort, PAF's design process relied on performance modelling tools that allowed the team to calibrate this union of skin and space, solid and void. The porosity of the *jaali*-clad facades, for instance, varies with orientation. The greater the solar exposure of a facade, the more opaque is the pattern of *jaali* on it. This variance, its visualisation and realisation, was made possible with solar modelling software.

This project is noteworthy for the manner in which programme, form and performance are integrated. It suggests that buildings in developing parts of Asia can successfully negotiate the past and present, walking the line between what users need and what they can afford. It advocates a return to local know-how and adoption of passive principles as preconditions for Greening. The result, in quantitative terms, is that PAF consumes half the energy that an equivalent building might, even if that building were assessment tool-compliant. In qualitative terms, it has become a vibrant hub of a thriving community of designers-to-be, elevating the way they see themselves.

2

191

| 1 | Exploded axonometric |
| 2–5 | Simulations of solar exposure and shading |

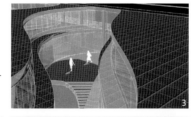

3

4

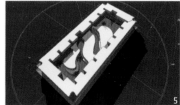

5

1_ *Jaali* are fretted screens that make up the outer skin of buildings, commonly seen in Mughal architecture of the region. They screen interiors from heat, dust and prying eyes. Stepwells are likewise indigenous to Rajasthan. Large wells – dug to a depth below the water table – are framed within an arrangement of terraces forming a public space.

May/August
April/September
March/October
February/November
January/December
June/July

6

7

Wellness
Microclimate and comfort: The underbelly

The underbelly is sunk 4 m below street datum so that cool, humidified air – heavier than warm, dry air – might be retained on-site. The earth around this space offers a cool thermal mass that reduces radiant temperatures. A mix of water and greenery creates a microclimate via evaporative cooling and transpiration that is substantially cooler than outside, particularly in summer. Cool air in this space, as it warms up, rises naturally, creating a convective flow that aids in cross ventilation.

Sinking the underbelly also keeps lines-of-sight within site, creating privacy for the students that gather there. Steps on the perimeter double up as seats, making this an ad hoc performance venue.

Hovering above this space is the teaching block, two storeys high with a footprint of 111 m by 50 m. Several curvilinear incisions break this architectural mass into alternating solids and voids. The solids contain studios and classrooms, the voids let daylight and air through. For part of the year when the sun angles are low, this configuration shades itself, limiting solar ingress to the spaces below.

8

9

30%
OF SITE IS COVERED IN PLANTS

4%
OF SITE IS COVERED IN WATER

10

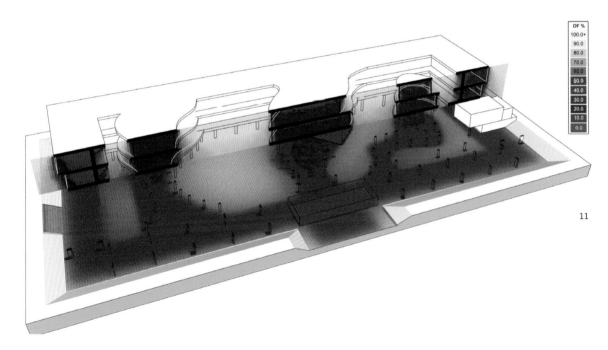

DF %
100.0+
90.0
80.0
70.0
60.0
50.0
40.0
30.0
20.0
10.0
0.0

11

100%
OF GROSS FLOOR AREA
WAS DESIGNED FOR NATURAL
VENTILATION OR FANS FOR

80%
OF ALL OPERATIONAL HOURS

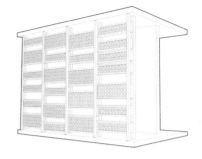

12

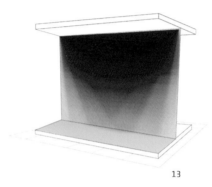

13

14

12   Section of facade with
     jaali
13–14   Solar exposure of partial
        facade without (left) and
        with (right) *jaali*
15–17   Views of *jaali*
18–19   Solar exposure of full
        facade without (top) and
        with (bottom) *jaali*
20–21   Daylight ingress and views

15

16

17

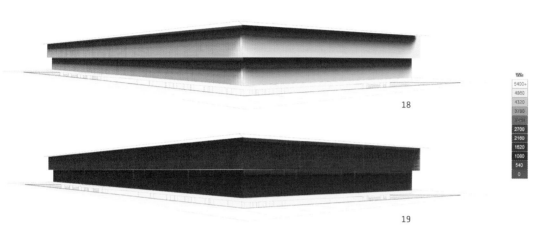

18

19

Wellness
Microclimate and comfort: *Jaali* and *matka*

The curvilinear inner courts contrast dramatically with the building's orthogonal exterior. On the outside PAF is wrapped in a layer of *jaali* that is set away from inner walls and windows. Aside from reduced heat gain, the *jaali* serves to modulate incoming natural light, which can be harsh much of the time. The floor plate is no more than 9 m wide at any point; in most locations an occupant is no more than 4.5 m from a window or opening. This all but eliminates daytime reliance on electrical lighting.

Of the more innovative local techniques adopted, the use of *matka* is interesting. *Matka* are traditional mud vessels for carrying water. Hundreds of 35 cm-wide *matka*, placed 2.5 cm apart, were cast into concrete slabs that are exposed to the sun. The gap between *matka* is filled with sand and then cast over with a binding layer of concrete. This sandwich of trapped air becomes a thermal barrier slowing down solar heat gain.

20

21

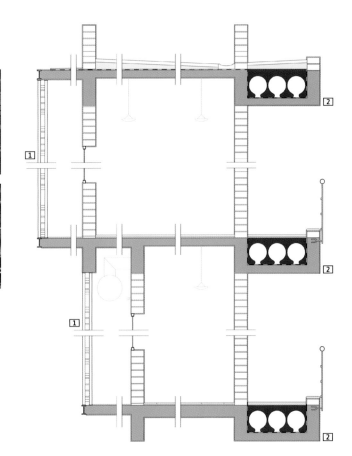

24

1 *Jaali* sunscreen
2 *Matka* insulation

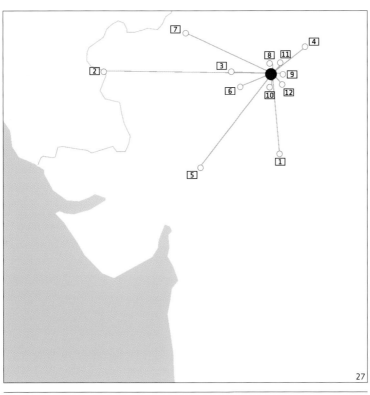

1	Grey Kota stone
2	Jaisalmer stone chips
3	Marble stone chips
4	Slate
5	Green marble
6	Granite
7	Gypsum
8	Concrete *jaali*
9	Concrete pavers
10	Aluminium
11	Commercial plywood
12	Earthen pots

27

Embeddedness
Materials and water

The material palette is a mix of stone, glass and concrete, almost all of which is locally sourced. Kota stone, granite, slate and Jaisalmer stone come from within Rajasthan. Aluminium and concrete come from within Jaipur city limits. The concrete *jaali* were cast on-site. *Matka* were bought in the markets of Jaipur.

Water is a precious commodity in desert climates. Since PAF relies on water year-round to induce thermal comfort, it must source most of what it needs on-site.

Recycled water from the sewage treatment plant is used for landscaping and flushing. Water in landscape elements found in the underbelly – needed for evaporative cooling – is sourced from the same plant. Rainwater captured is used to recharge the aquifer.

The design team also made a case for what not to build as a way of reducing construction cost. The underbelly, for instance, is subdivided with plants, walkways and water. It accommodates many programme needs without walls and slabs. The structural grid of the building was optimised for an almost column-free floor plate that increased flexibility and efficiency by 20%, and also reduced the demand for materials.

28

PROJECT TEAM

Developer
Pearl Academy of Fashion

Architect
Morphogenesis

Electrical engineer
Integral Designs

Structural engineer
NM Roof Designers Ltd

Plumbing
Tech Consultancy

Heating ventilation and air conditioning
Design Centre

Landscape consultant
Oracles

Main contractor
RG Colonizers Pvt Ltd

Building operator
Pearl Academy of Fashion

SUPPLIERS

Sanitaryware/fittings
Parryware

Flooring
Terrazzo Insitu
RG Colonizers Pvt Ltd

Furnishing
Geeken Seating Collection,
Inline India Ltd (Chic India
Furniture)

Furniture
Mike Knowles, InLine

Air conditioning
Voltas Limited, 3 star-rating

Lighting
Prvisa Luminaires by ONS
Impex

Paint
Asian Paints

Elevator
Schindler

Stone
Local procurement

Window frames
Jindal aluminium sections

Frameless glazing/plain float glass
Modi Guard

Cladding/facade
Concrete *jaali* (cast on-site by local artisans)

False ceiling
POP ceiling (manufactured on-site)
RG Colonizers Pvt Ltd

Rainwater harvesting
RG Colonizers Pvt Ltd

Sewage treatment plant
Brisanzia Technologies

AWARDS

2011
Winner, FuturArc Green Leadership Award, institutional category, BCI Asia Construction Information Pte Ltd

2010
Highly Commended Seal of Distinction, Cityscape Awards, Emerging Markets, Cityscape Global

2009
| *Winner, International Design Awards, architecture category*, International Design Awards
| *Winner, World Architecture Festival Awards, Barcelona, Best Learning Building, Highly Commended Seal of Distinction, Cityscape Architectural Awards, Dubai*, Cityscape Global
| *Citation, 20+10+X World Architecture Community Awards*, World Architecture Community
| *Finalist, ARCASIA Award*, Architects Regional Council, Asia
| *Best Sustainable/Green Architecture, ArchiDesign Awards*
| *The Institutional Architecture Award*, Architecture+Design & Spectrum Foundation

2008
Finalist, MIPIM Asia Awards, MIPIM Asia

2007
Special Award for Environmental Design, Cityscape Architectural Review, Dubai

---

PERFORMANCE[2]

Annual energy consumption
290 MWh

On-site energy sourcing (as % of total consumed)
Nil

Greenhouse gas emissions
Not available

Energy intensity
24.7 kWh/m^2/year
(54% less than a GRIHA-compliant equivalent building)

Annual water consumption
7,500 m^3

Water intensity
Not available

On-site water sourcing (as % of total consumed)
Grey water recycling:
100%

Materials (construction)
| Locally sourced Kota stone, 4,640 m^2 as flooring
| Locally sourced terrazzo, 5,900 m^2 as flooring
| Concrete *jaali*, 1,100 m^2, made by local artisans

198

29–31 Weather for Jaipur, India
32 Sun path over PAF
33 Exterior perspective

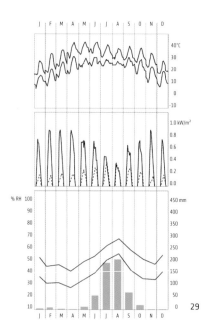

29

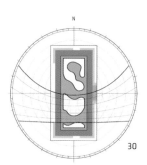

30

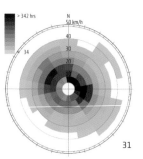

31

2_ Energy and water consumption figures are for a 12-month period from 2009 to 2010.

| Furniture made out of
compressed tetra pack
boards
| Locally sourced *matka* for
insulation

Comfort modes[3]
Thermal comfort
| Passive (natural
ventilation):
100% (for 80%
operational hours)
| Active (air conditioning):
50% (for 20% operational
hours)
Visual comfort
| Passive (daylight):
90%
| Active (artificial light):
10%

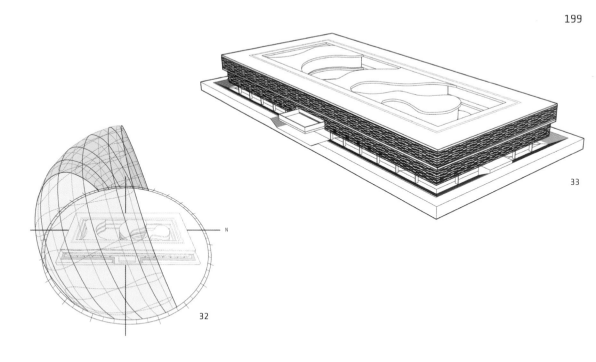

32

33

3_ Percentage of gross floor area that is
designed to be primarily reliant on passive
strategies or active systems

SAFE HAVEN BATHHOUSE & LIBRARY

OLD MARKET LIBRARY

THAILAND

SAFE HAVEN BATHHOUSE & LIBRARY

OLD MARKET LIBRARY

Ban Tha Song Yang
Tak Province 63150
Thailand

Min Buri
Bangkok 10150
Thailand

Location
17.55512° N
97.92594° E

Programme
Bathhouse
Library

Location
13.81046° N
100.72895° E

Programme
Library

Completion
January 2009

Occupancy
Serving a
community of
79 Karen refugee
orphans

Completion
May 2009

Occupancy
Serving a
community of
400 residents

Cost
Bathhouse:
US$3,800

Library:
US$4,900

Cost
US$4,500

**Operational
hours**
8,760/year

**Operational
hours**
8,760/year

Size
2 levels

Size
Up to 2 levels

Gross floor area
27 m²

Gross floor area
Bathhouse:
61 m²

Site area
Not available

Library:
28 m²

Type
Community

Site area
8,000 m²

Type
Community

1 Safe Haven Library: built
  by students from Norway
2 South facade of Safe
  Haven Bathhouse with
  a teak plantation in the
  background
3 Old Market Library: volunteers and builders from
  the Min Buri community
  during construction
4 Safe Haven Bathhouse:
  local workers preparing
  bamboo

Social sustainability does not get the same attention as environmental or economic sustainability in Asia. The preoccupation with growth and resource security often distracts powers-that-be from poorer communities in rural settings and urban slums. Whenever state agencies and non-governmental organisations attend to these, their interventions seem utilitarian, lacking insight into the needs and aspirations of the people they serve.

Norwegian architects, Andreas Grøntvedt Gjertsen and Yashar Hanstad, have been involved in humanitarian work in Asia through their design studio TYIN tegnestue. Since 2008 they have built several community projects in rural and urban settings in Thailand. In their accounting of these, they speak of an "architecture of necessity"[1]. The projects examine how basic (often pressing) needs might be met with little money and a healthy regard for human dignity.

The team starts by matching what is needed to what is available. Sanitation, flooding, weather-proofing and cost are factored in early, delineating what is built and how. In the way that elements subsequently come together – connecting a building's occupants to site, climate, community – the project speaks to their mind and spirit. Climate-moderating sunscreens, for instance, also offer privacy. Experts lead the process but the community almost always gets involved. Structure and space are simple but to these there are accents of colour, texture and materiality. These contemporary whimsical touches – set in rustic and run-down settings – are never jarring or patronising.

Besides the communities they serve, the projects are a learning platform. Some of TYIN's field projects in Asia were also hands-on workshops for students of architecture from Norway for whom the act of building,

so far away from what they were accustomed to, became a way of comprehending developing societies and their needs.

Two TYIN projects are featured. The first is a bathhouse and library in an orphanage close to the border of Thailand and Myanmar, in a small community that is home to Karen refugees. The Karen people are an ethnic minority who have been expelled from Myanmar but have no official status in Thailand. The other is the adaptive reuse of a 100-year-old building that was converted into a library for residents of Min Buri, a densely populated area of Bangkok, once a thriving commercial hub that is now an urban slum. Both are small, strategic injections, designed in part to meet everyday needs, in part to restore pride to a community struggling to find its place in society.

207

1_ TYIN tegnestue Architects.
   www.tyintegnestue.no

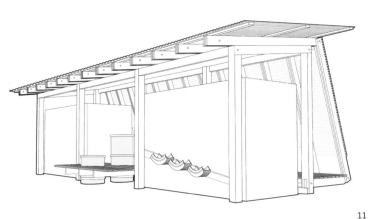

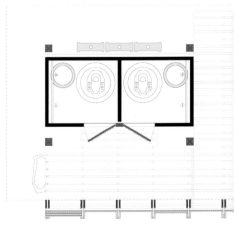

11

Safe Haven: Bathhouse
Embeddedness

5	Urinals made of old tyres and inexpensive plastic pipes
6-7	Bamboo screen for privacy and shade
8	Bathing space
9	The floor is raised and drains into a 1 m-deep trough filled with gravel and stones
10	Toilets made with old tyres and ready-made products from local shops
11	Front view
12	Plan
13	Back view
14	South facade

In January 2009 TYIN invited 15 Norwegian architecture students to participate in a workshop at the Safe Haven orphanage. The most pressing needs at the time were for a new bathhouse and library. Karen workers toiled alongside TYIN on the bathhouse. The students, with their professors, built the library.

The primary challenge of the bathhouse was the handling of sewage and drainage. On this site, there can be too much or too little rain, exacerbating the risk of disease especially if sanitation systems are compromised as a result of a downpour. The earlier bathhouse was often wet and dirty. In the new amenity, waste from the new toilets passes through pipes and ends up

buried underground. The raised wooden floors keep the space dry. The drainage system, consisting of a 1 m-deep trough filled with gravel, is designed to cope with the deluge of water in the wet season.

The bathhouse is a rectilinear structure with a western toilet, two pit toilets, washbasins and a bathing and washing area. Its intimate functions are concealed behind concrete block walls that make up the two enclosed spaces on either side of the building. Inside, toilets are made from old tyres and ready-made products purchased from local shops. Semiprivate spaces are found between these two blocks, accented by a tilted facade made of bamboo that leans over the front of the

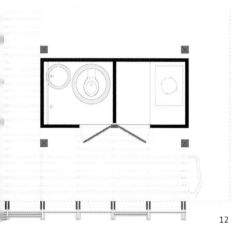

12

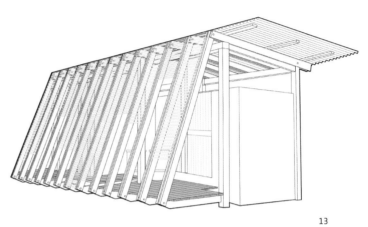

13

building acting as a weather shield and modesty screen. The central bathing area and circulation spaces are lifted off the ground to let excess water drain through onto the gravel pit below.

14

15	A patio divides the library into two parts
16	Bookshelves against the back wall
17	Computer area
18	Back of library with a play area and benches
19	Plan
20	Front of library is protected by bamboo and eaves
21	Loft

Safe Haven: Library
Embeddedness

The library, like the bathhouse, is a simple structure. A concrete block wall to one side acts as a thermal barrier and structural anchor. A tilted bamboo screen on the other side keeps the interior ventilated, shaded and daylit. The structure was made from local wood purchased nearby. Bamboo was sourced from the adjacent forest. The foundation is made of stones and boulders found on-site, some 17 m³ in total.

On the lower floor, the plan is subdivided by a patio. To one side of the patio is the reading space; on the other is a computer area. A flight of steps leads up to a loft that functions as a resting or sleeping area for the children.

18

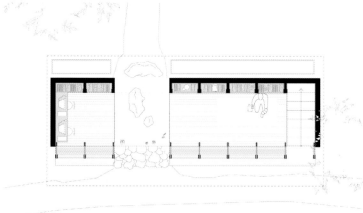

19

20

211

21

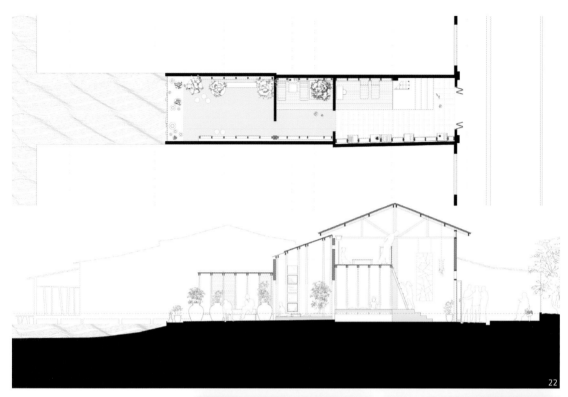

22

23

24

25

Old Market Library
Embeddedness

The library opens onto a covered walkway to the front and a small canal at the back. Connecting the two, a corridor runs lengthwise on the ground floor with reading spaces to one side. The high roof of the old building permits a loft space that is reached via a staircase near the front entrance. This is the ancillary space for reading and gathering.

A key concern of the design team was the annual rainy season when flood waters can rise by up to 50 cm above floor level. Keeping the water out would be difficult; the designers decided instead to elevate reading zones to ensure that the library is usable throughout the flooding period. Construction details were conceived with water in mind; the concrete sidewalls and aired connections prevent humidity and rot in the wood.

Another consideration was reliance on local and reused materials. The bookshelves are recycled wooden boxes from an earlier project; the cladding is old and decayed wood, found in the immediate surroundings. More robust materials that were needed were bought at a local second-hand shop.

Old Market Library
Advocacy

A key aspiration was to boost community bonding in the area, the library acting as an agent of positive change. The design process sought to engage the stakeholders. Initially this meant that the designers held regular meetings with nearby residents to find out what they wanted and to create awareness of the project. Residents were also surveyed for their views on the community, its past, present and future. As the project evolved, becoming more tangible, members of the community joined in as active participants. A regular group of volunteers soon started to work with TYIN.

28	Backyard
29	Box shelves made from recycled materials
30	Loft
31	Children of Min Buri community present conceptual models
32–33	Locals working with experts and volunteers

SAFE HAVEN BATHHOUSE

PROJECT TEAM
Client
Safe Haven orphanage
Architects
| Andreas Grøntvedt
  Gjertsen
| Yashar Hanstad

SUPPLIERS
All materials were bought in
local markets

OLD MARKET LIBRARY

PROJECT TEAM
Client
Old Market Community
Architects
| Pasi Aalto
| Andreas Grøntvedt
  Gjertsen
| Yashar Hanstad
| Magnus Henriksen
| Erlend Bauck Sole
Collaborators
Kasama Yamtree and Patama
Roonrakwit (CASE Studio
Architects)

SUPPLIERS
All materials were found in
the area or bought second
hand from local markets

SAFE HAVEN LIBRARY

PROJECT TEAM
Client
Safe Haven orphanage
Architects
Students from the Norwegian
University of Science and
Technology
| Pasi Aalto
| Jan Kristian Borgen
| Mari Folven
| Ragnhild Førde
| Sunniva Vold Huus
| Olav Fåsetbru Kildal
| Lene M.N. Kværness
| Oda Moen Møst
| Ørjan Nyheim

| Karoline Salomonsen
| Anne Sandnes
| Ola Sendstad
| Kristoffer B. Thørud
| Caroline Tjernås
| Anders Sellevold Aaseth
Collaborator
Rintala Eggertsson Architects
Professors
| Hans Skotte
| Sami Rintala
Sponsors
| Norsk Betongforening
| Bygg uten grenser
| Minera Norge
| Spenncon

| Norwegian University of
  Technology and Science,
  NTNU

216

34–36   Weather for Ban Tha
         Song Yang, Tak Province,
         Thailand
37–39   Weather for Bangkok,
         Thailand

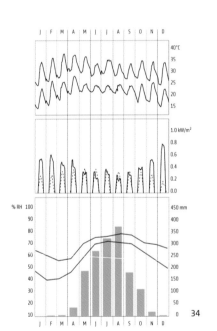

34

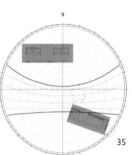

35

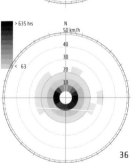

36

AWARDS

2011

| Honorable Mention, Architecture of Necessity, Virserum Art Museum Sweden (awarded to TYIN tegnestue)

| Finalist, Norsk Form Pris for Unge Arkitekter, Foundation for Design and Architecture, Norway (awarded to TYIN tegnestue)

| Shortlist, International WAN Awards, World Architecture News blog (awarded to TYIN tegnestue)

| Winner, Gold, International Architecture Awards, Chicago Athenaeum: Museum of Architecture and Design and the European Centre for Architecture, Art, Design and Urban Studies US (awarded to TYIN tegnestue)

| Finalist, Great Places Award, Environmental Design Research Association UK (awarded to TYIN tegnestue)

| Winner, Gold, Dedale Minosse Award, ALA-Assoarchitetti, Italy (awarded to TYIN tegnestue)

2010

| Winner, Gold, Best of TIDA, Eco and Conservation Award, Thailand Interior Design Association Thailand (Old Market Library)

| Winner, Silver, International Sustainability Award, Sustainable Building, Italy (awarded to TYIN tegnestue)

| Winner, Gold, Making Space Awards, Children in Scotland in association with Scottish Government, Architecture and Design, Scotland (awarded to TYIN tegnestue)

| Winner, Gold, The Earth Awards, Social Justice Award, UK (awarded to TYIN tegnestue)

2009

Winner, Gold, Building of the Year, Museums and Libraries International, ArchDaily blog (Safe Haven Library)

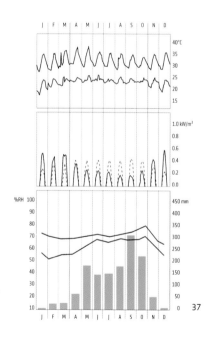

37

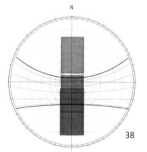

38

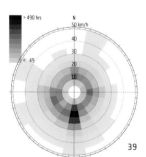

39

SAU MAU PING SOUTH ESTATE

HONG KONG,
PEOPLE'S REPUBLIC OF CHINA

Kwun Tong
Kowloon
Hong Kong
People's Republic of China

Location
22.31576° N
114.23507° E

Programme
5 housing blocks
3,995 apartment units

Completion
August 2009

Occupancy
11,000 residents

Cost[1]
US$112,500,000

Operational hours
8,760/year

Size
Up to 41 levels

Gross floor area
175,700 m²

Built-up area[2]
39,133 m²

Site area
49,000 m²

Site coverage
18%

Type
Residential

1_ Eight hundred and seventy-seven million
   Hong Kong dollars in US dollar equivalent
   based on international exchange rates on
   August 1st 2009 | International Monetary
   Fund. www.imf.org
2_ Including walls, gardens, walkways, circulation, pool decks and paved areas

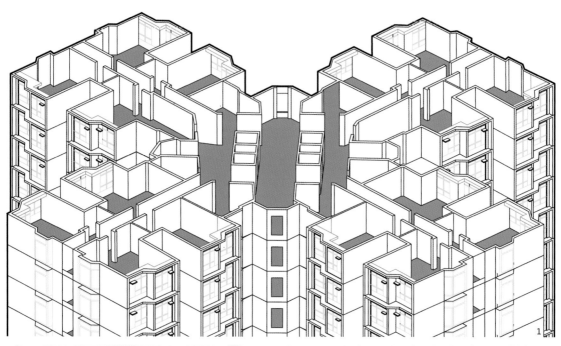

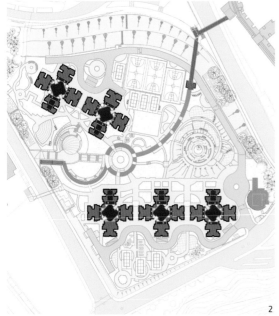

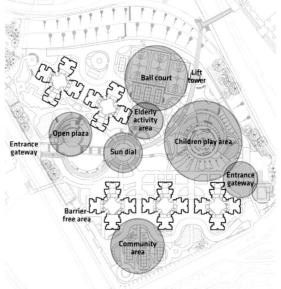

Ball court

Lift tower

Elderly activity area

Open plaza

Entrance gateway

Sun dial

Children play area

Entrance gateway

Barrier-free area

Community area

Affordable public housing is one of the most pressing needs in Asia. Some 20,000 new dwellings are needed each day, many for people who must rely on state assistance.[3] The response of state agencies is often at odds with the idea of liveability. The proliferation of repetitive, soulless residential towers across the region raises the question of what makes a *home*. Many have argued that this calls for a broader consideration of wellness, going beyond the hardware of the built environment towards softer attributes of *place* that lead to a shared sense of belonging.

The imperative to build public housing fast and cheaply will not go away. It must however be countered with a context-specific response to the needs of the community that the development will serve. Sau Mau Ping South (SMPS) estate suggests that the one need not be at odds with the other.

Since 1987, the Sau Mau Ping enclave in Kowloon has been redeveloped in phases. Work on SMPS – a cluster of five towers for 11,000 residents – started in 2004. Like most housing estates in Hong Kong, a tight budget means relying on off-site prefabrication. This raises the question: what sets it apart? Prefabrication has been known to lead to a quality of *sameness* that can be at odds with place-making. The design team looked to the project site for opportunities to craft identity.

The process proceeded on two fronts. At one end, experts studied wind and light using environmental simulation tools. They examined how these fluxes – channeled through the site – influence ventilation and daylighting. Their analyses resulted in an alignment of the five towers that aided air movement through the residential units. This also played a part in determining how the ground plane and its activities were laid out.

At the other end, members of the team looked for connectivity to nature and within community. The SMPS groundscape holds varied plant species and public spaces, the former catering to biodiversity, the latter to social needs. Both contribute to wellness. Public spaces are inclusive and accessible, including to those with disabilities. These spaces bear the mark of residents through installations of art and signage that were created by them. Greenery extends onto slopes and buildings; as a result, SMPS is one of the most heavily greened of housing estates in Hong Kong. The sloping topography, which might have been a constraint, is used to full advantage. Mounted within this landscape, wind turbines and photovoltaic panels – popping up like art installations – generate electrical power and awareness of environmental issues.

It is at this scale – in the visceral exchange between people and their environment – where it is apparent how this estate has sought to forge an identity and lifestyle. That SMPS has achieved this within constraints of budget and time is a noteworthy lesson for other public housing projects in Asia.

225

1	Sectional view of a typical residential tower
2	Site plan
3	Zoning of the ground plane

3_ Economist Intelligence Unit. (2011)

Solar heat
gain reduced
by 30%

4

5

226

8

9

10

11

12

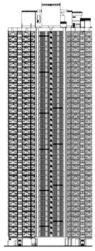

Wellness
Wind and light

A fluid dynamics study of the site identified strong summer winds – 3–5 m/s – from the southeast. This led to a particular alignment of towers that sought to channel airflow, creating a wind corridor through the site. This was done without compromising the ventilation needs of a completed estate behind SMPS. Blocks were positioned such that they also maximised internal shade, some shading others from the west sun.

Equipped with a working model of architectural form and environmental attributes, the team looked at the combined effect of air and solar exposure on the ground plane. This helped them decide positions for activity sites. In other words, comfort was a key consideration in determining the placement of activities.

Within towers, the windows are positioned such that they channel air through lift lobbies and corridors. The introduction of a wind scoop on the roof pushes air down to compensate for slower air speeds on lower floors. To optimise the entry of daylight into residential units, the depth of the window overhangs was adjusted with orientation.

4   SMPS towers
5   Improvement to envelope-shading resulting in higher thermal comfort for occupants
6   Detail of envelope-shading
7   Computational fluid dynamics simulation showing wind corridor resulting in an acceleration of wind speeds in summer months
8   Overshadowing at 8am in summer months
9   Overshadowing at 4pm in summer months
10 Computational fluid dynamics simulation showing wind in winter months
11 Overshadowing at 8am in winter months
12 Overshadowing at 4pm in winter months

On-grade greening

Slope greening

Roof greening

Concrete greening

Vertical greening

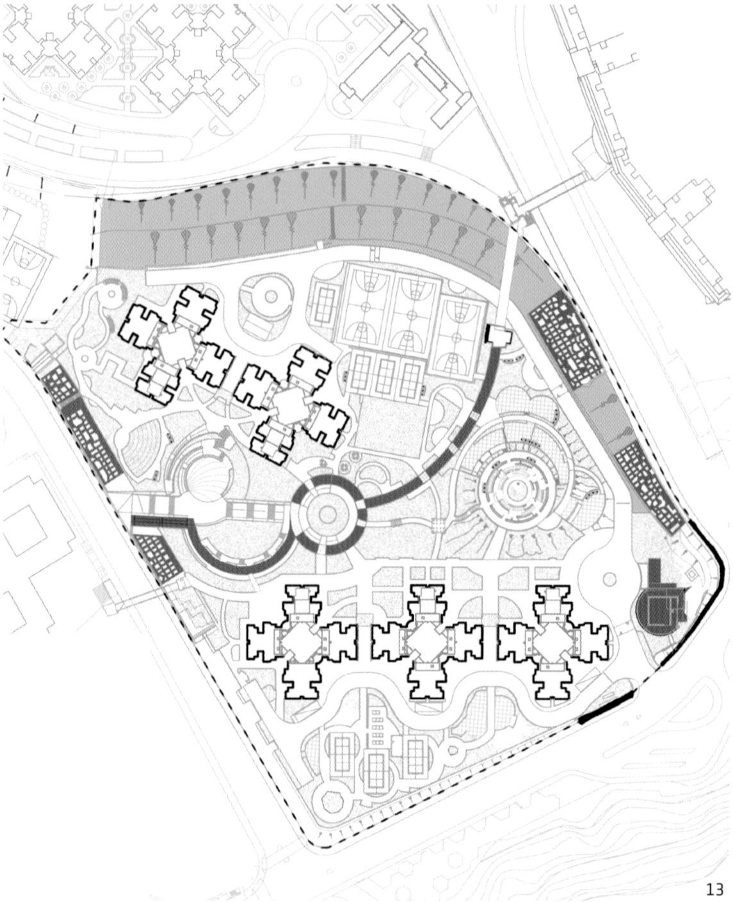

13

13   Landscaping of the SMPS
       site
14–17   Landscaping includes
       new ground cover,
       conservation and replant-
       ing of existing trees
       and building-integrated
       greenery on walkways and
       facades
18–19   Slope before and after
       restoration and planting

Wellness
Greenery

Three landscape strategies give
SMPS more greenery than any
other public housing estate in
Hong Kong.

1.   **Maximise ground cover**
       (10,225 m^2)

The ground plane is covered with
planters and lawns that line pedes-
trian pathways and activity zones.
A flowering garden was created at
the front of the wind corridor so
that scent from flowers would flow
through the estate.

15

16

17

18

19

229

2. Utilise urban slopes (7,200 m²)

Some 2,200 m² of concrete mesh stabilises existing slopes, reducing the need to remove soil and trees. This has led to the retention of 114 trees. The 42 trees that had to be moved were transplanted within the site. The slope once stabilised was turfed and planted with over 26,090 indigenous trees and shrubs that attract birds and butterflies.

3. Integrate with buildings (vertical, 205 m²; rooftop, 1,625 m²)

Plants extend onto rooftops of low-rise buildings and walkways as well as vertical wall surfaces. The development has the longest green covered walkway of any Hong Kong housing estate.

The green coverage of SMPS is some 21,430 m² in total, amounting to 43% of the overall site area. The estate is home to 5,529 trees, averaging one to every two residents. This is equivalent to a CO_2e reduction of 127.1 tonnes. The greenery has been estimated to reduce heat island effect by a factor of four (compared to an equivalent surface area of bare ground).

Efficacy
Materials

Prefabrication reduces construction cost and hastens project timeline. All facade walls, staircases and chutes for the SMPS project were prefabricated off-site. In total over 14,000 m³ of prefabricated concrete was used. The resulting building geometry, greatly simplified, meant that on-site wet work was also quickened. The symmetrical layout of tower blocks, for instance, resulted in 50% less wall formwork, compared with industry norms. The dividends were reduced construction waste and pollution.

Whereas many housing projects rely on prefabrication, few take a position on recycling. At SMPS recycled plastics were used for landscape furniture and decking, the latter amounting to some 650 m². An additional 8,300 m² of paving was made with recycled paver blocks. The concrete structure contains some 1,464 tonnes of pulverized fuel ash, a waste from other industries that reduces the demand for cement.

Advocacy
Community engagement

The *Action Seedling* programme is a campaign that calls for residents to look after seedlings during construction and later, when the project is completed, to plant them permanently around the estate. This programme has been implemented in several Hong Kong housing estates, including SMPS.

The *Artwork* programme at SMPS saw students from neighbourhood schools competing to decorate boulders that were brought in from a nearby quarry. A resident of the estate was invited to make calligraphic signs for the estate and its blocks. The most significant act of engagement was the post-occupancy survey in which 355 interviews were carried out with residents. The findings were generally positive. Overall satisfaction exceeded 90% of votes cast. Positive impressions of estate provisions and greenery were as high as 95%; comfort in outdoor areas was rated 'good' by 93%.

PROJECT TEAM
Developer
Hong Kong Housing Authority
Architect, building services engineer, civil engineer, geotechnical engineer, landscape architect, planner, quantity surveyor and structural engineer
Development & Construction Division, Housing Department, HKSAR Government
Environmental design consultant I
Ove Arup & Partners Hong Kong Ltd
Environmental design consultant II
Ecosystems Limited
Main contractor I
Hanison Construction Company Limited
Main contractor II
Chatwin Engineering Limited
Facility manager
Estate Management Division, Housing Department, HKSAR

SUPPLIERS
Thermal insulation
Henkel Adhesive Co Ltd
Hybrid light
EGL Energy
Wind turbine
New Energy Consulting Engineering Ltd

Green roof
Strongly International Ltd
Precast facades
Shen Zhen Sun Wah Concrete Products Co Ltd

AWARDS
2011
Winner, FuturArc Green Leadership Award, residential (multiple houses) category, BCI Asia Construction Information Pte Ltd
2010
Winner, Grand Award, Green building Awards, new building category, Hong Kong Green Building Council

PERFORMANCE[4]
Annual energy consumption
2,124.6 MWh (for public areas only)
Greenhouse gas emissions
Not available
Energy intensity
Not available

Annual water consumption
13,157 m³ (for public areas only)
Water intensity
Not available

Materials (construction)
Prefabrication
| Facade:
  13,099 m³
| Staircase:
  922 m³
| Refuse chute:
  22 m³

Materials (operation)
| Recycled paver blocks for external areas:
  8,312 m²
| Six concrete seats from nearby demolished estate reused as outdoor seating
| Recycled plastics at outdoor landscape furniture and decking:
  650 m²
| Pulverized fuel ash in concrete:
  1,464 tonnes

Wellness (occupant response)
| Overall satisfaction with estate:
  91.5%
| Satisfaction with estate provisions and greening adequacy:
  95.0%

| Satisfaction with pedestrian wind environment comfort level:
  93.0%

Comfort modes[5]
Thermal comfort
| Passive (natural ventilation):
  100%
| Active (air conditioning): Hoods are provided for the installation of air conditioning units at the discretion of tenants
Visual comfort
| Passive (daylight):
  100%
| Active (electrical lighting):
  None

232

27–29   Weather for Hong Kong, People's Republic of China
30   Elevation of a residential tower
31   Section across site

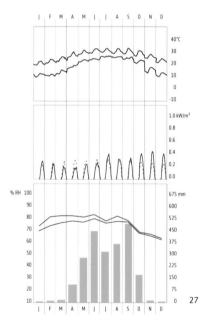

27

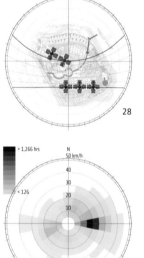

28

29

4_ Energy and water consumption figures are for the year 2011.
5_ Percentage of gross floor area that is designed to be primarily reliant on passive strategies or active systems

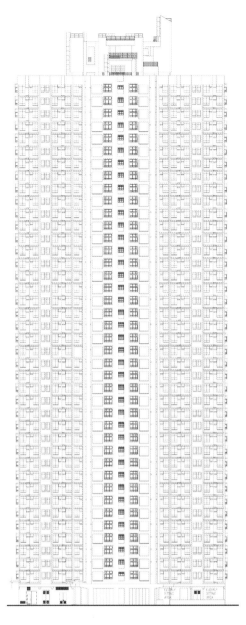

30

31

SONEVA KIRI

KOH KOOD,
THAILAND

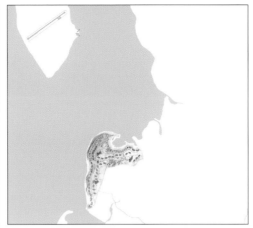

110 Moo 4
Koh Kood Sub-District, Koh Kood District
Trat Province 23000
Thailand

Location
11.69494° N
102.52974° E

Completion
2010

Cost
Not disclosed

Size
Up to 2 levels

Gross floor area
28,324 m² (guest villas only)

Site area
570,096 m²

Type
Hospitality

Programme
36 villas
7 restaurants
Gym
Spa
Staff residences and amenities

Occupancy
16,889 guest nights
97,635 staff nights

Operational hours
8,760/year

1 Food and beverage outlet
2 Main facility
3 Jetty
4 The Den
5 Eco Villa
6 Spa
7 Open air cinema and storm water pond
8 Food and beverage outlet
9 *Heart of House*
10 Eco Centre
11 Tennis and volleyball courts
12 Oxidation pond
13 Food and beverage outlet

1

Gestures of environmental concern are common in the hospitality sector in Asia. Guests are encouraged to use towels and bed sheets more than once. Some attention is paid to local sourcing, mostly fittings and finishes that guests come into contact with. There may be the odd herb garden on the premises somewhere.

At Soneva Kiri (SK) the question of ecological impact is probed deeper. It is tackled partly in how its buildings are designed, partly by how the resort behaves. There is at each property by Soneva – the group that owns SK – a Social and Environmental officer. They in turn answer to the group's Conscience officer who tracks the big picture from emissions to waste. Their job is to link the resort operations to externalities, specifically its impact on local communities and the planet.

This approach goes back to a world view espoused by the couple who owns the chain. *Slow Life* is their catchphrase that speaks of things sustainable, local, organic and wholesome (hence, S-L-O-W). Guests arriving at SK have their shoes taken from them because the world, according to Soneva, feels different when there is sand between one's toes. This sensitisation to things natural continues into the stay. Driftwood is used to fashion interior elements such as chairs and lamp shades. The villas are an ode to vernacular design and local craft. Trees that were there before the resort came along have been kept in place, becoming a part of the architecture. At the tree-top dining station, guests are hoisted up in baskets where, amidst tropical trees, they are served by staff rigged to cables.

Behind the glossy photo ops though there is hard-nosed commitment. All drinking water, for instance, is produced and bottled on-site. Almost all produce is local. At the *Heart of House* – a moniker for back-

of-house – there is considerable space for on-site sourcing and recycling. A pig farm and vegetable garden take all organic waste from kitchens. These provide food to the resort's kitchens and nearby villages. The SK team tracks greenhouse gas emissions annually including those resulting from flights to and from the resort (amounting to some 75% of its total). This is unusual amongst resorts; most do not look past operational energy use. Soneva then commits to the next step: it offsets 100% of its annual emissions by investing in carbon sequestration and renewable energy.

It is this willingness to account for impact – beyond site and neighbourhood – that differentiates the SK model from others in the hospitality sector. In the process SK redefines how high-end luxury in Asia can take the high road.

241

1   Site plan
2   Tree-top dining pod
3   Retained trees integrated
      into the architecture

4

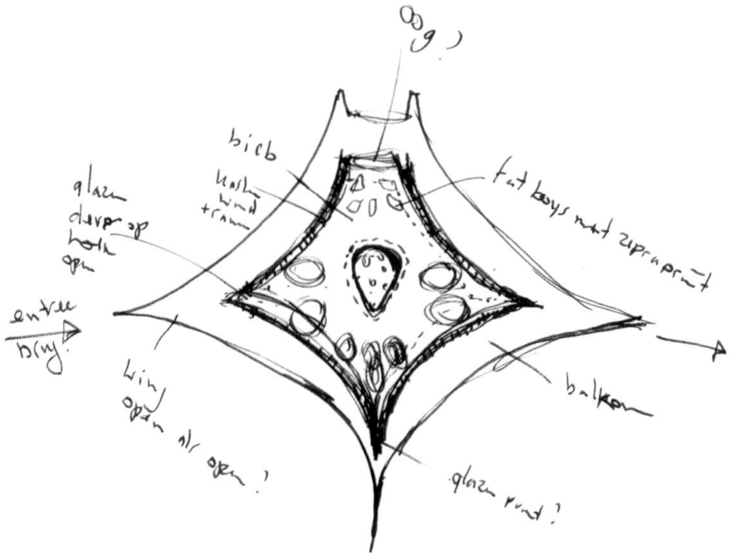

Embeddedness
The Den[1]

4 Early sketch showing form and layout
5 Model by 24H-architecture
6 Cluster of activity spaces
7 Manta ray form
8 Entrance ramp

Two innovative projects at SK embody the quest for embeddedness. The first, the Den, is a children's activity centre located on a rocky slope close to the sea. Its *biomorphic* form has been likened to a manta ray. The complex shape incorporates bioclimatic principles of wind, shade and light. The challenge here was bamboo, the construction material of choice.

Bamboo is widely used in Asia, and said to be one of the more ecologically-sound materials. It can be harvested after five years compared with 40 years before a tropical hardwood tree becomes useful to construction. The main structure of the Den uses *Pai Tong* bamboo (*Dendrocalamus asper*) in lengths up to 9 m and a diameter of 10–13 cm. The secondary roof and belly structure is made from *Pai Liang* bamboo (*Bambusa multiplex*) in 4 m length and a diameter of about 5 cm. Both come from plantations in the neighbouring Thai province of Prachinburi. All bamboo was treated with boron, a natural salt, to protect it from termites and other insects.

To help the international team of experts construct the form that had been imagined, a three-dimensional computer model and a scale model were first created. The 1:30 scale model was tested in the wind tunnel of Thammasat University in Bangkok. The *Pai Tong* bamboo was tested for strength in King Mongkut Institute of

1_ This section is written with inputs from 24H-architecture

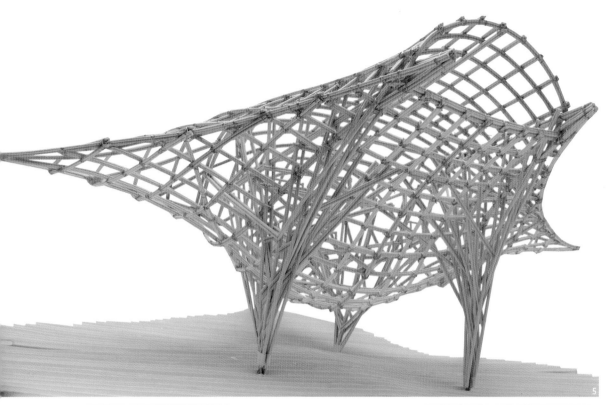

Technology in Bangkok. Construction on-site was carried out by Thai crafts-men from the Karen hill-tribe in the Mae Chaem district in Chiang Mai.

Embeddedness
Eco Villa

The Eco Villa is the other prototype at SK. It makes the case that luxury can be had for zero greenhouse gas emissions and 100% reliance on local know-how and materials,

The villa was erected by a team of Thai craftsmen that included mud brick experts, terracotta potters, master carpenters and stonemasons. Low embodied energy materials, recycled waste products and Green building techniques were used throughout. Foundations were made from sandstone boulders extracted from this and other sites. Some of the timber was harvested, dried and treated on-site. The rest was regionally sourced; mostly eucalyptus and rubberwood from plantations in a nearby province. A pottery kiln was

built on-site to produce terracotta pipes and spouts for rainwater collection. Soil from the site was mixed with rice husks and straw (both agricultural waste products) and molded into adobe mud bricks and plaster for the interior walls. Site-sourced sandstone was used for the exterior walls. Soil excavated to make way for a pond was used on the villa's green roof.

The pond is the villa's rainwater storage system *and* swimming pool. Rainwater is circulated through reed beds filled with aquatic plants that lower the nutrient content and cleanse it. Ultra violet light eliminates pathogens; waterfalls aerate the cleansed water. No toxic chemicals are used.

Daylight enters the villa via a central skylight. The villa's green roof, its thermal mass and operable openings keep it cool most of the time, reducing the need for air conditioning. All of the villa's energy needs are met by hybrid renewable system consisting of a wind turbine, photovoltaic solar panels and a micro hydro turbine.

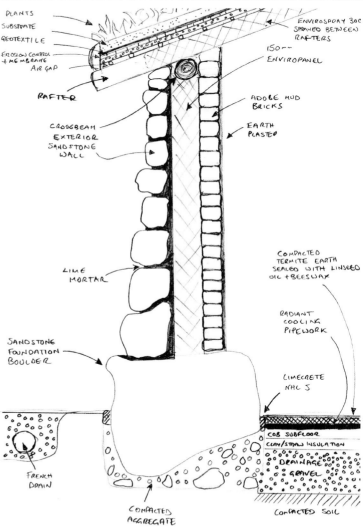

PLANTS
SUBSTRATE
GEOTEXTILE
EROSION CONTROL + MEMBRANE AIR GAP
RAFTER
CROSSBEAM EXTERIOR SANDSTONE WALL
LIME MORTAR
SANDSTONE FOUNDATION BOULDER
FRENCH DRAIN
COMPACTED AGGREGATE
ENVIROSPRAY 300 SPRAYED BETWEEN RAFTERS
150mm ENVIROPANEL
ADOBE MUD BRICKS
EARTH PLASTER
COMPACTED TERMITE EARTH SEALED WITH LINSEED OIL + BEESWAX
RADIANT COOLING PIPEWORK
LIMECRETE NHL 5
COB SUBFLOOR
CLAY/STRAW INSULATION
DRAINAGE GRAVEL
COMPACTED SOIL

Embeddedness and Efficacy
Resource loops

15   Organic waste from SK
      kitchens goes to a pig farm
16   On-site food production
17   Conversion of spent cook-
      ing oil into biodiesel
18   Rainwater collection and
      treatment
19   Storm water pond doubles
      up as open air cinema
20   Production of potable
      drinking water

Almost 100% of all water consumed is rain-capture that is treated on-site to potable standards. All wastewater coming from villas and kitchens goes to a treatment plant where it is recycled for garden irrigation. The resort's vegetable and herb gardens satisfy some 10% of the resort's food needs; 85% of food consumed is sourced locally or regionally.

All solid waste is separated. Over 8 tonnes of paper, plastic, metal and glass are recycled each year. In the same period some 1,500 litres of used cooking oil is converted to 1,200 litres of biodiesel that is then used to power some of the resort's pickup vehicles. Shredded garden waste is mixed with kitchen waste. Part of this goes to an earthworm farm that turns it into compost which then becomes fertiliser for the vegetable gardens. Part of it is fed to the resort's pigs, some 80 of them in 2011. In the same year 20 pigs were given to the local farmers as a gift.

A total of 6.8 tonnes of food waste and 3 tonnes of horticultural waste each year are used as pig feed or turned to compost.

247

21 Reliance on FSC-certified
 wood
22 Staff restoring mangrove
 swamp at SK
23 Reliance on locally sourced
 timber
24 Reforestation area
 near Chiang Mai, North
 Thailand
25 Area undergoing
 reforestation
26 Nursery supporting
 reforestation

Ecology
Emissions and habitats

In mid-2011, 200,000 trees were planted over 80 hectares of the Doi Pa Ma, Sri Lanna National Park near Chiang Mai. It was the first time that reforestation on this scale was carried out in Thailand. The cost to Soneva is about US$900,000 for each year of the programme. The resort chain worked with Plant a Tree Today Foundation[2] that organised the effort, engaging volunteers from the military, local community, local school groups and students from Chiang Mai University. Fourteen indigenous tree species were planted. In 2012 this number will be increased to 30. The goal is to create biodiversity and attract seed-disbursing birds that will lead to a viable ecosystem. The yearly planting will amount to

greenhouse gas offsets equaling some 160,000 tonnes CO_2e.

In South India, some years earlier, a 1.5 MW wind turbine was funded by Soneva and operated by The Converging World.[3] In its 20-year lifetime it will produce 80,000 kWh of electrical power – equal to some 70,000 tonnes of offsets. Revenue from this turbine will be put into a second wind turbine, doubling the mitigation effort. The cost to Soneva there was US$1.7 million.

These global efforts wouldn't mean much if SK had been built at the expense of local ecology. In the run-up to construction, wildlife corridors were defined and vulnerable areas protected from construction activities. Villas were built on land

2_ Plant a Tree Today Foundation.
 www.pattfoundation.org
3_ The Converging World.
 www.theconvergingworld.org

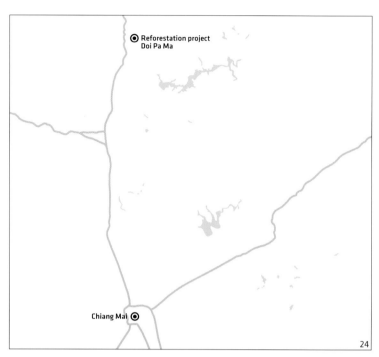

Reforestation project
Doi Pa Ma

Chiang Mai

24

25

26

where there were fewer mature trees. Sometimes a villa was moved to save a tree; sometimes the tree became a part of the building. Trees that could not be left in place were transplanted. Around 400 larger trees and palms were transplanted along with thousands of small plants. Almost all wood used in construction is FSC-certified or from plantation sources within Thailand. Staff at SK routinely engage in replanting exercises aimed at restoring a nearby mangrove area.

PROJECT TEAM

Developer

Soneva

Architects

| Habita (overall resort concept)
| 24H-architecture (the Den)
| Habita (Eco Villa)
| Joerg Stamm (bamboo bridge)

Interior design

Soneva Creative Department (all villas and the Den)

Bamboo consultant

| Ecobamboo LTDA (the Den)

Mechanical and electrical engineer, lighting consultant

EEC Lincolne Scott Co Ltd

Civil and structural engineers

| Planning and Design Co Ltd (overall resort)
| Planning & Design Co Ltd, Thailand (the Den)
| Ove Arup Thailand (wind-tunnel tests for the Den)

Quantity surveyors

| Page Kirkland Co Ltd, Thailand
| Davis Langdon & Seah Ltd, Thailand

Landscape consultants

| Green Architects International
| Louis Thompson (Eco Villa)

Main contractors

| K-Tech Co Ltd, Ritta Co Ltd (all villas)
| Birthright Co Ltd, Ritta Co Ltd (MEP)
| Craftsmen from Mae-Chaem village near Chiang Mai (Eco-Villa and the Den)

Building operator and facility manager

Soneva

SUPPLIERS

Bamboo supplier

Pimtha Co, Ltd Bangkok, Thailand (the Den)

Waterproofing membrane for green roof

de Boer (Eco Villa)

Air conditioning

Solcool (Eco Villa)

Magnapool mineral swimming pool system and biological wastewater treatment system

Janish and Janish (Eco Villa)

Energy design and installation

Suntechnics (Eco Villa)

AWARDS

2011

| Winner, Green Development Award, Thanachart Bank Thailand Property Awards
| Winner, PoolAsia Award, resort pool villa main category (criteria: environmentally friendly and fully integrated water treatment), PoolAsia

PERFORMANCE[4]

Annual energy consumption

4,400 MWh

On-site energy sourcing

| Diesel generator: 99%
| Photovoltaics (Eco Villa only): 10.7 MWh (6.5 kWp)
| Wind turbine (Eco Villa only): 0.5 MWh (1.7 kWp)

Greenhouse gas emissions

| Direct emissions:[5] 2,913 tonnes CO_2e
| Indirect emissions:[6] 13,899 tonnes CO_2e

Energy intensity

| 38.56 kWh/resident[7] night
| 55 kWh/m^2/year (Eco Villa only)

Annual water consumption

92,786 m^3

Water intensity

0.8 m^3/resident/year

On-site water sourcing

100% (of total resort needs, from central rainwater collection reservoir and deep well)

Materials (construction)

85% of materials for Eco Villa were sourced on-site (adobe bricks, timber, stonework, soil substrate for green roof)

Materials (operations)

| 80% of materials from replenishable or low-impact sources (for instance, paper, cleaning liquids, fertilisers and organic food)
| 10% of food consumed is grown on-site
| 85% of food consumed is locally/regionally farmed (from within a radius of less than 2,000 km from SK)
| 90% organic waste generated is reused on-site (as compost, livestock feed and biofuel)
| 85% solid waste is sent for recycling

250

27–29 Weather for Koh Kood, Thailand

Drawings of the Den:
30 Front elevation
31 Back elevation
32 Cross section
33 Side elevation
34 Long section
35 Plan, ground floor
36 Plan, entrance floor
37 Plan, first floor
38 Plan, roof structure
39 Plan, roof

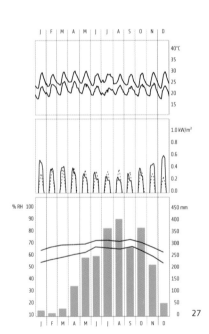

27

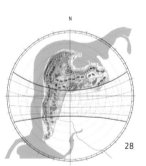

28

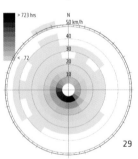

29

4_ Energy and water consumption figures are for the period July 2010 to June 2011.

5_ Greenhouse gas emissions arising from sources owned by resort/spa such as all on-site energy production and electrical power that is imported from local electricity suppliers

6_ Greenhouse gas emissions arising as a consequence of the operation of the resort/spa but from sources not owned or controlled by the resort/spa, for instance, staff and guest air travel, staff and guest ground travel, sea, air and road freight, food and other resources such as paper and water

7_ Resident refers to both hotels guests and staff, who stay on Koh Kood island for the duration of their shift.

On-site food sourcing
(as % of total consumed)
10%

Comfort modes[8]
Not available

30

31

32

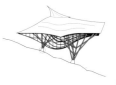

33

34

35

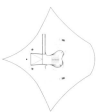

36

37

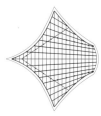

38

39

8_ Percentage of gross floor area that is
    designed to be primarily reliant on passive
    strategies or active systems

THE MET

BANGKOK,
THAILAND

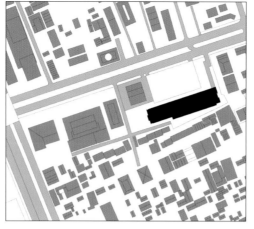

125 South Sathorn Road
Thungmahamek, Sathorn
Bangkok 10120
Thailand

Location
13.72221° N
100.53415° E

Completion
December 2009

Cost
US$132,000,000

Size
66 levels

Gross floor area
124,885 m²

Built-up area[1]
4,631 m²

Site area
11,361 m²

Site coverage
40.7%

Type
Residential

Programme
370 residential units

Deck on 9th floor:
Barbecue areas
Aerobics room
Game room
Gym
Pocket gardens
50-m swimming pool
Children's pool
Jacuzzi
Pool deck
Outdoor showers
Changing rooms
Steam and sauna
Hot and cold pools

Deck on 28th and 47th floors:
Terraces with sky gardens
Barbecue areas
Gym
Children's playrooms
Function rooms
Libraries

Occupancy
1,500 residents

Operational hours
8,760/year

253

1_ Including walls, gardens, walkways, circulation, pool decks and paved areas

Density

Sited in one of Bangkok's busiest commercial districts, The Met speaks of the challenge of rising densities in cities. Asian urbanism, at its current pace, often overlooks the importance of shared space and greenery as conditions that are necessary for well-being. Pressure to build to high plot ratios – often as much as 10 – leaves little space for community or nature. In public housing these are assigned to whatever space is left on the ground; in private developments there might be a podium deck with pool and gym. There is also a tendency, in the way these buildings are designed, to compromise natural ventilation and daylight access with deep floor plates, which in turn increases reliance on electromechanical systems that has its own cost and environmental impact.

Built 66 storeys high, The Met packs 1,500 persons onto its 1.1 hectare site. Compared to its neighbours – some of the more exclusive residential towers in Bangkok – The Met seems massive. If not for its design, it might also have seemed crowded and unfriendly.

What distinguishes this development from others is its interstitial spaces and greenery. Decks, balconies and planted surfaces interrupt the architectural form, breaking it down into subclusters of mid-sized communities. These same elements create a microclimate that makes it possible for residents to *not* have to rely on air conditioning and electrical lighting.

The Met is one of several high-density prototypes in Asia. These projects[2] are distinguished by a signature *street-in-the-sky* that extends the ground plane up, linking stacks of apartments across with layers of community space and greenery. They are noteworthy for how they deliver comfort.

Air and light

The design of The Met was guided by a belief that each inhabitant is entitled to natural air and light. The building is sliced in several directions to create interstitial spaces. The living spaces of every apartment unit look outward facing the city skyline;

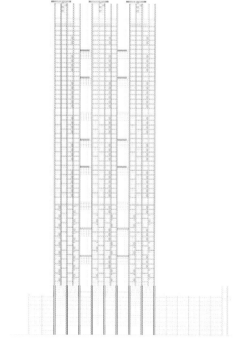

1

259

1   North elevation
2   Table 2: Comparison of two high-density residential developments in Southeast Asia

	Plot ratio	Gross floor area (m²)	Storeys	Units	Density (persons/ha of site area)	Community space (m²/person)	Community space (% of GFA)
The Met, Bangkok, 2009	10	124,885	66	370	1,363	8.3*	10
The Pinnacle@Duxton, Singapore, 2009	9	253,957	50	1,800	2,664	5.3	14

* 4.2 if normalised to public housing standards for occupancy

2

2_ The Pinnacle@Duxton (2009, Singapore), Linked Hybrid (2009, Beijing, China) and Skyville@Dawson (2015, Singapore)

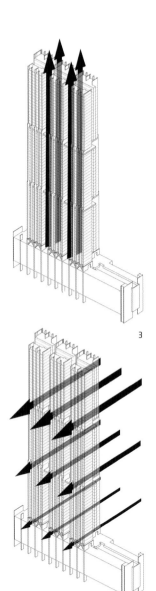

3

4

back-of-house service spaces open onto an internal void that connects the tower vertically. This central space brings air and light into the building's core by breaking down an otherwise hulking mass.

Residents are offered the option of air conditioning. The hoped-for scenario – in this democratisation of comfort – is that well-conceived passive strategies will lower cooling loads and have fewer occupants reaching for the thermostat.

Ensuring that passive principles work effectively in a building of this size meant that several conventions of real estate had to be challenged. The typical compact tower – a central service core and deep floor plate – is substituted with what is really an ensemble of six towers linked by decks and bridges. What is lost here is the efficiency of a single service shaft; instead there are three cores, each supporting two apartments on every floor. This fragmentation, and the resulting duplication of cores, has two consequences. It offers residents privacy, allowing each unit to operate

independently, letting occupants decide when and where they interact with neighbours. It also permits air movement. Pressure differentials around the building force air through and up the tower. As a result when two opposite-facing windows are opened in an apartment, air moves through the unit, front to back or vice versa.

This idea of returning to known principles of passive comfort is hard to sell in tropical cities of Asia where air conditioning is now easily available and energy is not expensive. Many residential towers in Bangkok do not even try. Air conditioning is assumed to be the only viable response to the combination of heat and humidity, noise and pollution. It is also assumed that all consumers want this all the time. The fact that The Met has found many interested buyers so quickly is significant. Bangkok's real estate sector appears to have taken notice. The Met has become an advocate of *fresh air architecture* for Thailand and tropical conditions elsewhere.

5

6

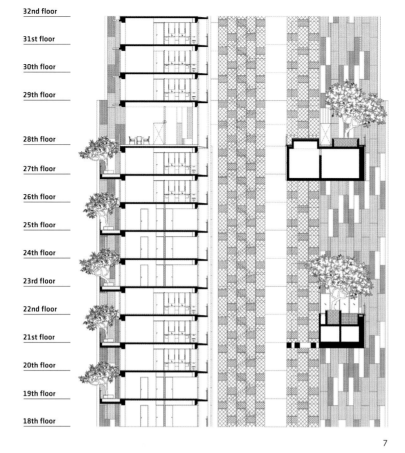

32nd floor
31st floor
30th floor
29th floor
28th floor
27th floor
26th floor
25th floor
24th floor
23rd floor
22nd floor
21st floor
20th floor
19th floor
18th floor

7

3–4   Permeability of form
       enables airflow through
       the width and height of
       the tower
5–6   Interstitial spaces
7   Section across 18th to
       32nd floors showing
       intermediate decks and
       greenery
8   Apartment with pool and
       landscaping

65%
OF RESIDENTS SAY THAT
THE MET'S DESIGN ENCOURAGES
A SENSE OF COMMUNITY

60%
SAY THAT THEY ARE SATISFIED
WITH THE GREENERY THAT
HAS BEEN INTEGRATED INTO
THE DEVELOPMENT

9-11   Greenery and community
         spaces
12   Measurement of noise
         levels at five locations
13   Integration of community
         decks
14   Integration of greenery

Wellness
Community space and greenery

Three decks cut across the width of the tower on levels 9, 28 and 47, acting as vertically distributed layers of community space. These hold a gym, swimming pool, children's playrooms and function rooms. There are also many insertions of landscaping: vertically planted screens over east and west facades and podium walls, frangipani trees peeking out of private balconies. On the ground and ninth levels, there are several formal arrangements of water and plants.

In the post-occupancy survey of Met residents,[3] 65% say that these spaces do in fact encourage neighbourly interactions.[4] Three considerations affect which deck is preferred by the inhabitants: wind, views of the skyline and noise from the street. The most used deck is on the ninth floor where many of the amenities are located. The second most used is the 47th floor where views are the best and noise levels lowest. This is also where wind speeds are the highest, some 50% higher than on the ninth level. When asked if greenery was satisfactory, 60% of the residents said yes.

3_ All survey readings and measurements reported here were conducted over a three-day period in July 2011. | Lim, L.W.I. (2011)

4_ This figure, interestingly, is higher at The Met than at The Pinnacle@Duxton, where the same question was asked in the survey. Fifty-five per cent of the residents there said that community spaces encourage interaction between neighbours. This challenges the assumption that residents of private housing interact less with each other – or value this type of interaction less – than in public housing projects. | Lim, L.W.I. (2011)

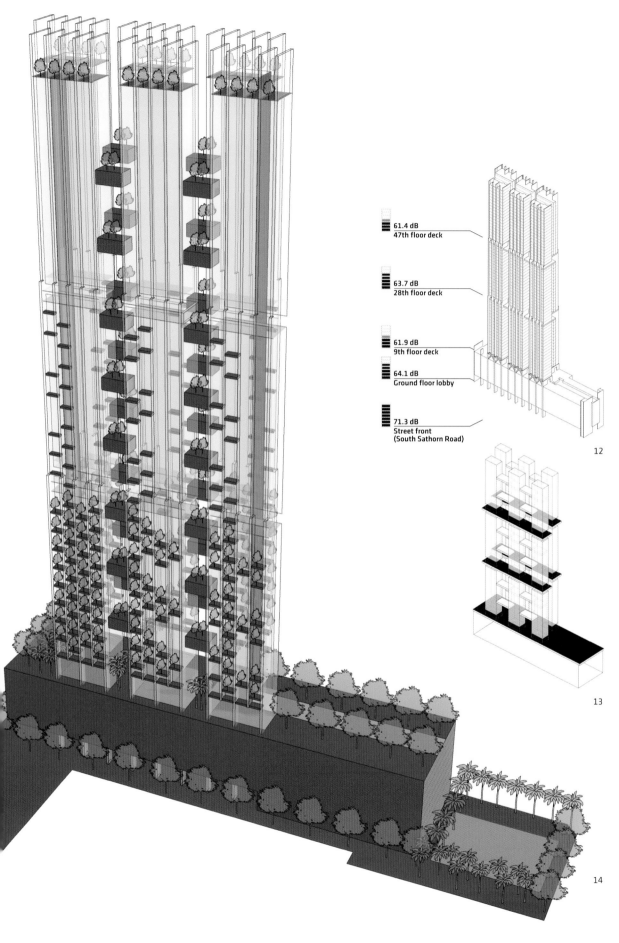

61.4 dB
47th floor deck

63.7 dB
28th floor deck

61.9 dB
9th floor deck

64.1 dB
Ground floor lobby

71.3 dB
Street front
(South Sathorn Road)

12

13

14

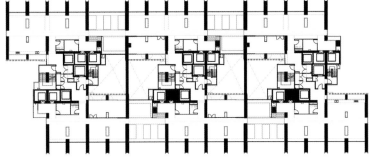

80%

OF RESIDENTS SAY THAT THEY
ARE GENERALLY COMFORTABLE
OR VERY COMFORTABLE IN THEIR
HOMES

45%

SAY THAT THEY HAVE LOW
TO MODERATE DEPENDENCE ON
AIR CONDITIONING

15   Plan of 28th floor
16–17 Apartment interior
18   Measurement of airflow
      and dry bulb temperature
      in three apartments

Wellness
Climate and comfort

Asked if they are generally comfortable in their apartments, 80% of residents answered yes. Nevertheless, 45% said that they had low to moderate reliance on air conditioning.[5] This could be a matter of habit or a lifestyle choice. The proportion is nonetheless good for a building of its type and location; many of The Met's neighbours are hermitically sealed and fully air-conditioned.

The Met's approach to passive comfort starts with its permeable form that lets air and light through. Its widest facades are oriented north and south which have the lowest solar exposure at this latitude. Windows are shielded by *brise-soleil*, fins that run vertically and horizontally on facades. Recesses, balconies and voids create pockets of shade without cutting off breezeways. Vertical movement of air through its central void was measured at an average of 0.7 m/s. Air speeds within three apartment units located at different points along the tower's height averaged 0.6 m/s, often higher. Indoor air temperatures, during midday peaks were several degrees cooler than simultaneous conditions on the ground. All living spaces at the front of the unit are substantially daylit; reliance on electrical light is lowest here and highest in back-of-house service spaces. Ninety-five per cent of those surveyed felt that daylight access was just right or more than needed.

5_ The same questions at The Pinnacle@ Duxton had the same level of overall satisfaction but only 35% of residents said they relied on mechanical cooling. | Lim, L.W.I. (2011)

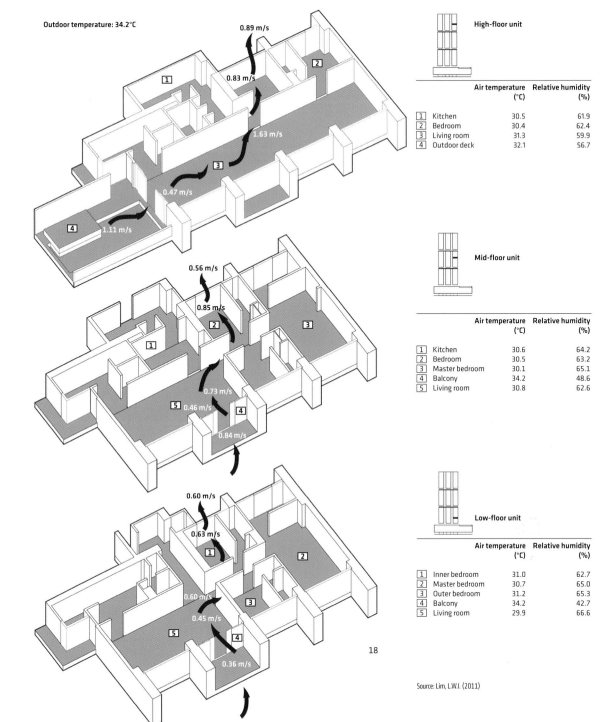

Outdoor temperature: 34.2°C

0.89 m/s
0.83 m/s
1.63 m/s
0.47 m/s
1.11 m/s

High-floor unit

		Air temperature (°C)	Relative humidity (%)
1	Kitchen	30.5	61.9
2	Bedroom	30.4	62.4
3	Living room	31.3	59.9
4	Outdoor deck	32.1	56.7

0.56 m/s
0.85 m/s
0.73 m/s
0.46 m/s
0.84 m/s

Mid-floor unit

		Air temperature (°C)	Relative humidity (%)
1	Kitchen	30.6	64.2
2	Bedroom	30.5	63.2
3	Master bedroom	30.1	65.1
4	Balcony	34.2	48.6
5	Living room	30.8	62.6

0.60 m/s
0.63 m/s
0.60 m/s
0.45 m/s
0.36 m/s

Low-floor unit

		Air temperature (°C)	Relative humidity (%)
1	Inner bedroom	31.0	62.7
2	Master bedroom	30.7	65.0
3	Outer bedroom	31.2	65.3
4	Balcony	34.2	42.7
5	Living room	29.9	66.6

18

Source: Lim, L.W.I. (2011)

PROJECT TEAM
Developer
Pebble Bay Thailand Co Ltd
Architect
| WOHA Architects Pte Ltd,
Singapore
| Tandem Architects LLC,
Thailand
Mechanical and electrical
engineer
Lincolne Scott Ng Pte Ltd,
Singapore
Civil and structural engineer
Worley Pte Ltd, Singapore
Environmental impact
assessment consultant
ERM-Siam Co Ltd, Thailand
Quantity surveyors
KPK Quantity Surveyors
(1995) Singapore Pte Ltd
Landscape consultant
Cicada Pte Ltd, Singapore
Main contractor
Bouygues Thai Ltd
Facility manager
CB Richard Ellis Co Ltd,
Thailand

AWARDS
2011
| Winner, RIBA Lubetkin
Prize, Royal Institute of
British Architects
| Winner, International
Architecture Award,
Chicago Athenaeum

and the European Centre
for Architecture, Art,
Design and Urban Studies
| Winner, Green Good Design
Award, the Chicago
Athenaeum and the
European Centre for
Architecture, Art, Design
and Urban Studies
2010
| Winner, the International
Highrise Award, City of
Frankfurt, Deutsches
Architekturmuseum and
DekaBank
| Winner, the Jorn Utzon
Award for International
Architecture, Australian
Institute of Architects
| Winner, RIBA International
Awards, Royal Institute of
British Architects
| Winner, BCI Green Design
Award, residential
architecture (multiple
houses) category, BCI Asia
Construction Information
Pte Ltd
2009
| Bronze Award Winner,
Emporis Skyscraper Awards,
Emporis
| Design of the Year,
President's Design Award,
DesignSingapore Council

and Urban Redevelopment
Authority
| Finalist, World Architecture
Festival Awards, housing
category, World
Architecture Festival
| Finalist, CTBUH Best Tall
Building Award, Council
on Tall Buildings and Urban
Habitat
| Winner, Asian Habitat
Award for Planning and
Designing, Asian Habitat
Society
2006
Winner, MIPIM Architectural
Review Future Project Awards,
tall buildings category,
The Architectural Review

PERFORMANCE[6]
Annual energy consumption
3,142 MWh
On-site energy sourcing
(as % of total consumed)
None
Greenhouse gas emissions
Not available
Energy intensity
25 kWh/m²/year

Annual water consumption
107,199 m³
On-site water sourcing
(as % of total consumed)
None

Water intensity
71.5 m³/person/year

Wellness (design)
| Space for community use
(expressed as % of total
gross floor area):
10%
| Surface area for building-
integrated planting
(expressed as % of total
site area):
100%
These figures were attained
for a developmental plot
ratio of 10

Wellness
(occupant response)
| 80% said that they are
generally comfortable or
very comfortable in their
homes
| 60% said that the thermal
condition is comfortable or
very comfortable
| 45% said that they have
moderate to low depend-
ence on air conditioning
| 85% said that the daylight
levels are just right or
slightly bright

19–21   Weather for Bangkok,
Thailand
22   Sun path over The Met
23   Axonometric view

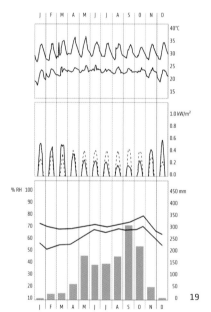

19

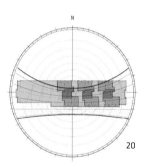

20

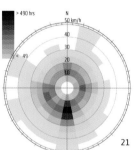

21

6_ Energy and water consumption figures
are for the year 2011.

Comfort modes[7]
Thermal comfort
| Passive (natural
  ventilation):
  99%
| Active (air conditioning):
  1%
Visual comfort
| Passive (daylight):
  95%
| Active (electrical light):
  5%

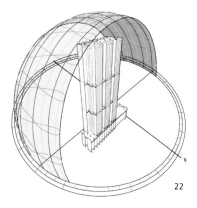

22

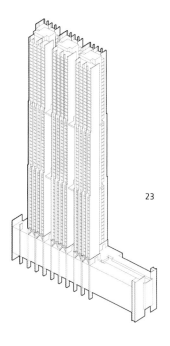

23

7_ Percentage of gross floor area that is
   designed to be primarily reliant on passive
   strategies or active systems

VANKE CENTRE

SHENZHEN,
PEOPLE'S REPUBLIC OF CHINA

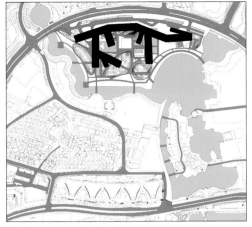

33 Huan Mei Road
Dameisha, Yantian District
Shenzhen 518083
People's Republic of China

Location
22.60078° N
114.29944° E

Completion
September 2009

Cost
Not disclosed

Size
6 levels

Gross floor area
105,638 m^2

Built-up area[1]
61,725 m^2

Site area
61,725 m^2

Type
Mixed use

Programme
Conference centre (8,292 m^2)
Condominiums (25,704 m^2)
Hotel (11,113 m^2)
Restaurants, bar and lobbies (4,600 m^2)
SoHo offices (13,591 m^2)
Spa (3,400 m^2)
Vanke Headquarters (13,874 m^2)
Public green space (47,288 m^2)

Occupancy[2]
370 persons

Operational hours[2]
2,340/year

1_ Including walls, gardens, walkways, circulation, pool decks and paved areas
2_ Vanke Headquarters only; this was the
   first phase of the Vanke Centre to be
   completed and occupied.

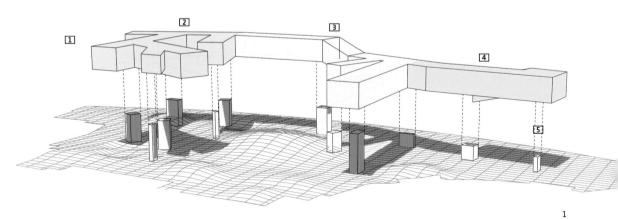

1

1 Ocean views
2 Office
3 Apartments
4 Hotel
5 Stairs and elevators

35 M

Ocean views

2

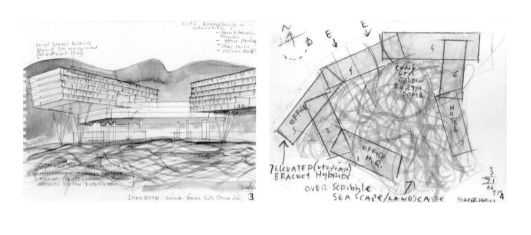

The Vanke Centre (VC) in Shenzhen has been dubbed a *horizontal skyscraper*; its jagged snake-like footprint is as long as some buildings are tall. The illusion that this is a tall building resting on its side is underscored by the fact that it hovers some 15 m off the ground, held aloft by eight structural supports that connect the building above with subterranean spaces below. The ground plane in-between, designed as an undulating landscape, is a public park. Of the 52,000 m² of landscaping created on this 61-hectare site, almost 92% is accessible to the people of Shenzhen. Much of it also serves to channel storm water run-off and recycle grey water. To be understood, this juxtaposition of public space and private interest must be seen in the context of Shenzhen and Chinese cities in general.

Shenzhen struggles with much of what plagues many fast-growing cities in China. Wealth and entrepreneurship thrive; infrastructure and public space lag behind. With more than 9 million residents piled on an average of 16,000 people/km², Shenzhen is the fourth densest city in Asia.[3] Many ordinary residents struggle with pollution, crowding and a lack of public amenities. It is no small gesture that, in this context, a commercially successful enterprise like China Vanke – the country's third largest developer of residential properties – acts explicitly in the public's interest by contributing to shared space and infrastructure.

It is worth noting that the architect, at early stages of design, could have opted for more conventional forms. Skyscrapers of the vertical kind are popular in Chinese cities where the height of a new building is seen to represent the wealth and status of its developer. There are also many low-to-mid height mixed-use developments that are laid out like small neighbourhoods. Either option – the high tower or low clusters – could have been argued for in the interest of the developer. Either could have been made compliant with LEED and accrued the benefits of a Green label.

The design team chose instead to create a new architectural typology that would synergise several objectives. In creating a park, the VC site takes on social and ecological roles. Keeping the building low has meant that the energy needed for the movement of people and goods during construction and in operation could be reduced. The building's altitude above ground is calibrated such that daylight and views are still possible. Wind flows freely across the site and through the building, offsetting the demand for air conditioning during the cooler months. Its ambling roofscape – the building's fifth facade – is layered with photovoltaics and greenery. There are many other considerations and insertions that enable VC to do well on an assessment tool checklist. Ultimately, it is its stance on community and ecology that makes it stand out.

275

1   The building hovers over a public park
2   Lifting the building off the ground permits views, light and air
3–5   Conceptual sketches by architect

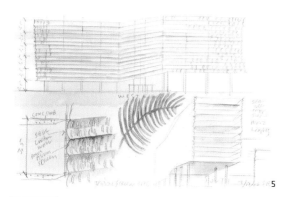

3_ United Nations Human Settlements Programme. (2010)

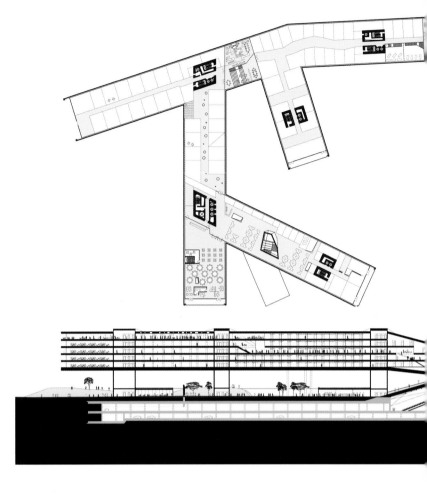

276

6   Building plan and section
7   Scale model
8   View of completed
    building

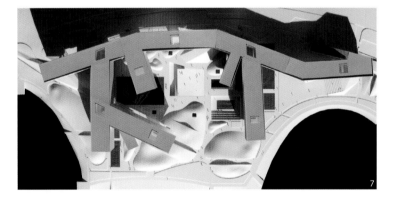

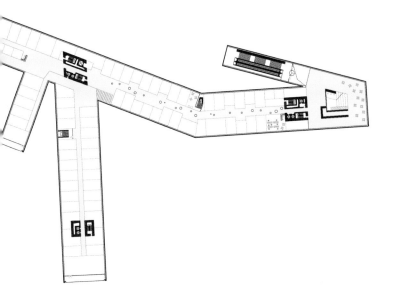

6

8

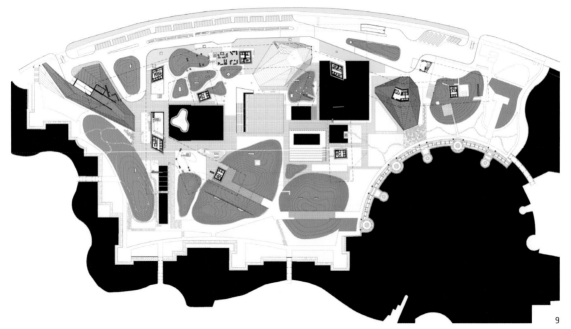

■ Water bodies
▧ Plants on patches and mounds
▨ Grasscrete
□ Grass
▦ Black/white granite and marble
▨ Stone paver
▨ Gravel

Embeddedness and Ecology
Water

9   Site plan with greenery
         and water bodies
10–11   Water bodies frame the
         building
12–13   Water features under the
         building
14   Roof plan with photovol-
         taics and greenery
15–16   Indoor electro-mechanical
         fittings
17   Roof-mounted
         photovoltaics

The story of the VC's landscape is the story of water. The site is in effect part of the municipal storm water management system. The sunken gardens, courtyards, ponds and planted mounds that have been created by VC offer a circulatory path that regulates and redistributes storm water throughout its site. Its lagoon acts as a bioswale and retention pond that is connected to several adjacent creeks. Gutters redirect overflow into a series of ponds and wetlands that are planted with marsh grasses and lotus. The system as a whole is designed to minimise run-off, erosion and environmental damage. With elements of rainwater storage and grey water recycling, no potable or municipal water is used for VC's maintenance or irrigation needs.

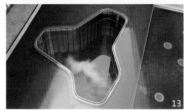

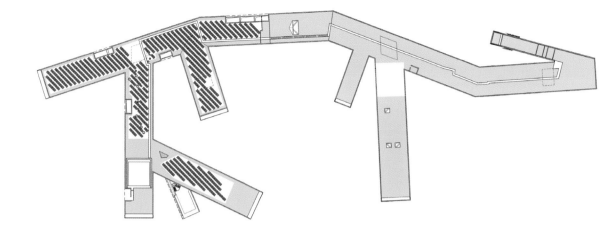

Photovoltaic panel area (1,930 m^2)
Green roof area (8,586 m^2)
Hardscape roof (5,854 m^2)

Embeddedness and Efficacy
Energy

The building's response to climate has yielded specific energy dividends. The 1,400 m^2 of photovoltaic arrays on the roof meet 12.5% of the total electric energy demand for Vanke Headquarters. It is estimated that during the cool season when natural ventilation is an option, mechanical systems can be switched off for at least 60% of the time. The facade-shading system, even in the closed position, lets in enough light for routine office functions in up to 75% of spaces, eliminating the need for electrical lighting.

Electro-mechanical systems are generally designed to high performance standards. These include a couple of strategic procurements. The ice storage system, for instance,

means that chillers are rarely switched on during the day. Ice made at night is later used to cool the building's interior. This reduces vc's demand on Shenzhen's grid during daytime peaks. Primary air handling units are fitted with heat recovery wheels. As air is exhausted from the building, it is used to preheat or pre-cool incoming fresh air. This system has a 70% heat recovery rate. The ventilation system adjusts fresh air intake to occupancy by monitoring build-up of CO_2 within a room. Daylight sensors adjust artificial lighting levels to available daylight. Occupancy sensors switch off lights when a space is unoccupied.

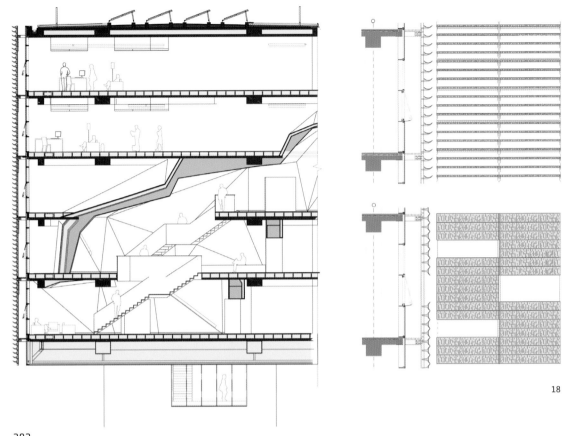

18

Wellness
Climate and comfort

Within the park several specially cooled pools run on geothermal energy, acting as sources of radiant cooling. This creates a microclimate that enhances visitor comfort in summer. These cooling ponds are linked to vc's grey water system.

Designing for comfort continues in the building with climate-responsive systems and occupant controls. Large operable windows 2 m wide offer natural ventilation and cross breezes during the cooler months of the year. From November to March when the outdoor conditions in Shenzhen are calm, these windows can take over from mechanical cooling systems in much of the building, in particular the condominium. The narrow plan depth ensures that cross-ventilation works. It also means that almost all occupants have access to daylight. One hundred per cent of regularly occupied rooms and areas receive daylight above 270 lux. Ninety per cent of interior spaces have direct views to the exterior.

Each of vc's 26 facades is different. The porosity of each facade was fine-tuned to the intensity of solar exposure so that daylight entry would not be compromised by solar heat gain. Some are fixed, others are controlled by sensors, opening and closing according to the sun. The least perforated of these facades, even in the closed position, will allow 15% light transmittance, yet reduce up to 70% solar heat gain at its peak.

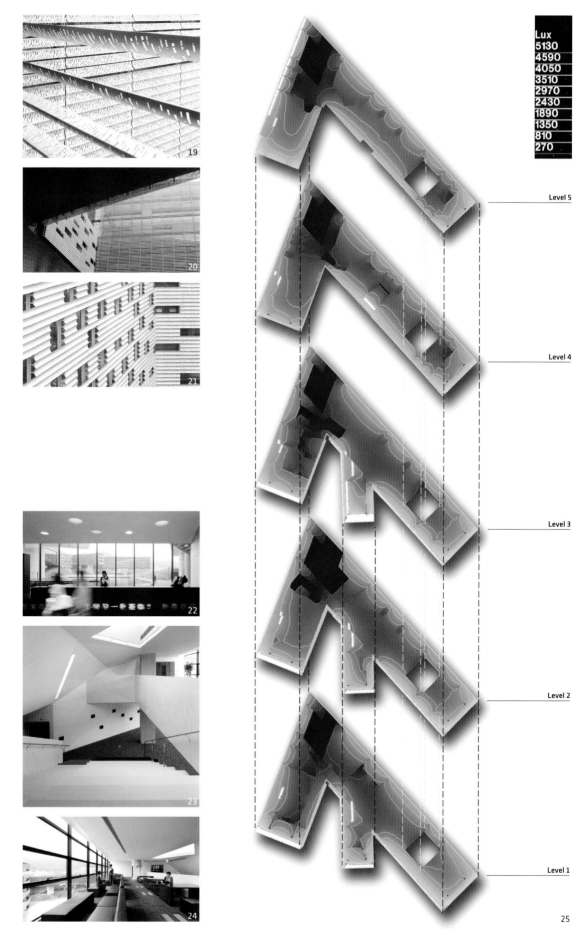

Lux
5130
4590
4050
3510
2970
2430
1890
1350
810
270

Level 5

Level 4

Level 3

Level 2

Level 1

19

20

21

22

23

24

PROJECT TEAM
Developer
Shenzhen Vanke Real
Estate Co
Architect
Steven Holl Architects
**Associate architect,
structural engineer[4] and
mechanical engineer**
China Construction Design
International
Structural engineer[5]
China Academy of Building
Research
Landscape architect
Shenzhen Institute of
Environmental Sciences
**Sustainable design
consultant**
Ove Arup & Partners Hong
Kong Ltd
Facility manager
Shenzhen Vanke Real Estate
Co Ltd
Climate engineer
Transsolar Energietechnik
GmbH
Lighting consultant
L'Observatoire International
Curtain wall consultant
Shenyang Yuanda Aluminum
Industry Engineering Co Ltd
Landscape consultant
Steven Holl Architects

Main contractor
The First Construction
Engineering Limited Company
of China Construction, Third
Engineering Bureau
Building operator[6]
Shenzhen Vanke Real
Estate Co

SUPPLIERS[7]
**Structural system (steel
tension cable)**
CSCEC
Metalwork (curtain wall)
Shenyang Yuanda Aluminum
Industry Engineering Co Ltd
Glass
Southern Glass
Wetlands
Shenzhen Academy of
Environmental Science
Green roof
Bai Yue Tech grass roof by
Zhu Min
**Cabinetwork, furniture,
and panelling (with custom
bamboo)**
Dasso
Paints and stains
ICI-Dulux
**Fixed auditorium seating
(with bamboo and green
mohair)**
Poltrona Frau Pitagora
Chairs
Vitra MVS collection

**Surfacing (kitchenette
countertops)**
Dupont (Corian)
Elevators/escalators
Hitachi UAX 1000
Carpet
Interface FLOR Menagerie
**Office furniture (with
bamboo desktop)**
CRC Logic workstation
Floor and wall tiles
Cimic
Plumbing (waterless urinal)
Sloan
Photovoltaics
Changzhou Trina Solar Energy
(TrinaSolar PV module)
Lighting
NVC custom T5 pendant
uplight, custom T4, and
exterior LED
Chillers
Carrier

AWARDS/CERTIFICATION
2011
| Winner, American
Architecture Award,
Chicago Athenaeum,
Museum of Architecture
and Design
| Winner, New York Honour
Award, American Institute
of Architects

| Winner, Institute Honour
Award, American Institute
of Architects
2010
| Winner, Green Good Design
Award, Chicago
Athenaeum, Museum of
Architecture and Design
and the European Centre
for Architecture, Art,
Design and Urban Studies
| Winner, Good Design is
Good Business Award,
Architectural Record, China
| Winner, BCI Green
Leadership Award,
commercial category,
BCI Asia Construction
Information Pte Ltd
| Merit Award, Hong Kong
Green Building Awards,
new buildings category
(Asia-Pacific), Hong Kong
Green Building Council
| Certified, Platinum, LEED
new construction 2.2,
United States Green
Building Council[8]

PERFORMANCE[9]
Energy consumption
2,057.3 MWh
On-site energy sourcing
| Photovoltaics:
266.7 MWh

284

26–28 Weather for Shenzhen,
People's Republic of China
29 Sun path over VC

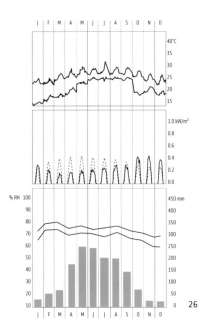

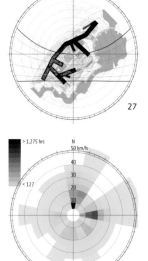

4_ Construction Documents and
Construction Administration
5_ Schematic Design and Design
Development
6_ Vanke Headquarters only
7_ Structure, Facade and Landscape apply
to whole development. Interior finishes
apply to Vanke Headquarters and
Conference Centre only

8_ Vanke Headquarters only
9_ Performance figures cited here for Vanke
Headquarters only. Energy and water
consumption figures are for the period
October 2009 to September 2010.

| Natural gas[10]:
1,334,340 kBtu

Greenhouse gas emissions
1,810.5 tonnes CO_2e

Energy intensity
144.5 kWh/m²/year

Annual water consumption
44,485.5 m³

Water intensity
120 m³/person/year

**On-site water sourcing
(system capacity)**
| Rainwater harvesting
system:
1,200 m³
| Grey water recycling:
150 m³/day

Materials (construction)
| 62% of structural materi-
als, by cost, were sourced
locally or regionally (within
a radius of less than 800 km
from project site)
| 28% of structural materi-
als, by cost, have full or
partial recycled content
| 59% of wood is FSC-
certified

Wellness (design)
95.6% of gross floor area
offers view to outdoors

Comfort modes[11]
Thermal comfort
Passive (natural ventilation):
20% (of operating period
in a year)
Visual comfort
Passive (daylight):
96.5%
(of gross floor area)

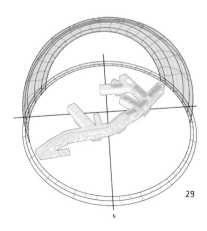

29

N

10_ Based on gas caloric value of 8,000 Kcal/kg
in Shenzhen
11_ Percentage of gross floor area that is
designed to be primarily reliant on passive
strategies or active systems

YAMUNA
CORPORATE OFFICE
KIRLOSKAR
BROTHERS LTD

PUNE,
INDIA

Pune, India

Yamuna
Corporate Office
Kirloskar
Brothers Ltd

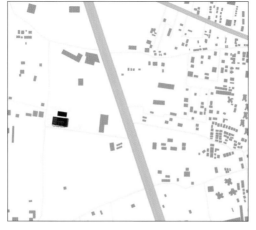

Survey no.98, Hissa no. 3–7
Taluka Haveli, District Pune
Baner 411045
India

Location
18.56049° N
73.76544° E

Completion
May 2009

Cost
US$11,118,500

Size
Up to 4 levels

Gross floor area
11,900 m²

Site area
20,200 m²

Site coverage
25%

Type
Workplace

Programme
Offices (80% of gross floor area)
Clubhouse (20% of gross floor area)

Occupancy
545 staff
25 visitors/day approximately

Operational hours
2,650/year

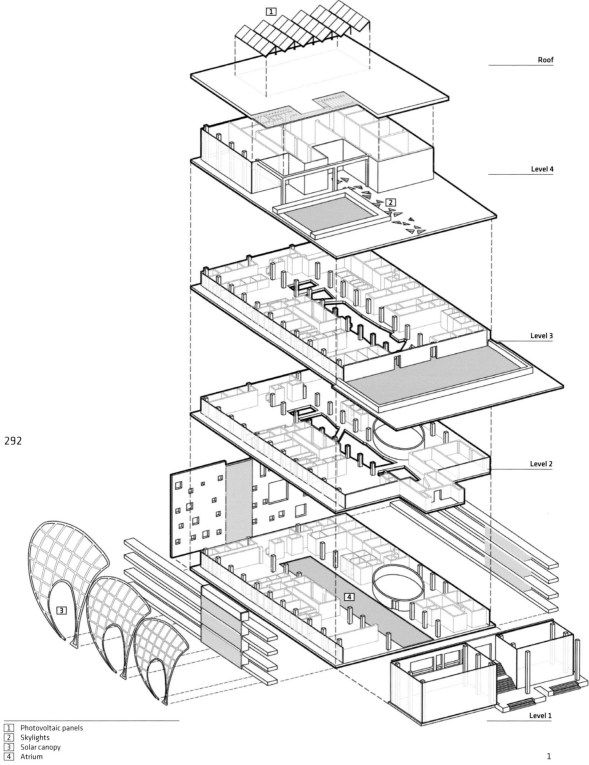

292

Level 4

Level 3

Level 2

Level 1

1. Photovoltaic panels
2. Skylights
3. Solar canopy
4. Atrium

1

At a point on an interstate highway on the outskirts of Pune, three tear-drop-shaped canopies flanking the corporate office of Kirloskar Brothers Ltd (KBL) become visible. They allude to the business of water pumps the company is known for. These elements on the building's south facade are more than a symbol. They reduce solar heat gain and temper daylight ingress, thereby improving the comfort of occupants.

As a corporate workplace with a high Green rating, KBL is often held up as an example of the business-case for Greening and for what an assessment tool-led approach can offer. Its other accomplishment – exemplified by the canopies – is in the people-centric approach to design that takes this building beyond the conventions of Greening.

There is, for example, a generosity of space and attention paid to user needs, both physical and psychological. The ergonomics of workstations and their placement in relation to view and light were carefully considered during the early design phase. Whereas many office buildings in India have deep plans and large windows, KBL has narrow floor plates and windows that vary in size with solar exposure. And while many large Indian corporations say they care for their employees, KBL offers amenities that are not commonly seen. Next to the office block, the KBL clubhouse is equipped with guest rooms for overnight stays, a gym, pool and cafeteria. The goal here, it seems, is to create a home away from home.

The problem with such ambitions is that they increase building size and with it, day-to-day consumption. Private sector offices in India reportedly consume 258 kWh/m^2/year, more than double the figure for public sector office buildings.[1] Much of this goes to air conditioning, which is supplied to some 75% of the building's gross floor area.[2] Despite KBL's higher-than-average reliance on mechanical cooling – 90% of gross floor area is cooled – it consumes 105 kWh/m^2/year, less than even public sector equivalents.

This level of performance, for a building so reliant on mechanical cooling, can be attributed in part to the adoption of certification as an early goal in the design process which called for high standards of systemic efficiency. Simulation tools used in the process enabled the design team to integrate these systems with principles of passive design, pushing performance further.

Wellness is however the theme that connects the dots on the drawing board. Integration of form and system is what makes this more than a raw assembly of Green features. This project illustrates how a strong design sensibility, augmented by an assessment tool, adds up.

293

1   Exploded axonometric of office block
2-3 Canopy over south facade

1_ Kumar, S., Kapoor, R., Rawal, R., Seth, S. & Walia, A. (2010)
2_ Kumar, S., Kamanth, M., Deshmukh, A., Seth, S., Pandita, S. & Walia, A. (2010)

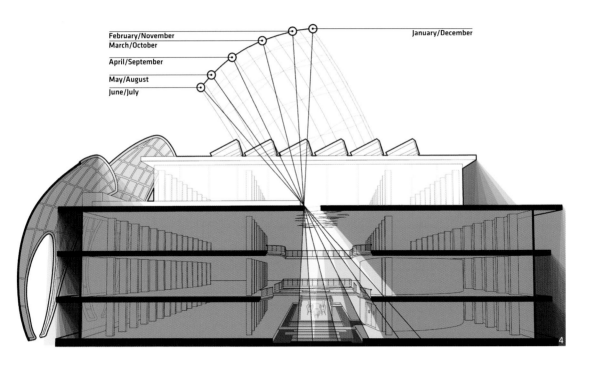

February/November
March/October
April/September
May/August
June/July

January/December

4

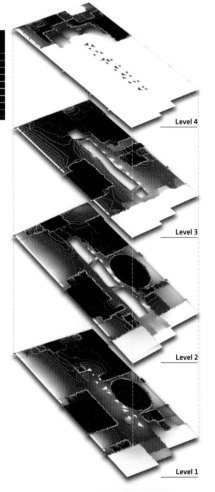

Lux
950
850
750
650
550
450
350
250
150
50

Level 4

Level 3

Level 2

Level 1

6

7

8

5

85%

OF EMPLOYEES EXPRESSED
SATISFACTION WITH THE
ENVIRONMENT

20%

INCREASE IN EMPLOYEE
PRODUCTIVITY WAS RECORDED
SINCE THE BUILDING BEGAN
OPERATION

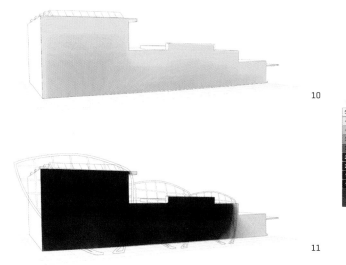

10

9

11

Wellness
Space and connectivity

The space per employee at KBL is 17 m²/person. In India this is typically about 13 m²/person,[3] often less. The 30% bonus alleviates the sense of crowding common in office buildings. With it, KBL offers its occupants a choice of settings beyond their personal workspace – lounges, tea corners, roof terraces, gardens and an atrium.

The atrium is the central organising space of the office block that breaks down its mass, reducing the distance between any employee and a window or skylight. The array of triangular skylights dotting the atrium roof increases the proportion of occupants with access to daylight to 80%. An equal number also have views to the outdoors. This degree of indoor-outdoor connectivity calls for careful calibration of envelope design. The building has large windows to the north and south, the latter shielded from low-angle winter sun by the canopies. On the east and west facades, windows are kept small to reduce heat gain. The skin also repels heat with double-glazing on windows and light-reflecting finishes on walls and roof.

Design and operation of the building's systems exceed international standards for fresh air intake and CO_2 monitoring, which improves the health of occupants in air-conditioned spaces. The control of these systems is partly left to the occupant via desktop light switches and individualised temperature controls.

3_ Kumar, S., Kamanth, M., Deshmukh, A., Seth, S., Pandita, S. & Walia, A. (2010)

4	Solar ingress and shading
5	Daylight distribution within office block
6–8	Atrium interior and roof-top skylights
9	Daylit interior space
10–11	Solar exposure of south facade without (top) and with canopies (bottom)

80%
OF ALL MATERIALS USED
ARE SOURCED REGIONALLY

20%
OF ALL MATERIALS USED
HAVE RECYCLED CONTENT

ALMOST
10%
OF ALL ENERGY CONSUMED
IS PRODUCED ON-SITE

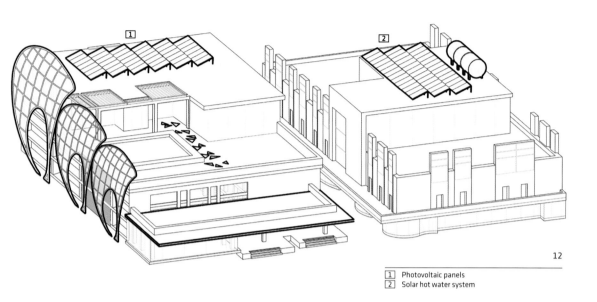

12

1 Photovoltaic panels
2 Solar hot water system

12 Location of photovoltaic
arrays and solar hot water
system
13 Photovoltaic arrays
14 Solar hot water system
15 Material-sourcing map
16–19 Local and regional stones
used as indoor and
outdoor finishes
20 Biodiesel tanks
21 Water recycling equipment

Embeddedness
Materials, energy, water

Rooftop photovoltaic panels and solar hot water systems offset some 2.5% of total electrical power demand and almost all of the hot water needs. Biodiesel generators (in place of more common diesel generators) satisfy over 7% of electrical power needs. An on-site sewage treatment plant generates enough water for all irrigation needs or about one third of the total water demand. On-site composting of food waste generates fertiliser for landscaping. Regional sources make up 80% of all materials used in construction. Twenty per cent of all materials used have recycled content. More than half of all wood used is from certified sources.

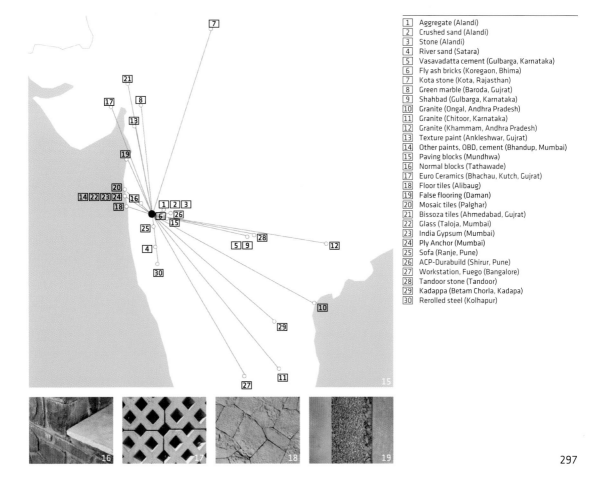

1 Aggregate (Alandi)
2 Crushed sand (Alandi)
3 Stone (Alandi)
4 River sand (Satara)
5 Vasavadatta cement (Gulbarga, Karnataka)
6 Fly ash bricks (Koregaon, Bhima)
7 Kota stone (Kota, Rajasthan)
8 Green marble (Baroda, Gujrat)
9 Shahbad (Gulbarga, Karnataka)
10 Granite (Ongal, Andhra Pradesh)
11 Granite (Chitoor, Karnataka)
12 Granite (Khammam, Andhra Pradesh)
13 Texture paint (Ankleshwar, Gujrat)
14 Other paints, OBD, cement (Bhandup, Mumbai)
15 Paving blocks (Mundhwa)
16 Normal blocks (Tathawade)
17 Euro Ceramics (Bhachau, Kutch, Gujrat)
18 Floor tiles (Alibaug)
19 False flooring (Daman)
20 Mosaic tiles (Palghar)
21 Bissoza tiles (Ahmedabad, Gujrat)
22 Glass (Taloja, Mumbai)
23 India Gypsum (Mumbai)
24 Ply Anchor (Mumbai)
25 Sofa (Ranje, Pune)
26 ACP-Durabuild (Shirur, Pune)
27 Workstation, Fuego (Bangalore)
28 Tandoor stone (Tandoor)
29 Kadappa (Betam Chorla, Kadapa)
30 Rerolled steel (Kolhapur)

29%
OF ALL WATER IS FROM ON-SITE
RECYCLED SOURCE

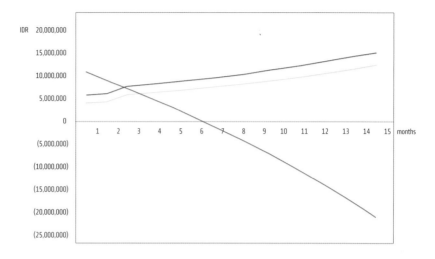

| IDR | 20,000,000 |
| 15,000,000 |
| 10,000,000 |
| 5,000,000 |
| 0 |

months: 1 2 3 4 5 6 7 8 9 10 11 12 13 14 15

(5,000,000)
(10,000,000)
(15,000,000)
(20,000,000)
(25,000,000)

──────── Running cost for chilled water
system
──────── Running cost for VRV system
──────── Simple payback for additional
initial capital investment

24

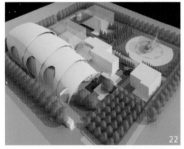

22

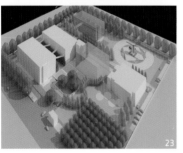

23

Site selection/brief formulation	Decision made to seek Green building certification
Concept design	Concept design stage commences with industry benchmarks of performance. This is accompanied by a study of architectural response to climate and passive strategies
Detailed design/contract documentation	Selection and integration of electro-mechanical systems Tools applied include life cycle assessment (of air conditioning options), daylight simulations and energy modelling
Construction	Documentation of construction activity, including local sourcing and construction waste management
Post-commissioning	Employees are surveyed before and after completion to assess effects on well-being, satisfaction and productivity Post-occupancy audits of indoor environmental quality, energy and water use are carried out

25

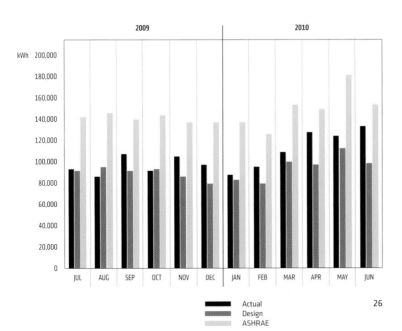

2009 | 2010

kWh

Actual
Design
ASHRAE

26

27

28

Integration
Aligning process to outcome

The decision to seek certification was perhaps the single most important driver of the design process. It defined what had to be measured and created awareness of benchmarks and targets. It clarified roles and accountability within the team, described metrics for quantification of performance, and obliged the team to seek expert input that might not otherwise have been considered.

Even though KBL is now discussed mostly in the language of assessment tool metrics – energy saved, waste diverted, water recycled – it is noteworthy that the design process started with form and envelope as primary responses to climate and site. Early sketches show two options for the office block: one with a more extensive use of canopies, another with a two-block configuration for permeability to daylight. The final outcome was a hybrid of the two. This vision of how the building might become a maker of comfort was important as integrator.

PROJECT TEAM

Developer
Kirloskar Brothers Ltd, Pune

Architect and project manager
Venkataramanan Associates

Heating, ventilation and air conditioning consultant
RS Kulkarn

Electrical consultant
Abhiyanta Electrical Consultants & Engineers

Plumbing and fire fighting consultant
ACE Consultants

Structural consultant
J+W Consultants

Landscape consultant
Ravi & Varsha Gawandi

LEED consultant
Environmental Design Solutions

Contractors
| Civil
  B.G. Shirke
| Interior
  Vector Projects India Ltd
| Heating, ventilation and air conditioning
  Servicool
| Intelligent building management system
  Sauter Race
| Electrical
  Pratibha Electricals

| Plumbing
  Ameet Consultants & Engineers

Owner and operator
Kirloskar Brothers Ltd, Pune

Facility manager
ISS Integrated Facility Services Pvt Ltd

SUPPLIERS

Modular furniture
Fuego furniture Pvt Ltd

Modular ceiling
Armstrong

Fly ash bricks
C'Cure Building Products Pvt Ltd

Glass
Saint Gobain

Grass pavers
Concrete Solutions

Gypsum boards
India Gypsum

Vitrified tiles
EURO Ceramics Ltd

Acoustic panelling and ceiling
Anutone

Aluminium composite panels
Durabuild Tech Pvt Ltd

Carpet
C&A (A Tandus company)

Certified wood
FSC wooden flooring from ECO Wood & Kahrs

Solar hot water system
AKSON

Solar photovoltaic system
| Kirloskar Brothers Ltd
| Vistar Electronics Pvt Ltd

Biodiesel generator
Kirloskar Oil Engines Ltd

Variable refrigerant volume system
Daikin

Heat recovery wheel
Desiccant Rotors

AWARDS/CERTIFICATION

2011
Award for Excellence in Architecture, interiors category, Indian Institute of Architects

2010
Winner, Emerson Cup (India & South East Asia), new building category, Emerson Climate Technologies

2009
LEED Platinum, new construction category, Indian Green Building Council

PERFORMANCE[4]

Annual energy consumption
1,253 MWh

On-site energy sourcing (% of total consumed)
| Biodiesel generator:
  7.1%

| Photovoltaic panels:
  2.5%

Greenhouse gas emissions
| 1,026 tonnes CO_2e/year
| 1.88 tonnes CO_2e/person/year

Energy intensity
| 105.3 kWh/m^2/year
| 2.3 MWh/person/year

Annual water consumption
18,457 m^3

On-site water sourcing (% of total consumed)
Grey and black water recycling: 29%

Water intensity
43 m^3/person/year

Materials (construction)
| 80% of site and contours left undisturbed
| 80% of materials are regionally sourced (against the Indian Rupee value of all materials procured)
| 20% recycled content in materials used (against Indian Rupee value of all wood-based building materials procured)
| 53% of wood is FSC-certified (against Indian Rupee value of all materials procured)

300

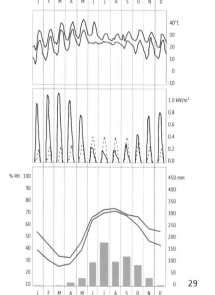

29

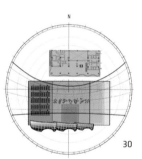

30

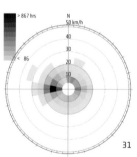

31

4_ Energy and water consumption figures are for the period June 2009 to June 2010.

| 99% of construction waste and debris diverted from landfill (as proportion of total weight of waste/debris)

| Floor area with view to outdoors: 92.9%

Materials (operations)
100% food waste is reused (composted for horticulture on-site)

Wellness
(occupant response)
| 60% of staff relies on shared transport provided by KBL
| 85% of staff express satisfaction with indoor environmental quality
| 20% increase in productivity from 2008 to 2010 (the new building became operational in 2009)

Comfort modes[5]
Thermal comfort (% of gross floor area)
| Passive (natural ventilation): 10%
| Active (air conditioning): 90%
Visual comfort
| Occupants with access to daylight: 83.3%

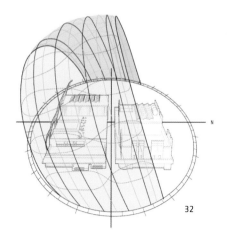

32

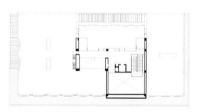

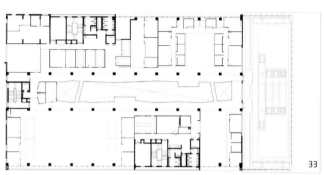

33

5_ Percentage of gross floor area that is designed to be predominantly reliant on passive or active design

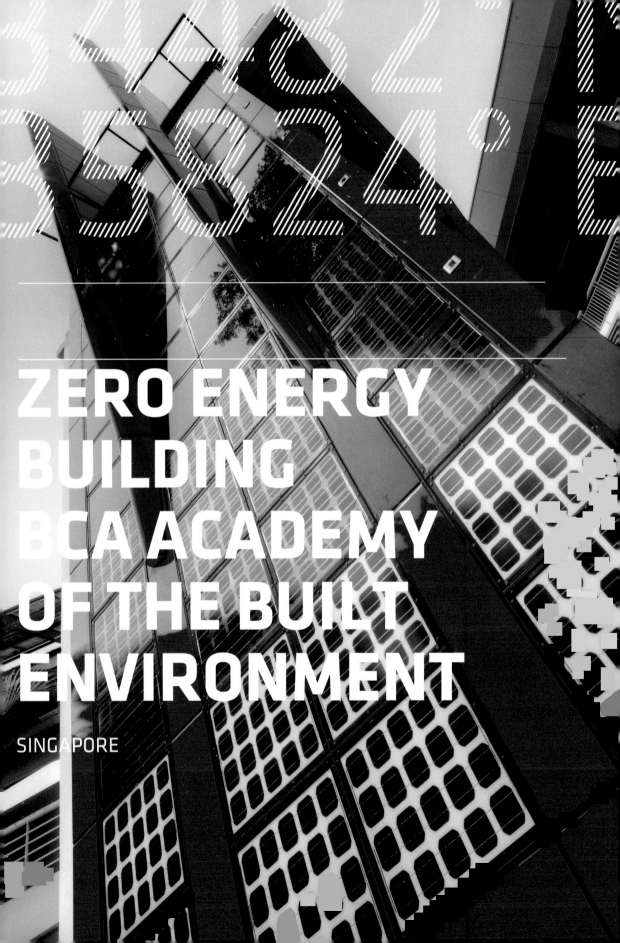

ZERO ENERGY BUILDING
BCA ACADEMY OF THE BUILT ENVIRONMENT

SINGAPORE

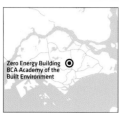

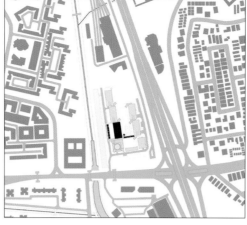

200 Braddell Road
Singapore 579700

Location
1.34482° N
103.85824° E

Completion
September 2009

Cost[1]
US$7,639,000

Size
3 levels

Gross floor area
4,500 m²

Site area
Land occupied by the BCA Academy
as a whole:
50,745 m²

Land occupied by the Zero Energy
Building only:
4,590 m²

Type
Workplace/education

Programme
Offices (67% of gross floor area)
Classrooms (33% of gross floor area)

Occupancy
80 staff
200 visitors/day

Operational hours
2,860/year

1_ Eleven million Singapore dollars in US
dollar equivalent based on international
exchange rates on September 1st 2009 |
International Monetary Fund. www.imf.org

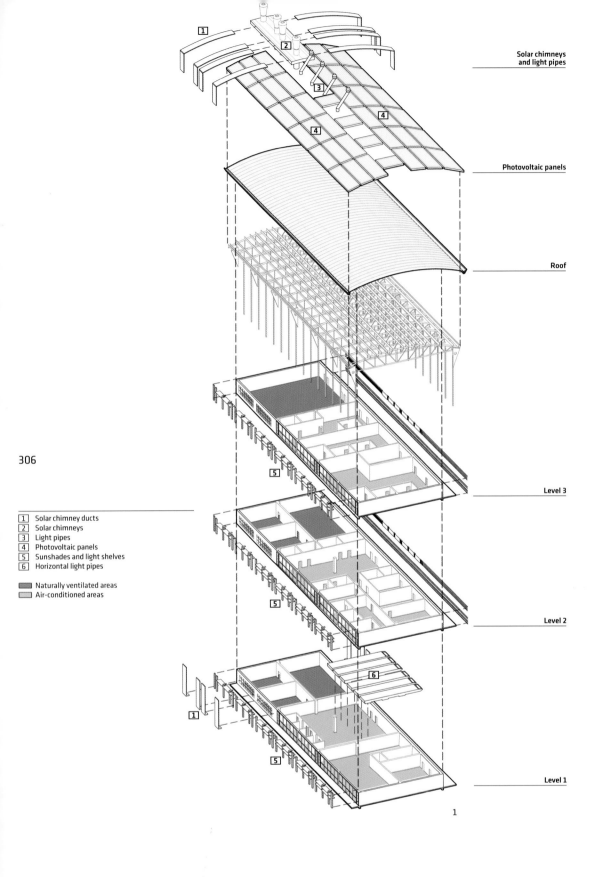

306

Solar chimneys
and light pipes

Photovoltaic panels

Roof

Level 3

Level 2

Level 1

1. Solar chimney ducts
2. Solar chimneys
3. Light pipes
4. Photovoltaic panels
5. Sunshades and light shelves
6. Horizontal light pipes

Naturally ventilated areas
Air-conditioned areas

1

Designing for *zero energy* in Asia is, in effect, an act of advocacy. It is to make the case for what might be done past the current conventions of Greening. Singapore announced in 2007 that its first zero energy building would be a retrofit. The city-state had set targets of 80% Green certification of *all* its buildings[2] and a 35% reduction in energy use by 2030.[3] To achieve this, the performance of its existing stock of buildings had to be improved.

For a zero energy building to be convincing, it must walk the line between pragmatism and forward-thinking. Integration of renewable technologies is important (despite current high cost); equally important is how energy demand is reduced at little or no cost.

The Zero Energy Building (ZEB) at the BCA Academy of the Built Environment is foremost a test-bed of ideas meant to persuade the building sector that this order of performance is possible. Its developer – the Building Construction Authority (BCA) of Singapore, the government department responsible for regulating the building sector – teamed up with research partners and consultants to cherry-pick technologies and ideas, and reframe the design-construction process. The Authority assigned a part of its own training academy for the retrofit. The real challenge though lay in breaking down mindsets that affect process and getting the design team to think about performance anew.

Since its completion ZEB's performance has been monitored. It has met the target of *net zero* energy – in other words, the energy it takes from the grid is less than what is put in. The numbers, before renewables, are particularly interesting. Whereas a building of the same use and occupancy would consume some 115 kWh/m^2/year, ZEB consumes 42. The 60% saving exceeds the 35% national energy target. This outcome can be traced

to several questions asked early in the design process. How, for instance, is comfort delivered? The building is only 45% air-conditioned and 49% reliant on electrical lighting; the rest is passive-run. Where electro-mechanical reliance is a must, the system gives many of its users control over how much cooling or lighting they get at their desktop.

Are there new ways of delivering passive comfort? At ZEB there is more than the obligatory window and sunshade. It has light and air-directing devices – not often seen in Singapore – that deal with the constraint of its deep floor plate. It relied on simulation tools and building information modelling software that allowed its team to visualise how these would be integrated into the building's fabric.

Many of the innovations in design are also visible. The envelope is an ensemble of fins, protrusions and plants that is engaged in an exchange of air, heat and light. Its appearance sets it apart from other buildings in the BCA Academy (for that matter, much of Singapore). It also sends an important signal that performance of this order is really about forging a relationship with the natural world.

307

1 Exploded axonometric
2–4 Facade- and roof-mounted elements responding to climate

2_ Keung, J. (2011, 13–16 September)
3_ Inter-Ministerial Committee on Sustainable Development. (2009)

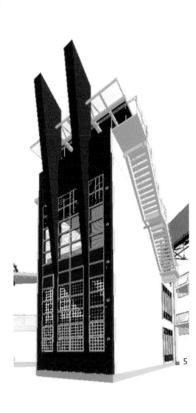

5

6

7

5   Integration of photovoltaics with staircase was aided by BIM software

6   Roof-mounted photovoltaic arrays and solar chimney

7   Facade-mounted photovoltaic arrays on sunshades

8–9 Data on electrical power consumption and generation for typical day (top) and consecutive months (bottom)

Efficacy and Embeddedness
Energy

The photovoltaic (PV) installations at ZEB are representative of what and how-to integrate renewable technologies. The main roof and linkway canopies hold some 90% of all arrays. Parts of a car park canopy and some sunshades are fitted with PV as well. A vertical face of a staircase (leading to a visitors' deck on the roof) displays five different types.

Across ZEB there are three grid-connected systems (190 kWP) with silicon wafer (polycrystalline), thin film (amorphous silicon) and hybrid (heterojunction with intrinsic thin layer) technologies. There are also three stand-alone systems (2 kWp) made up of silicon wafer (monocrystalline), thin film (amorphous silicon) and non-silicon (copper indium gallium selenide). The diversity allows researchers to assess which technology works best under Singapore skies.

The output from these arrays peaks at midday, when the energy generated is more than what is needed at the time. Monthly totals show that ZEB produces slightly more than it needs in most months. The amount produced in a year exceeds what is consumed by a convincing margin.

The systems that consume energy were picked for their efficiency. These back-of-house elements – chiller and cooling towers, variable speed drive for pumps, single coil twin fan (SCTF) air distribution[4] – are interfaced with front-of-house features with user controls. In its

4_ The SCTF is an innovative air distribution system that delivers an overall energy saving of about 12%. It also facilitates a high standard of indoor air quality and occupant comfort.

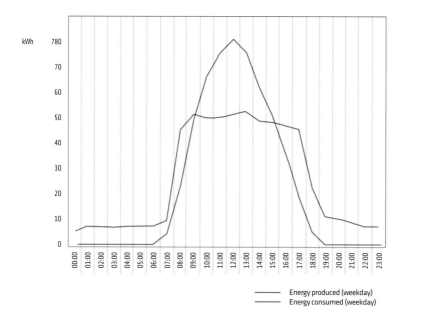

kWh

Energy produced (weekday)
Energy consumed (weekday)

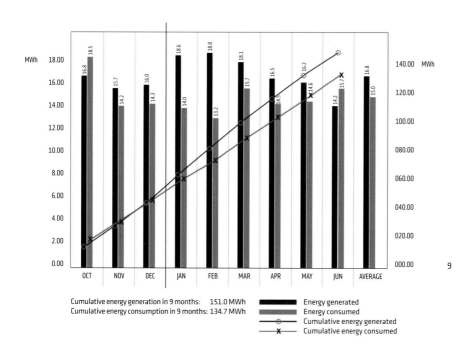

Cumulative energy generation in 9 months: 151.0 MWh
Cumulative energy consumption in 9 months: 134.7 MWh

Energy generated
Energy consumed
Cumulative energy generated
Cumulative energy consumed

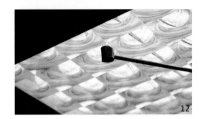

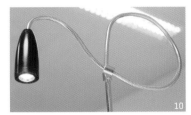

10 Desktop lighting
11 Floor-mounted air conditioning diffuser
12 Light pipe and light sensor
13 Table 4: Summary of
photovoltaic installations
at ZEB
14–15 Cooling towers
16 Air conditioning chillers

occupied spaces, air is released at low speeds from floor-mounted diffusers. Occupants also have personalised ventilation nozzles which bring cool air to their desktops.

Like air conditioning, indoor lighting strives to be responsive.

Artificial lighting is closely tied to daylight and occupant behaviour. Daylight sensors, motion sensors, dimming controls and task lights ensure that lights are switched on only when needed.

	Location	Installed capacity (kWp)	PV technology	Area installed (m^2)
Grid-connected photovoltaics	Main roof	142.50	Polycrystalline	1,037.0
	Linkway	20.50	Polycrystalline	149.0
	Carpark	15.40	Amorphous	259.0
	Viewing gallery	3.40	HIT bifacial	22.0
	Lower roof	7.20	Polycrystalline	52.0
	Sunshade	1.00	Amorphous	20.0
Stand-alone photovoltaics	Railing level 2	0.42	Polycrystalline	4.7
	Railing level 3	0.19	Amorphous	4.7
	Staircase level 1	0.36	Monocrystalline	4.1
	Staircase level 2	0.54	Monocrystalline	6.2
	Staircase level 3	0.22	Amorphous	4.1
	Staircase level 4	0.24	Amorphous	6.2
	Staircase level 5	0.23	CIGS	4.1

Source: Anupama, R.P., Wittkopf, S.K., Huang, Y., Nandar, L., Ang, K.S., Prasad, D., Scartezzini, J.L., & Toh P.S. (2010, 21–23 April)

13

311

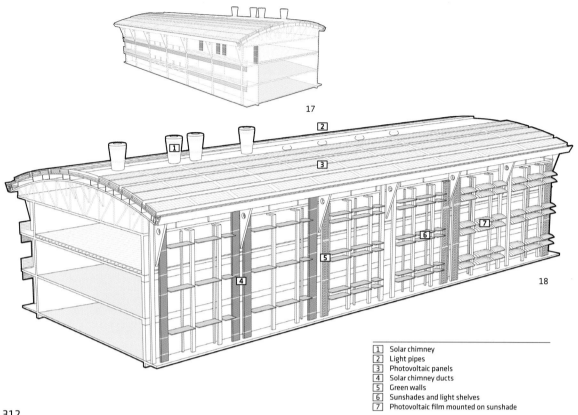

17

18

1	Solar chimney
2	Light pipes
3	Photovoltaic panels
4	Solar chimney ducts
5	Green walls
6	Sunshades and light shelves
7	Photovoltaic film mounted on sunshade

Wellness
Climate and comfort

To reduce thermal gains, ZEB deploys several strategies and features. The vertical green walls and green roofs absorb part of the sun's energy. Some is repelled by sunshades and low-e glass windows. Daylight is admitted in a controlled manner via light shelves and light pipes. Mirrored ducts transmit light horizontally from facade to middle of the floor plate.

To aid ventilation solar chimneys expel warm air which rises naturally to the roof on upper floors. On lower floors, this air is conveyed via ducts that are exposed to the sun's heat. When the sun is out, warm air in these ducts rises resulting in a convective pull that draws air across the floor plate. With these chimneys and ducts at work, air speed within the classrooms was measured at around 0.5 m/s.

An occupant survey[5] found that the thermal chimneys and shading devices make a significant difference to comfort in naturally ventilated classrooms. Interestingly, light shelves do not have the same unequivocal response. The increase in light levels is felt to be an increase in heat gain even though this is not supported by change to indoor temperature suggesting that this perception is, in part, psychological.

5_ Wong, N.H. & Tan, E. (2011)

19

20

21

22

23

24

25

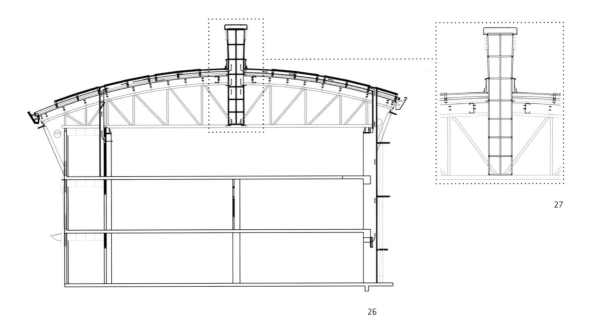

27

26

26–27 Detail of solar chimney
        integrated with roof
28–30 Solar chimney, views from
        outside and inside

28

29

30

31

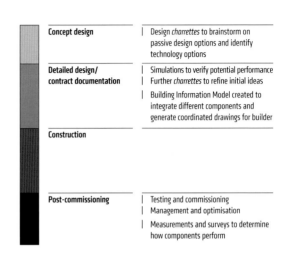

32

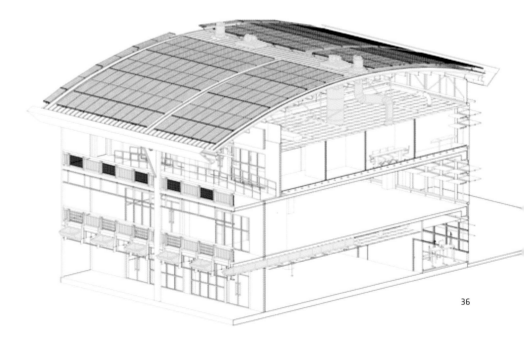

33

34

Concept design		Design *charrettes* to brainstorm on passive design options and identify technology options
Detailed design/ contract documentation		Simulations to verify potential performance
		Further *charrettes* to refine initial ideas
		Building Information Model created to integrate different components and generate coordinated drawings for builder
Construction		
Post-commissioning		Testing and commissioning
		Management and optimisation
		Measurements and surveys to determine how components perform

35

36

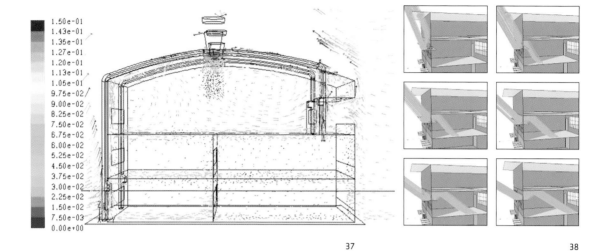

37

38

Integration
Passive and active systems

Integration of process was managed from the start. It began with *charrettes* at which team members gathered to brainstorm strategies and technologies. These sessions relied on assessments of climatic exposure, site conditions and material constraints of the existing shell and structure. With the initial ideas in place, the question became one of connectivity and synergy. Performance modelling was carried out by various experts to test viability and performance of systems in relation to one another. With these, the team reconvened to discuss, amend and streamline objectives.

As the project moved ahead, a Building Information Model (BIM) was created to aid the documentation and construction phase. This model combined information from different disciplines and trades – architectural, structural, electro-mechanical – allowing everyone to see how things come together. It focused, in particular, on the creation of new object libraries for PV elements (facade, roof, railing, canopy, shading, windows), solar active glazing (electrochromic glazing) and daylight redirection systems (light pipes, mirror ducts).[6] It permitted the coordination of sizes and tolerances for fabrication and installation. The model also aided the production of construction drawings which were later used by the builder and subcontractors.

31–32	Mirrored ducts
33–34	Light pipe
35	Table 5: Summary of design process
36	Integration of mirrored ducts and light pipes aided by BIM software
37	Simulations with computational fluid dynamics software showing solar chimney and stack effect in action
38	Simulations showing effectiveness of light shelves

6_ Wittkopf, S.K. & Huang, Y. (2011)

PROJECT TEAM
Developer
Building & Construction
Authority (BCA), Singapore
Architect
DP Architects Pte Ltd
Project manager, mechanical and electrical engineer, civil and structural engineer
Beca Carter Hollings & Ferner
SEA Pte Ltd
Quantity surveyor
Davis Langdon & Seah
Singapore Pte Ltd
Principal investigator (for green building technologies)
National University of
Singapore
Main contractor
ACP Construction Pte Ltd
Building operator
Building & Construction
Authority (BCA), Singapore

SUPPLIERS
Building management system
Quantum Automation Pte Ltd
Chillers
Johnson Controls (Singapore)
Pte Ltd
Electrical
KC Teck Engineering Pte Ltd

Energy-efficient air conditioning system
| Hitachi Plant Technologies
   Ltd
| Enhanced Air Quality
   Pte Ltd
Illuminance sensors
Renewpowers Technology
Pte Ltd
Mirror duct reflective materials
| Aluminium alloy
   Alanod Aluminium,
   Germany
| Mirror acrylic
   Dama Enterprise Pte Ltd
| Mirror polycarbonate
   Heliobus AG
   Sittertalstrasse
Solar tracking system
Solar Tracking Skylights Inc.
Light pipes
SolaLighting Ltd
Light pipes (with rotating mirror)
Monodraught Ltd, UK
Light pipes (without rotating mirror)
Eurolite Technologies Pte Ltd
Light shelf system
Facade Treatment
Engineering Sdn Bhd
Photovoltaic integrator
Grenzone Pte Ltd
Plumbing and sanitary
Qianda Engineering Pte Ltd

Roof greenery system
Garden and Landscape Centre
Pte Ltd
Solar chimney and mirror ducts
ACP Construction Pte Ltd
Testing chambers glazing
| Type 1 (electrochromic
   glass, untinted)
   Sage Electrochromics, US
| Type 4 (photovoltaic
   glass)
   SolarGy Pte Ltd
Vertical greenery system
| Garden and Landscape
   Centre Pte Ltd
| Consis Engineering Pte Ltd
| Shimizu Corporation

AWARDS/CERTIFICATION
2011
| Winner, *Distinguished
   Award, Minister for National
   Development's Research
   and Development Award*
   Ministry of National
   Development, Singapore
| Winner, *Special Submissions
   (for single coil twin fan),
   ASEAN Energy Awards,
   Energy Efficiency
   Competition*
   ASEAN Centre for Energy
2010
| Winner, *Prestigious
   Engineering Achievement*

Award, The Institution of
Engineers, Singapore
| Winner, *BCI Green
   Leadership Award*,
   institutional category,
   BCI Asia Construction
   Information Pte Ltd
2009
*Certified, Green Mark
Platinum, new building
category*, Building
Construction Authority,
Singapore

PERFORMANCE[7]
Annual energy consumption
194 MWh
On-site energy sourcing
Photovoltaics: 100%
Greenhouse gas emissions (energy taken from grid)
92.4 tonnes CO_2e/year
Greenhouse gas emissions offset (energy put into grid)
96.6 tonnes CO_2e/year
Energy intensity (before photovoltaics)
42 kWh/m^2/year (63.5%
better than a building of
similar use and operations)

Annual water consumption
Not disclosed

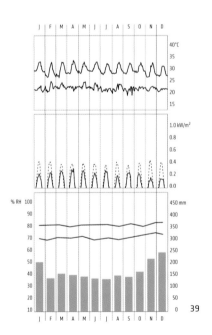

39

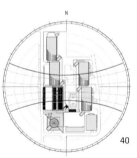

40

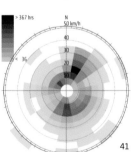

41

7_ Energy and water consumption figures
    are for the period October 2010 to
    September 2011.

**On-site water sourcing
(as % of total water
consumption)**
Nil

Materials (construction)
| 98% of all materials used
  were sourced within
  1,000 km from project site
| 85% recycled nylon fibre
  content in all carpets
| 100% of hardcore used
  was from construction
  waste
| 100% metal roofing sheet
  and steel reinforcement
  were sent for recycling in
  scrap yards

Wellness (design)
92.9% of gross floor area
offers view to outdoors

Comfort modes[8]
Thermal comfort
| Passive (natural
  ventilation):
  55%
| Active (air conditioning):
  45%
Visual comfort
| Passive (natural light):
  51%
| Active (electrical lighting):
  49%

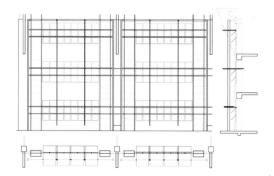

42

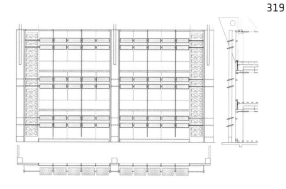

43

8_ Percentage of gross floor area that is
   designed to be primarily reliant on passive
   strategies or active systems

The publisher and author thank the project consultants, building owners and operators who offered images, drawings and data on their projects, and the photographers who gave permission to reproduce their images. Each of the in-depth case studies featured in this book had one or more submitting parties that assembled materials and sought clearance for their use. This book would not have been possible without them.

The author also acknowledges the many individuals who offered their time and support, in particular, the panel of reviewers who commented on the front-of-book essay.

Submitting parties
| Alexandra Health Pte Ltd
| Alila Hotels and Resorts
| Building & Construction Authority, Singapore
| CPG Consultants Pte Ltd
| Development & Construction Division, Housing Department, Hong Kong, SAR Government
| Green School, Bali
| IEN Consultants Sdn Bhd
| Morphogenesis
| Ove Arup & Partners Hong Kong Ltd
| Soneva
| Steven Holl Architects
| TYIN Tegnestue
| Venkataramanan Associates
| WOHA
| 24H-architecture

Reviewers
| Ray Cole
| Cheah Kok Ming
| Chrisna du Plessis
| Candice Lim
| Gregers Reimann
| Jalel Sager

Supporters
| Akshay Chalikwar
| Chang Joy Lee
| Firus Faisal
| Dindayal Gulabani
| Harsha Gulabani
| Khin Thida Kyaw
| Matthias Krups
| Robert Krups

ADB. (2009, April). *The Economics of Climate Change in Southeast Asia: A Regional Review.* Asian Development Bank. Retrieved from http://www.adb.org/publications/economics-climate-change-southeast-asia-regional-review

ADB. (2010, August). *Key Indicators for Asia and the Pacific 2010.* Asian Development Bank. Retrieved from http:/www.adb.org/ publications/key-indicators-asia-and-pacific-2010

ADB. (2010a, November). *Climate Change in Southeast Asia: Focused Actions on the Frontlines of Climate Change.* Asian Development Bank. Retrieved from http://www.adb.org/publications/climate-change-southeast-asia-focused-actions-frontlines-climate-change

ADB. (2010b, November). *Climate Change in South Asia: Strong Responses for Building a Sustainable Future.* Asian Development Bank. Retrieved from http://www.adb.org/publications/climate-change-south-asia-strong-responses-building-sustainable-future

ADB. (2010c, November). *Climate Change in East Asia: Staying on Track for a More Sustainable Future.* Asian Development Bank. Retrieved from http://www.adb.org/publications/climate-change-east-asia-staying-track-more-sustainable-future

ADB. (2011, May). *Basic Statistics 2011.* Asian Development Bank. Retrieved from http://www.adb.org/publications/basic-statistics-2011

ADB. (2011, August). *Asia 2050: Realizing the Asian Century.* Asian Development Bank. Retrieved from http://www.adb.org/publications/asia-2050-realizing-asian-century

ADB, HCMC People's Committee & DONRE. (2009, 25 April). *HCMC Adaptation to Climate Change, Volume 2: Main Report, Draft 4.* Prepared by the International Centre for Environmental Management. Retrieved from http://www.icem.com.au/documents/climatechange/hcmc_cc/hcmc_ccdraftreport_vol2_main_report.pdf

Anggadjaja, E. (2011, 13–16 September). Regional study on sustainable building policies in Southeast Asia. *Paper presented at the 2011 International Green Building Conference.* Singapore.

Anupama, R.P., Wittkopf, S.K., Huang, Y., Nandar, L., Ang, K.S., Prasad, D., Scartezzini, J.L., & Toh P.S. (2010, 21–23 April). Building integrated photovoltaic of Singapore's zero-energy building. *Paper presented at the International Conference on Applied Energy.* Singapore.

Architecture and Building Research Institute, Ministry of Interior, Taiwan. www.abri.gov.tw

Baird, G. (2010). *Sustainable Buildings in Practice: What the Users Think.* New York, USA: Routledge.

BCI Asia. (2008). *Green Building Market.* Building Construction Information, Asia.

BEAM Society, Hong Kong. www.beamsociety.org.hk

Bell, P.A., Greene, T.C., Fisher, J.D. & Baum, A. (1996). *Environmental Psychology* (4th ed.): Harcourt Brace College Publishers, USA.

Bernstein, P.G. (2010). Digital technology in architectural education: transient or transformative? *FuturArc, 17,* 36–37.

BREEAM, UK. www.breeam.org

Buchanan, P. (2000). *Ten Shades of Green: Architecture and the Natural World.* New York, NY: New York League of Architects.

Building and Construction Authority, Singapore. www.bca.gov.sg

Butler, R.A. (2005, 16 November). *World Deforestation Rates and Forest Cover Statistics, 2000–2005.* Retrieved from http://news.mongabay.com/2005/1115-forests.html

CII-Sohrabji Godrej Green Business Centre. www.greenbusinesscentre.com

Cole, R.J. (2012a). Regenerative design and development: current theory and practice. *Building Research & Information, 40:1,* 1–6.

Cole, R.J. (2012b). Transitioning from green to regenerative design. *Building Research and Information, 40:1,* 39–53.

Deuble, M. & de Dear, R. (2010, 9–11 April). Green occupants for green buildings: the missing link? *Paper presented at the conference on Adapting to Change: New Thinking on Comfort. Cumberland Lodge.* Windsor, UK.

du Plessis, C. (2012). Towards a regenerative paradigm for the built environment. *Building Research and Information, 40:1,* 7–22.

EarthCheck. (2010). *Benchmarking Assessment of Alila Villas Uluwatu.* Alila Hotels and Resorts.

Earthcheck. www.earthcheck.org

Economist Intelligence Unit. (2011). *Asian Green City Index: Assessing the Environmental Performance of Asia's Major Cities.* Siemens AG, Munich, Germany. Retrieved from http://www.siemens.com/press/pool/de/events/2011/corporate/2011-02-asia/asian-gci-report-e.pdf

Environmental Protection Administration, R.O.C. (Taiwan) (2009). *Towards Low Carbon Cities in Taiwan.* Retrieved from onunfccc.epa.gov.tw

Fa'atulo, W.R. (2010). *Perceiving Architectural Sustainability: Architects and Non Architects in Singapore* (Masters dissertation). National University of Singapore, Singapore.

Forman, R.T. (2002). The missing catalyst: design and planning with ecology roots. *Ecology and Design: Frameworks for Learning.* Johnson, B.R. & Hill, K. (Eds). Washington, USA: Island Press.

Fowler, K.M. & Rauch, E.M. (2006). *Sustainable Building Rating Systems.* Pacific Northwest National Laboratory, USA.

Gifford, H. (2008). *A Better Way to Rate Green Buildings: LEED Sets the Standard for Green Buildings but Do Green Buildings Actually Save Any Energy?* Retrieved from www.henrygifford.com

Global Footprint Network. www.footprintnetwork.org

Gopal, K. (2011). Sustainable cities for India: can the goal be achieved? *FuturArc*, *20*, 74-77.

Green Building Index, Malaysia. www.greenbuildingindex.org

Green Rating for Integrated Habitat Assessment, India. www.grihaindia.org

Guggenheim, D. (Director) & Bender, L. (Producer). (2006). *An Inconvenient Truth* [DVD]. United States: Paramount Home Entertainment.

Hamilton, A. (2011). Droughtbusters. *Time*, Oct 3, 2011. 47-50.

Hardy, J. & Stones, R. (2010). The FuturArc interview. *FuturArc*, *17*, 38-43.

Heringer, A. (2008). Home-made family houses. *FuturArc*, *11*, 44-51.

Hui, C.M.S. (2011, 18-21 March). Green roof urban farming for buildings in high-density urban cities. *Paper presented at the Hainan China World Green Roof Conference 2011*. Hainan, China

Human Development Reports, United Nations Development Programme. hdr.undp.org

Indian Green Building Council. www.igbc.in

Institute of Building Environment and Energy Conservation, Japan. www.ibec.or.jp

Inter-Ministerial Committee on Sustainable Development. (2009). *A Lively and Liveable Singapore: Strategies for Sustainable Growth*. Ministry of the Environment and Water Resources and Ministry of National Development, Singapore.

International Living Buildings Institute. (2008). *Living Building Challenge Version 1.3*. International Living Buildings Institute, Seattle, Washington, USA. Retrieved from http://ilbi.org/

International Monetary Fund. www.imf.org

IPCC. (2007). *Climate Change 2007: Synthesis Report. Contribution of Working Groups I, II and III to the Fourth Assessment Report of the Intergovernmental Panel on Climate Change*. Pachauri, R.K & Reisinger, A. (Eds.). IPCC, Geneva, Switzerland.

Jayakar, D. (2010). Greener than Green! *Inside Outside, February 2010*, 168-177.

Jayaraman, V. (2011). *Indian Regional Architecture: Influence of Global Green Agenda* (Masters dissertation). National University of Singapore, Singapore.

Kerr, T. (2008). The Green future of buildings, *FuturArc*, *10*, 26-32.

Keung, J. (2011, 13-16 September). Singapore: small nation but big vision for the built environment. *Paper presented at the 2011 International Green Building Conference*. Singapore.

Keynes, J.M. (1987). In Moggridge, D. (Ed.) *The Collected Writings of John Maynard Keynes: The General Theory and After. Part 1 - Preparation, Volume 13*. Cambridge, U.K.: Cambridge University Press.

King, B. (2008). Beyond oil. *FuturArc*, *10*, 97.

Kishnani, N. (2002). *Climate, Buildings and Occupant Expectations: A Comfort-Based Model for the Design and Operation of Office Buildings in Hot Humid Conditions* (Doctoral thesis). Curtin University of Technology, Perth, Australia. Retrieved from http://espace.library. curtin.edu.au/R/?func=dbin-jump-full&object_ id=12749&local_base=GEN01-ERA02

Kishnani, N. (2010). Singapore architects take a stand. *FuturArc*, *18*, 132-133.

Kishnani, N. (2011). *Green Building Design: Training Guide for Vietnam*. United Nations Environment Programme & the Ministry of Construction, Vietnam.

Kishnani, N. & Lim, C. (2010). Uncommon sense. *FuturArc*, *19*, 54-63.

Kofoworola, O.F. & Gheewala, S.H. (2009). Life cycle energy assessment of a typical office building in Thailand. *Energy and Buildings*, *41 (2009)*, 1076-1083.

Koh, H.Y. & Kishnani, N. (2009). Reinventing Eden: introducing nature into urban Singapore. *Paper presented at the International Tropical Architecture Conference*. Bangkok, Thailand

Kumar, S., Kamanth, M., Deshmukh, A., Seth, S., Pandita, S. & Walia, A. (2010). *Performance Based Rating and Energy Performance Benchmarking for Commercial Office Buildings in India*. USAid ECOIII.

Kumar, S., Kapoor, R., Rawal, R., Seth, S. & Walia, A. (2010). *Developing an Energy Conservation Building Code Implementation Strategy in India*. USAid ECOIII.

Lazarus, P. (2012). BIM: value and challenge. *FuturArc*, *24*, 78-81.

Le, V.C. & Lee, B.L. (2010). Wind and water bar. *FuturArc*, *19*, 52-53.

Lee, E.L. (2011). The FuturArc interview. *FuturArc*, *21*, 36-41.

Lewis, R. & Carmody, L. (2010, March). *Green Building in Asia*. Responsible Research. Retrieved from http://www.responsibleresearch.com/Green_Building_in_Asia-Issues_for_ Responsible__Executive_Summary_.pdf

Li, B. (2011, 13-16 September). Low carbon and Green buildings in China. *Paper presented at the 2011 International Green Building Conference*. Singapore.

Lim, C. & Lee, B.L. (2011a). Green village. *FuturArc*, *23*, 60-63.

Lim, C. & Lee, B.L. (2011b). Panyaden school. *FuturArc*, *23*, 70-73.

Lim, C. & Lee, B.L. (2012). JCube. *FuturArc*, *24*, 72-73.

Lim, L.W.I. (2011). *High-Rise, High-Density Living: the Skyscraper as the Future Model of City Living in Asia* (Masters dissertation). National University of Singapore, Singapore.

Lim, Y.A. & Kishnani, N.T. (2010). Building integrated agriculture: utilising rooftops for sustainable food crop cultivation in Singapore. *Journal of Green Building*, 5 (2): 105-113.

Lohnert, G., Dalkowski, A. & Sutter, W. (2003). Integrated design process: a guide for sustainable and solar-optimised design. *IEA, Task 23, Optimisation of Solar Energy Use in Large Buildings, Subtask B, Design Process Guidelines*. Berlin, Germany: International Energy Agency.

Low, C. (2008). Eco-tower extraordinaire. *FuturArc, 10*, 38-43.

Lyle, J.T. (1994). *Regenerative Design for Sustainable Development*. New York, USA: Wiley.

McGraw Hill Construction. (2008). *Global Green Building Trends; Market Growth and Perspectives from Around the World*.

McKinsey & Company. (2008). *Pathways to a Low Carbon Economy*. Retrieved from https://solutions.mckinsey.com/ClimateDesk/default.aspx

Merryweather, M. (2011). Ho Chih Minh City under the wrecking ball. *FuturArc, 21*, 64-71.

Michiya, S.T. & Tatsuo, O. (1998). Estimation of life cycle energy consumption and CO_2 emission of office buildings in Japan. *Energy and Buildings 28 (1998)*, 33-41.

Ministry of Construction of the People's Republic of China & National Head Office for Quality Supervision, Inspection and Quarantine of the People's Republic of China. (2006, 7 March). *Evaluation Standard for Green Building*. National Standard of the People's Republic of China (P GB/T 50378-2006).

Murakami, S. & Ikaga, T. (2008). *Evaluating Environmental Performance of Vernacular Architecture through CASBEE*. Japan GreenBuild Council & Japan Sustainable Building Consortium (Eds.) Institute for Building Environment and Energy Conservation, Japan. Retrieved from http://www.ibec.or.jp/CASBEE/english/document/Vernacular_Architecture_brochure.pdf

National Geographic Society. (2009, September). Plugging into the sun. *National Geographic Magazine*, 40.

Ng, E. (2012, 2 March). More measures being considered to tackle climate change. *Today Online*. Retrieved from www.todayonline.com

Nguyen, V.S. (2009, January). *Industrialization and Urbanization in Vietnam: How Appropriation of Agricultural Land Use Rights Transformed Farmers' Livelihoods in a Peri-Urban Hanoi Village*. EADN Working Paper No. 38, 2009.

Nicholls, R.J., Hanson, S., Herweijer, C., Patmore, N., Hallegatte, S., Jan Corfee-Morlot, Jean Chateau & Muir-Wood, R. (2007). *Ranking of the World's Cities Most Exposed to Coastal Flooding Now and in the Future*. OECD Environment Working Paper No. 1, 2007.

Nicol, J.F. & Humphreys, M.A. (2002). Adaptive thermal comfort and sustainable comfort standards for buildings. *Energy and Buildings, Vol. 35*: 95-101.

Orr, D.W. (1992). *Ecological Literacy*. Albany, NY: State University of New York, Albany.

Plant a Tree Today Foundation. www.pattfoundation.org

Public Utilities Board, Singapore. (2011, July). *ABC Waters Design Guidelines*. Retrieved from www.pub.gov.sg/abcwaters/abcwatersdesignguidelines/Pages/ABCDesignGuidelines.aspx

Rastogi, M. (2011). The FuturArc interview. *FuturArc, 22*, 40-47.

Read-Brown, A., Bardy, F. & Lewis, R. (2010, September). *Sustainability in Asia: ESG Reporting Uncovered*. Morales, R., Carmody, L. & Lyon, E. (Eds.). Responsible Research. Retrieved from http://www.responsibleresearch.com/Sustainability_in_Asia___ESG_Reporting_Uncovered.pdf

Reed, R., Bilos, A., Wilkinson, S. & Schulte, K.W. (2009). International comparison of sustainable rating tools. *Journal of Sustainable Real Estate*, Vol. 1, No.1-2009. Retrieved from http://www.costar.com/josre/JournalPdfs/01-Sustainable-Rating-Tools.pdf

Rees, W.E. (1999). The built environment and the ecosphere: a global perspective. *Building Research & Information, 27*: 4, 206-220.

Rees, W.E. (2008). Human nature, eco-footprints and environmental injustice. *Local Environment, 13(8)*, 685-701.

Roger, S. & Evans, L. (2011, 31 January). World carbon dioxide emissions data by country: China speeds ahead of the rest. *Guardian*. Retrieved from www.guardian.co.uk

Sachs, J.D. (2011, 29 August). *The Economics of Happiness*. Retrieved from http://www.project-syndicate.org/commentary/the-economics-of-happiness

Sager, J. (2011). A matter of life and death? Towards biophilic living interiors. *FuturArc, 23*, 28-35.

Singapore Institute of Architects. (2010). *Twelve Attributes of a Sustainable Built Environment*. Retrieved from http://www.sia.org.sg/resources/2010/12AttributesOfGreenArchitecture.pdf

Sinclair, C. (2012). The FuturArc interview. *FuturArc, 25*, 30-35.

Singer, P. (2011). *Can We Increase Gross National Happiness?* Retrieved from www.project-syndicate.org

Sivarajan, S. (2011). *A Study into the Advent and Growth of Green Building Practices in India*. (Masters dissertation). National University of Singapore, Singapore.

Smith, B.J., Tang, K.C. & Nutbeam, D. (2006). WHO health promotion glossary: new terms. *Health Promotion International Advance Access*, World Health Organization, Geneva, Switzerland, Oxford University Press. Retrieved from http://www.who.int/healthpromotion/about/HP%20Glossay%20in%20HPI.pdf

Sng, P.L. (2011). *In What Way Can the Green Building Contribute to Human Wellness in the Singapore Context?* (Masters dissertation). National University of Singapore, Singapore.

Solidance. (2011). *Asia Pacific's Top 10 Green Cities*. Ellson, J. (Ed.) Retrieved from www.solidance.com

Steele, J. (2005). *Ecological Architecture: a Critical History*. London, United Kingdom: Thames and Hudson Ltd.

Suteethorn, K. (2009). Urban agriculture: ecological functions for urban landscape. *Paper presented at the 2009 Incheon IFLA APR Congress*. Incheon, Korea.

Sze, T.Y. (2011). *New Regionalism in Tropical Architecture: the Re-Convergence of Formal and Performance-Based Paradigms in the Ecological Age* (Masters dissertation). National University of Singapore, Singapore.

Tan, S.Y. (2012). *The Practice of Integrated Design: The Case Study of Khoo Teck Puat Hospital* (Masters dissertation). BCA Academy-University of Nottingham, Singapore.

The Converging World. www.theconvergingworld.org

The World Bank. data.worldbank.org/indicator

TYIN Tegnestue Architects. www.tyintegnestue.no

Ulrich, R.S. (1984). View through a window may influence recovery from surgery. *Science, 224*, 420–421.

United Nations Environment Programme. (2007). *Buildings and Climate Change; Status, Challenges and Opportunities*. Sustainable Buildings and Climate Initiative, UNEP. Retrieved from http://www.unep.org/ publications/search/pub_details_s.asp?ID=3934

United Nations Environment Programme. (2009). *Buildings and Climate Change: Summary for Decision-Makers*. Sustainable Buildings and Climate Initiative, UNEP. Retrieved from http://www.unep.org/sbci/ pdfs/SBCI-BCCSummary.pdf

United Nations Environment Programme. (2010). *The 'State of Play' of Sustainable Buildings in India*. Sustainable Buildings and Climate Initiative, UNEP. Retrieved from http://www.unep.org/pdf/SBCI_State_of_play_ India.pdf

United Nations Human Settlements Programme. (2010). *The State of Asian Cities 2010/11*. UN-HABITAT Regional Office for Asia and the Pacific, Fukuoka, Japan. Retrieved from http://www.unhabitat.org/pmss/listItemDe-tails.aspx?publicationID=3078

United Nations Statistics Division. unstats.un.org

US Green Building Council. www.usgbc.org

Van der Ryn, S. & Cowan, S. (2007). *Ecological Design*, 2nd Edn. Washington, DC: Island Press. Vietnam Green Building Council. www.vgbc.org.vn

Wittkopf, S.K. & Huang, Y. (2011). *Advanced Daylighting and Building Integrated Photovoltaics for High Performance Buildings in the Tropics: Zero Energy Building @ BCA Academy*. Solar Energy Research Institute of Singapore (SERIS), Singapore.

Wong, N.H. & Tan, E. (2011). *Future Green School: Zero Energy Building @ BCA Academy*. National University of Singapore, Singapore.

Wong, V. (2011, 2 June). As world millionaires multiply, Singapore holds its lead. *Bloomberg Businessweek*. Retrieved from www.business-week.com

World Green Building Council. www.worldgbc.org

World Resources Institute. (2005). *Millennium Ecosystem Assessment Report*. Washington, USA: Island Press.

Wu, Z. (2011). *Evaluation of a Sustainable Hospital Design Based on its Social and Environmental Outcomes* (Masters dissertation). Cornell University, Ithaca, NY, USA.

Yeang, K. (2006). *Ecodesign: A Manual for Ecological Design*. London, UK: John Wiley and Sons.

Yoong, E. (2008). Pusat Tenaga Malaysia's Zero Energy Office. *FuturArc, 10*, 64–67.

CREDITS

GRAPHICS

PICTURES